Caroline

Lord Russell of Liverpool

സ്റ്റസ്റ്റസ്റ്റസ്റ്റസ്റ്റസ്റ്റസ്റ്റസ്റ്റസ്റ്റസ്റ്റസ്റ്റസ്റ്റ

Caroline
The Unhappy Queen

സ്റ്റസ്റ്റസ്റ്റസ്റ്റസ്റ്റസ്റ്റസ്റ്റസ്റ്റസ്റ്റസ്റ്റസ്റ്റസ്റ്റ

Illustrated

ROBERT HALE · LONDON

© *Lord Russell of Liverpool 1967*
First published in Great Britain 1967

Robert Hale Limited
63 Old Brompton Road
London SW7

SBN 7091 0200 3

Printed in Great Britain
by Ebenezer Baylis and Son, Ltd.
The Trinity Press, Worcester, and London

Contents

Illustrations

ଜ୍ୟଜ୍ୟଜ୍ୟଜ୍ୟଜ୍ୟଜ୍ୟଜ୍ୟଜ୍ୟଜ୍ୟଜ୍ୟଜ୍ୟଜ୍ୟଜ୍ୟଜ୍ୟଜ୍ୟଜ୍ୟଜ୍ୟ

The portrait of Mrs. Fitzherbert was supplied by
the Mansell Collection. The other illustrations were
supplied by the Radio Times Hulton Picture Library.

Acknowledgements

I am most grateful to Her Majesty the Queen for graciously giving me permission to make use of material from the Royal Archives.

I also wish to express my thanks to Mr. S. S. Wilson, C.B.E., Keeper of Public Records, for giving me access to certain documents; to Mr. C. S. D. Dobson, Librarian to the House of Lords, for helping me with the research into the parliamentary debates on the Bill of Pains and Penalties and to Sir Charles Petrie Bart for allowing me to quote from *The Life of George Canning* and *The Modern British Monarchy*.

As usual my thanks are due to my wife for the ungrateful task of typing out the manuscript and for much other help and advice during the writing of the book.

ONE

A Marriage of Convenience

ᘛᘚᘛᘚᘛᘚᘛᘚᘛᘚᘛᘚᘛᘚᘛᘚᘛᘚᘛᘚᘛᘚᘛᘚᘛᘚᘛᘚᘛᘚᘛᘚᘛᘚᘛᘚ

"I SHALL never marry," the Prince of Wales, later to become the Prince Regent and subsequently George IV, once said to the first Earl of Malmesbury. He did not think that he was suited to a marriage of convenience and who would contradict him. In the end it was only the combination of overwhelming debts and the need for a legitimate grandchild to George III which drove him into a marriage which, from the outset, had little chance of success.

Although his future bride appears to have been moderately good-looking she had no other physical attractions. Her mother, the Princess Augusta, was a coarse woman with a vulgar mind and the daughter's underclothes were said to be as filthy as her mother's follies. "I knew," wrote Lord Malmesbury, though he did not explain how he got the information, "that she wore coarse petticoats, coarse shifts and thread stockings and these were never well washed or changed often enough." Nor was that all, there was madness on both sides of her family.

But whatever the truth may have been about the Princess's personal cleanliness, and in the eighteenth century this did not count for very much, she had been in her youth, and continued to be in later life despite her many detractors, an attractive, lively and engaging personality.

Indeed had she never married her dissolute husband, who was to become her evil genius, and had accepted one of the several offers of marriage which she had received before George III selected her as his daughter-in-law, life could not conceivably have turned out to be more tragic than it did.

Her father, Charles William, Duke of Brunswick and husband of George III's sister, the Princess Augusta, adored his daughter and spoiled her. She, in her turn, always remembered him with love and admiration, but with awe, as well she might for he was no ordinary man. "My father," she used to say, "was a hero: they married me to a zero."

There could, however, never have been any reasonable possibility that the marriage of this rather frivolous and irresponsible young girl to such a useless and selfish degenerate as the Prince of Wales would ever be successful. The kindest thing that could be said of him was that he was not the marrying sort. Thackeray's assessment of him was much less charitable.

This George, what was he? I look through all his life and recognize but a bow and a grin. I try to take him to pieces and find silk stockings, padding, stays, a coat with frogs and a fur collar, a star and a blue ribbon, a pocket handkerchief prodigiously scented, one of Truefitt's best nutty brown wigs reeking with oil, and a black stock under waistcoats, more underwaistcoats and then nothing.[1]

It could be said that Thackeray's summing-up failed to mention any of the Prince's good qualities, if indeed there were any, but an estimate of his character, made a hundred years later by an objective historian, does not put him in a more favourable light:

He was a clever versatile lazy man . . . attractive and rude by turns,

[1] *The Four Georges* by William Makepeace Thackeray.

but always a liar, always selfish, bad in his private and public conduct and without the least understanding of his age. He was a fair judge of character and could turn a pleasant phrase, but he never concerned himself with anything which did not ultimately affect his own pleasure. . . . He was a poor argument for his own cause and the English Monarchy could hardly have survived a successor of his kind. It may be said that he showed in his private life signs of his father's madness[1] and that in his selfishness and low behaviour he was no worse than four of his six brothers. It is difficult to find other arguments in his favour.[2]

Nevertheless, although nothing can excuse the way in which he treated his wife, his upbringing and the circumstances of his youth were partly responsible for his decadent character. He had feared and hated his grandmother and no one was more pleased than he was when she died. He also hated both his parents and disliked on principle everything which his father enjoyed. George III's chief hobby was agriculture, on account of which he earned the nickname of Farmer George, but the Prince preferred the city lights, and when, at the age of eighteen, he was given a little freedom he seized it with both hands. His father was a Tory, so George became a Whig.

He had never been allowed to mix with other children so he had no companions of his own class, but when he was allowed to set up a home of his own in Buckingham House he was introduced to the wrong people by his uncle the Duke of Cumberland, who "found a satisfaction in turning the Prince's apartments into a combined gambling den, pawnshop and brothel."[3]

[1] He had a mania for hoarding hardly less strong than his love of extravagant spending. He kept all his coats, boots and pantaloons over a period of fifty years. After his death bundles of love-letters, women's gloves and locks of hair were found amongst his papers. He also left banknotes scattered in five hundred pocket-books, about £10,000 of loose money in his boxes.

[2] *The Age of Reform* (*The Oxford History of England*) by E. L. Woodward.

[3] *Charles James Fox*, by Drinkwater.

When he was but seventeen years old, Perdita, the actress whose maiden name was Mary Darby, became his mistress. She was four years older than her lover and had been married since 1774, when she was only sixteen years of age, to a waster named Robinson who neglected her and led a life of dissipation which soon landed him in a debtor's prison. Perdita, who by this time had given birth to a child, kept things going by doing any kind of menial job which came her way. Through David Garrick, who had taken some interest in the girl before her marriage, she made her debut on the stage at Drury Lane in the part of Juliet, with William Brereton as Romeo. She became a star on the first night and, but for her appearance before the Prince of Wales at a command performance of *The Winter's Tale*, almost exactly three years later, she would, undoubtedly, have had a successful career on the stage. The Prince, however, fell madly for her and the young woman foolishly deserted the stage and became his mistress. In less than eighteen months, however, he had found a new one and Mrs. Robinson was paid £5,000 for handing over the passionate love letters which the Prince had written to her over the signature of Florizel, and given a life pension of £5,000 a year, which she continued to draw until her untimely death fifteen years later at the early age of forty.

A year after he had rid himself of Perdita the Prince came of age and established himself at Carlton House, where he continued to live a life of dissipation aided and abetted by Charles James Fox and a number of other Whig politicians. As Sir Edward Parry has written:

One wonders how men like Fox, Burke and Sheridan could associate with such a character as George, Prince of Wales. But politics make us acquainted with strange bedfellows. . . . He treated his political friends as he treated the women he ruined to give him pleasure, but grave statesmen should not have been seduced by his advances and one cannot grieve over their betrayal. In the same way some of the Court ladies who sought for his patronage had full warning of the price they would pay for it and one can pass over their stories of neglect and desertion without wasting pity on them.

His meeting with Maria Fitzherbert, however, was something much more serious. He was then twenty-two and she was about twenty-eight. As far as it was possible for him to love anybody the Prince loved Mrs. Fitzherbert, but when a rumour came to the ears of Fox that his royal friend was considering marriage with her he became greatly alarmed and wrote a long letter in which he tried to dissuade the Prince from doing anything so foolish and dangerous.

In a short reply written on the following day, the Prince assured Fox that he need have no fears as there was no truth in the rumour. "Believe me," he wrote, "the world will soon be convinced that there not only is not, but never was, any ground for these reports which of late have been so malevolently circulated."

Nevertheless four days later the Prince and Maria were married according to the rites of the Church of England in the drawing room of her house in Park Street, Mayfair.[1]

How long the Prince would have continued living with Mrs. Fitzherbert, had it not been that by 1794 he was hopelessly in debt, it was impossible to say, but there is reason to suppose that before then he had already begun to tire of her and had started an intrigue with Lady Jersey. In June of that year, however, Mrs. Fitzherbert received a curt note from the Prince that he would never enter her house again.

Two months later the King was delighted to be able to write to William Pitt and give him the good news that he had long been waiting to receive:

I have this a.m. seen the Prince of Wales who has acquainted me with his having broken off all connection with Mrs. Fitzherbert and his

[1] The marriage certificate is in the Royal Archives at Windsor Castle.

desire of entering into a more creditable line of life by marrying, expressing at the same time that his wish is that a niece of the Princess of Brunswick is the person. Undoubtedly she is the person who naturally must be the most agreeable to me. I expressed my approbation of the idea, provided his plan was to lead to a life that would make him appear respectable and consequently render the Princess happy. He assured me that he perfectly coincided with me in my opinion. I then said that until Parliament assembled no arrangement could be taken except by sounding my sister that no idea of any other marriage may be encouraged.

For the King to have told Pitt that it was the Prince's wish that he should marry Caroline was, perhaps, putting it a little too strongly. The only other bride considered eligible was Princess Louise of Mecklenberg-Strelitz, but the Prince would not entertain the idea of marrying her although his mother tried to persuade him. His decision in favour of Caroline, however, appears to have been a question of Hobson's choice, for his private opinion on the subject is said to have been, "one damned German *frau* is as good as another." One of his friends believed that Lady Jersey may have had a hand in influencing his choice, for Princess Louise was the better-looking of the two and, had the Prince of Wales married her, Lady Jersey's position as one of his mistresses might more easily have been in jeopardy.

Having informed Pitt of the Prince's welcome decision the King lost no time, and, on 14th November, Lord Malmesbury, who was already in Germany on a special mission to the Court of Berlin, received instructions to demand the hand of the Princess Caroline of Brunswick for his son. He was given no discretion whatsoever but it is clear from the entries in his diaries that, while publicly he confined himself strictly to carrying out His Majesty's command, in private he did all he could to prepare the rather wilful and independent girl for what was to come.

On his arrival in Brunswick a fortnight later he was immediately asked by the Duke and Duchess to dine with them so that he should have the earliest opportunity of meeting the Princess. At dinner he sat next to his hostess, but when not actually engaged in conversation with her he appears to have wasted no time and kept the Princess under a watchful eye, for he wrote a detailed description of her in his diary before he retired to bed. "She appeared," he wrote, "to be much embarrassed when I was presented to her but during the evening she gave every indication that she was vastly happy with her future expectations." She had "a pretty face not expressive of softness," and although "she did not have a graceful figure she had a good bust and *des épaules impertinentes.*"[1]

Her mother talked of nothing else but the offer of marriage and was delighted at the prospect, though for the wrong reason. All the German princesses, she told Malmesbury, had learnt English in the hope of becoming Princess of Wales, but she had never imagined that the choice would fall on her daughter because she knew that her brother, King George III, was against marriages between first cousins.

As the days went by, during which time Malmesbury had several long conversations with the Duke of Brunswick on another subject, his opinion of Caroline changed for the better. He found that she improved on acquaintance and was "gay, cheerful and sensible." On 3rd December, the day fixed for the final interview before the signing of the marriage treaty, a letter arrived from the Prince of Wales enclosing a portrait of himself and precise instructions to leave for England with the Princess as soon as possible. On the following morning the treaty was signed and a dinner and ball were held that evening to celebrate the occasion.

The instructions which the Prince had given Malmesbury by letter were in flat contradiction to those which he had received

[1] *Diaries and correspondence of James Harris, First Earl of Malmesbury,* edited by his grandson, 1844.

from the King. Nevertheless, Malmesbury wrote to the Prince to the effect that he and his charge would set out for England on the 11th, provided that before then he received confirmation that the fleet which was to escort them across the channel had already sailed. But it was not to be. Nearly four months were to elapse before the Princess and her escort entered the Thames and anchored off Gravesend.

During this time the Princess had many talks with Lord Malmesbury about the future and received a lot of sound advice which she appears to have taken without offence. On several occasions, also, both the Duke and his mistress, Mademoiselle Hertzfeldt, warned Malmesbury about the Princess's faults, such as they were. They amounted, however, to little more than indiscretion and a habit of saying too much at the wrong time. Caroline, the Duke said, was not difficult but, perhaps, a little lacking in judgment. "Try and persuade her," he told Malmesbury, "not to be free in giving opinions of persons and things aloud." All this was confirmed by Mademoiselle Hertzfeldt. Caroline had to be dealt with strictly as she was inclined to be tactless and lose her temper. Some guidance should be given her as to her behaviour after her arrival in England, and, in Mademoiselle Hertzfeldt's opinion, Lord Malmesbury would be the most suitable person to give it. He took the hint and advised Caroline, "to avoid familiarity, to have no confidantes, to avoid giving any opinion, to approve but not to admire excessively, and to be perfectly silent on politics and party." She took all this in good part and hoped that Lord Malmesbury would continue to advise her after she reached England.

Eventually, on Easter Sunday 1795, the Princess disembarked at Greenwich about noon. The royal coaches had not yet arrived since one of the ladies-in-waiting, Lady Jersey, had delayed the start, doubtless deliberately, by not being ready in time. When, at last, she did arrive Lady Jersey professed herself as being "very much dissatisfied with the Princess's mode of dress," and expressed herself in such terms that Lord Malmesbury thought it his duty to speak "rather sharply" to her. She also said that she could not sit in a coach with her back to the horses and hoped that she might be allowed to sit facing them. Lord Malmesbury told her in no uncertain terms that this was strictly forbidden by the King, and that as she must have known that riding backwards in a coach disagreed with her, she ought never to have accepted the appointment of a Lady of the Bedchamber, who ought never to sit forward, and that if she was likely to be sick he would put Mrs. Aston into the coach with the Princess. That did the trick, and Lady Jersey and Mrs. Harcourt, who had accompanied the Princess on her journey across the channel, "sat backwards and the Princess sat by herself forward." After these unpleasant preliminaries the cortège eventually reached the Duke of Cumberland's apartments in Cleveland Row at about half past two.

The King and the Prince of Wales were at once informed of Caroline's arrival and the Prince came to meet her. What happened then is best described in Lord Malmesbury's own words.

I, according to the established etiquette, introduced (no one else being in the room) the Princess Caroline to him. She, very properly, in consequence of my saying to her it was the right way of proceeding, attempted to kneel to him. He raised her (gracefully enough) and embraced her, said barely one word, turned round, retired to a distant part of the appartment, and, calling me to him, said, "Harris I am not well; pray get me a glass of brandy." I said, "Sir had you not better have a glass of water?"—upon which he, much out of humour, said with an oath, "No: I will go directly to the Queen," and away he went. The Princess, left alone during this short moment, was in a state of astonishment; and on my joining her, said, "Je le trouve très gros, et nullement aussi beau que son portrait." ("I find him very fat and not half as handsome as his portrait.")

Caroline can hardly be blamed for being somewhat astonished.

She had heard a good deal about the Prince, including much to his discredit, but this was more than she had expected. His callous rudeness was still first and foremost in her mind at dinner when her behaviour disgusted the Prince and was the beginning of a dislike which soon developed into hatred.

Three days later, in the Chapel Royal, St. James's, the wedding took place at eight o'clock in the evening with all the appropriate pomp and circumstance, but it was obvious to anyone who had eyes to see that it was a marriage in name only—indeed on the previous day many bets were taken at all the leading West End clubs that it would never take place. The Prince arrived, apparently drunk, though his state may have been due more to the state of nervous apprehension he was in than the amount of drink which he had taken, although this was more than was good for him. Whatever may have been the Princess's feelings after the shock of the first meeting with her future husband she managed to disguise them, and chatted happily with the Duke of Clarence while waiting at the altar for the Prince's arrival. Throughout the ceremony she conducted herself with complete decorum but he behaved most strangely and on one occasion he suddenly rose from his knees and looked anxiously around as though he was going to make a bolt for it. The King quickly left his place, went up to his son and told him to kneel down again.

The obvious tension was not relieved when the Archbishop of Canterbury paused while reading the passage, calling upon any persons who knew any just impediment why these two persons should not be joined together in holy matrimony to say so or forever hold their peace, and looked intently at the King and the Prince of Wales. It is more than likely that he had heard rumours of the Prince's marriage to Mrs. Fitzherbert, but in that event only two proper courses were open to him: either to refuse to conduct the ceremony of marriage or to gabble through the dangerous injunction and hope that nothing embarrassing would happen.

Luckily nothing did, and the service ended without incident and the guests went to Buckingham House for the reception, which was later followed by a family supper party. What happened after that is wrapped in mystery, and perhaps it is better so, but Caroline, later describing the wedding night to Lady Bury, told her that the Prince spent it "sleeping under the grate where he fell and where I left him."

Somewhere, sometime during the night, however, it would appear that the Prince managed to consummate the marriage despite his condition—although there were many rumours, though no real evidence, to the contrary—for in nine months' time almost to the day Caroline gave birth to a girl, the unhappy Princess Charlotte. Early next morning the newly weds were heard shouting at each other in the Princess's room, the door was flung open and the Prince, mad with anger and still fully dressed but dishevelled, rushed out and disappeared into his own room.

Two days later they both went to Windsor and from there to Kempshott, a house in Hampshire which had previously belonged to Mrs. Fitzherbert. To take his new wife, the future Queen of England, to spend her honeymoon in the house which had previously belonged to his former mistress and morganatic wife was bad enough, but that was not the only insult she had to bear. Lady Jersey stayed with them, and the Prince when he was not with her spent the rest of the time drinking and gambling with some of his most dissolute friends.

During the first few weeks after their return to Carlton House Lord Malmesbury dined with them frequently. It was hardly surprising in the circumstances that the Princess's behaviour on some of these occasions was not all that could be desired. She had no friends at Court whatsoever and could hardly be blamed for having little or no consideration for her husband's feelings. After one of these dinners at which the Prince of Orange was a guest the Prince of Wales took Malmesbury aside and asked him what he thought of Caroline's behaviour. He admitted that it left much to be desired but told the Prince that the Duke of Brunswick had warned him about it and had told him that she had been brought up very strictly and that it was necessary *de la tenir serrée*. To this the Prince replied that he could see it "but too plainly; but why Harris did you not tell me before or write to me from Brunswick?" Malmesbury said that what the Duke had said was only intended as a friendly warning and that it did not cast "any real slur or aspersion on the Princess." The reason why he had not informed the Prince about this by letter, Malmesbury said, was that he had not been sent to Brunswick "on a discretionary commission, but with the most positive commands to ask Princess Caroline in marriage and nothing more." Nevertheless, he continued, "had I discovered notorious or glaring defects or such as were of a nature to render the union unseemly, I should have felt it as a bounden duty to have stated them but it must have been to the King and to no one else." The Prince seemed to understand this, although with bad grace.

During the next few months there was to be no respite for poor Caroline. In June 1795, only two months after the marriage had taken place, the House of Commons was asked to increase the Prince's allowance to £125,000 per annum, and a Royal Commission was set up to liquidate his debts, which by then amounted to no less than £639,890. It is not surprising that the King told Lord Eldon, the Lord Chancellor, that he felt sure that he would be the last King of England.

It was bad enough for Caroline to realize that the sole reason for her marriage was that the Prince of Wales should settle down to a respectable married life in order that the British Parliament might be persuaded to liquidate the debts of the heir to the throne. Had there been any chance that the marriage would be a happy one this cross might not have been so hard to bear, but she was now tied for the rest of her life to a worthless despicable husband. As she told Lady Charlotte Bury, one of her ladies-in-waiting: "Judge what it is to have a drunken husband on one's wedding day and one who spent the greater part of his bridal night under the grate where he fell and where I left him. If anybody were to say to me at this moment, will you live your life all over again or be killed, I would choose death, for you know sooner or later we must all die, but to live a life of wretchedness twice over—oh, *mein Gott*, no!"

Meanwhile she awaited the birth of her child with mixed feelings which she laid bare in a letter that she wrote to a friend of hers in Germany on 1st December 1795.

I expect speedily to be the mother of an infant. I know not how I shall be able to support myself in the hour of solitude but I trust in the benevolence of Heaven. The Queen seldom visits me and my sisters-in-law are equally attentive. Yet the English character I admire, and when I appear in public nothing can be more flattering than the reception which I meet with. I am surrounded with miserable and evil principles: and whatever I attempt is misrepresented. The Countess[1] still continues here. I hate her and I am confident that she does me no less. My husband is very partial to her and so the rest you will be able to divine.

On 7th January 1796 the child was born amid general rejoicing. Even the Prince of Wales was delighted, not because of any fatherly feelings towards his daughter but because he felt that he had fulfilled his part of the bargain by presenting the nation with an heir to the throne and would henceforth be free to live his own life without having to show, even in public, any consideration for his wife. He lost no time in letting her know this, and sent a message to Lord Cholmondley to the effect that he intended to have nothing more to do with her. She told the bearer of this message that she was not prepared to accept a verbal dismissal and

[1] The Countess of Jersey.

that her husband must put his decision in writing and that if there were to be a separation it must be final. To this he was only too ready to agree and wrote accordingly. Caroline replied on the 6th May as follows:

The avowal of your conversation with Lord Cholmondeley neither surprises nor offends me; it merely confirmed what you have tacitly insinuated for this twelve months. But after this it would be a want in delicacy, or rather an unworthy meanness in me, were I to complain of these conditions which you impose upon yourself. I should have returned no answer to your letter if it had not been conceived in terms to make it doubtful whether this arrangement proceeds from you or from me; and you are aware that the honour of it belongs to you alone.

The letter which you announce to me as the last, obliged me to communicate to the King, as to my sovereign and my father, both your avowal and my answer. You will find enclosed the copy of my letter to the King. I apprise you of it that I may not merit the slightest reproach of duplicity from you. As I have, at this moment, no protection but His Majesty I refer myself solely to him upon this subject; and if my conduct meet his approbation I shall be in some degree, at least, consoled. I retain every sentiment of gratitude for the situation in which I find myself, as Princess of Wales, enabled by your means to indulge in the free exercise of a virtue dear to my heart—I mean charity. It will be my duty to act upon another motive—that of giving an example of patience and resignation under every trial. Do me the justice to believe that I shall never cease to pray for your happiness and to be

Your much devoted
Caroline.

Thus did their marriage come to an end, except in name only, and she can have had no genuine regrets that it was over. From the very first night it had been sheer purgatory. She had been living most of the time under the same roof as one of her husband's mistresses in whose presence and in the presence of many of his friends she was constantly and degradingly humiliated. In his *Memoirs of George the Fourth* Huish gave this description of life in Carlton House:

> It may be looked upon, at this time as a Pandora box filled with treachery and vice. The immediate associates of the Prince, male and female, were persons distinguished for their immorality of conduct, their licentiousness and debauchery. Scenes of the most indecent nature were daily and nightly practised under its roof which, as it was now the residence of a virtuous wife and mother, ought to have been uncontaminated by the presence of the harlot or libertine.

When she complained of what went on to the Queen she was merely told that the Prince had every right to choose his own friends and that it was a constant embarrassment to him that his wife lived with him in London. No wonder Caroline loathed her mother-in-law.

The King, however, who was Caroline's uncle as well as her father-in-law, was extremely upset at his son's treatment of her, and did all he could to maintain the rights to which she was entitled as Charlotte's mother. As he wrote to Lord Eldon, "Caroline's injuries deserve the utmost attention of the King as her own conduct has proved irreproachable." He prevailed upon the Prince to allow Charlotte to remain under her mother's care and this she did until after her eighth birthday.

TWO

Montague House

⤎⤏

In 1797 the Princess of Wales was made to leave Carlton House and eventually to live at Montague House, Blackheath, where she remained until she decided to go abroad in 1814. While living there she became acquainted with Sir John and Lady Douglas, who were frequent visitors. It was through this meeting that the Delicate Investigation came about, an inquiry made by a tribunal composed of a number of the Prince of Wales' friends into his wife's conduct, acting upon a scandalous report made to the Prince by Lady Douglas and her husband in December 1805.

The news of the Princess's separation from her husband soon became general knowledge and the reaction of the people in London was most sympathetic. Wherever she appeared in public she was greeted with cheers and on her first visit to Covent Garden Opera House the whole audience gave her a standing ovation. Something else also happened which must have given her considerable satisfaction, the dismissal of Lady Jersey, whose only comment was that the Prince was a "sequence; King, Queen and Knave." While he was still living with Caroline he had wanted his mistress under the same roof, not that he really cared much for her, but for the purpose of outraging his wife. Now that they had parted all he wanted was that Mrs. Fitzherbert should return to him. Eventually he got his way, but not until she had obtained a ruling from the Pope, of which, incidentally, His Holiness kept no record, that Mrs. Fitzherbert was the Prince's lawful wife and that his marriage to Caroline was not legal.

Once Caroline was installed at Montague House she soon settled down to a more normal life and entertained a large number of friends, although all those who regularly visited her there well knew that by so doing they would lose the goodwill and the patronage of their future King. This does not appear to have worried them unduly, however, for the Prince was generally regarded with loathing and contempt, except by some of his Whig cronies, and there was always the possibility that his excesses would remove him from the scene before he could succeed his father. Lawyers, artists and writers were all frequent guests of the Princess, as well as statesmen and politicians. The Queen and her daughters never visited Caroline but the King often did. Her daughter, Charlotte, was not allowed to live with her, having been moved to Windsor on the Prince's orders. She was, however, allowed to visit her mother once a week.

A German writer, Herr Campe, who, incidentally, translated Daniel Defoe's *Robinson Crusoe* into German, visited the Princess in 1802 and in a book entitled *Travels in England* described the life she led there, and, in particular, the charitable work which was her main occupation. When he was at Montague House one of the things which his hostess showed him with great pride was her large vegetable garden. "This," she said, "is my principal concern. Here I endeavour to acquire the honourable name of a farmer and that, as you see, not merely in jest. The vegetables which I raise here in considerable quantity are carried to town and sold. The produce amounts annually to a handsome sum." But it was the purpose to which this handsome sum was applied which most interested Herr Campe. The Princess "had no court, no officers of state, no chamberlains, and no maids of honour because she had no occasion for them," nor was the money used to educate her daughter or for her own personal expenses but "to educate eight or nine poor orphan children to whom she had the condescension to supply the place of a mother. Her own was the child of the State and, according to the constitution of the country, must not, alas, be educated by herself. These poor children, on the other hand, were boarded by her with honest people in the neighbourhood." Herr Campe then described the charming and affecting scene when the Princess introduced some of her foster children to him. "They seemed," he wrote, "perfectly ignorant of the high rank of their foster mother . . . the sight of a stranger somewhat abashed them but their bashfulness soon wore off and they appeared to be perfectly at home." With her they behaved quite naturally. "People find fault with me," Caroline said, "for not doing more for these children after I have taken them under my care. I ought, in their opinion, to provide them with more elegant and costly clothes . . . but I only laugh at their censure for I know what I am about. It is not my intention to raise these children to a rank superior to that in which they are placed: in that rank I mean them to remain and to become useful, virtuous and happy members of society. The boys are destined to become expert seamen and the girls skilful, sensible, industrious housewives, nothing more."

This charitable work which so impressed Herr Campe was unfortunately soon to land the Princess in a great deal of trouble, for her newly acquired friends, the Douglases, were to become her bitterest enemies.

One of the children who had been introduced to Herr Campe on the occasion of his visit to Montague House was William Austin, who had been born in the Brownlow Street Hospital on 11th July 1802. His father, Samuel Austin, was a dockyard labourer, and as the family were extremely poor the Princess took interest in them and eventually decided to adopt the baby William. The child was brought to live at Montague House where his mother came and saw him whenever she liked. Caroline, however, became very fond of William and treated him just as she would her own child. That was the truth, the whole truth, and nothing but the truth, but in 1806 the Prince of Wales, who since their separation had never ceased spying on his wife in order to discredit her and hold her up to calumny, submitted evidence to a Commission consisting of Lord Erskine, who was then the Lord Chancellor; Lord Grenville, the First Lord of the Treasury; Lord Spencer, Secretary of State; and Lord Ellenborough, that Austin was, in fact, the illegitimate son of the Princess.

Sir John and Lady Douglas, who came to live in Blackheath in 1801, were very friendly with Admiral Sir William Sidney Smith, under whom Sir John had previously served, and just before his departure for Italy and Sicily on an important mission for which he had been specially selected by Nelson, Sir Sidney was living with the Douglases. The Admiral, who was very good company and never stopped talking, principally about himself, was a frequent visitor to Montague House and having been introduced to the Princess of Wales by the Douglases became a great favourite there and she never tired of listening to his rambling reminiscences.[1]

Lady Douglas was of humble origin, being the child of a private soldier and of the illegitimate daughter of a Bath lawyer, and she was, doubtless, flattered when she got to know the Princess and began to be invited with her husband to many of the parties given at Montague House. It later came to the Princess's knowledge, however, that Lady Douglas had said some scandalous things about her and she sent word that in future she would no longer be *persona grata* in the Princess's home. This was very unwise of her as

---

[1] See *Knight of the Sword* by the author, 1964.

she had been warned by many of her friends that Lady Douglas was a dangerous vindictive woman and would leave no stone unturned to try and damage Caroline's reputation. This warning proved to be only too true.

The Douglases, incensed by the ultimatum from Montague House, began a campaign of slander against the unfortunate Princess, who consulted her brother-in-law, the Duke of Kent. A year later the Prince learned of the Duke's visit to Caroline, sent for him, and was then told the whole story. About twelve months ago, the Duke said, he had received a note from the Princess requesting him to visit her at Blackheath in order to assist her in arranging a difficult matter between her, Sir Sidney Smith, and the Douglases, the details of which she would inform him when he called to see her. The Princess told him at their interview that she supposed he knew that for some years she had been on quite friendly terms with Charlotte Douglas but that later she had intimated through a Mrs. Vernon, one of her Ladies, that Lady Douglas's presence at Montague House would no longer be welcome. This had resulted in her receiving a request in the joint names of Sir Sidney, Sir John and Lady Douglas for an audience to demand an explanation of what they considered to be an unwarranted affront.

The Princess, not wishing to be personally involved, had asked the Duke to intervene on her behalf and to take whatever steps he judged best to put an end to the matter. The Duke told her that as he knew neither Sir John nor his wife he could not, in the first instance, address himself to them but, as he knew Sir Sidney slightly, he would, if she agreed, approach him and see whether the affair could be amicably settled. Eventually he saw the Admiral, who told him of the real reason why an audience with the Princess of Wales had been requested. The Douglases had received, Sir Sidney told the Duke, a most scandalous anonymous letter which, from the handwriting and style, Sir John and he were both convinced had been written by the Princess herself. The contents of the letter were not, at this interview, disclosed, though they were later. Knowing, however, the unfortunate effect which the disclosure of this information would have if the facts became public, and the use to which the Prince of Wales would enthusiastically put it, for his own spiteful purposes, the Duke urged Sir Sidney to persuade the Douglases to take no further action and let the matter drop. The Admiral said that it would not be too easy to persuade Sir John to do this but that he would do his best.

A few days later Sir Sidney called on the Duke and told him that he, personally, would do nothing further but that the only promise he had been able, with great difficulty, to extract from Sir John amounted to no more than that "he would under existing circumstances remain quiet if left unmolested but he could not pledge himself not to bring the subject forward hereafter when the same motive might no longer operate to keep him silent."

It did not take Sir John long, however, to break his promise, for soon afterwards he and his wife signed a statement which was eventually handed to the Prince of Wales and formed the basis of the allegations which the Commission were asked to investigate. This document, which was headed "Statement of Lady Douglas" and consisted of more than 20,000 words, was of a most scandalous and defamatory nature and covered the entire period of the Douglases' acquaintanceship with the Princess. The two most serious allegations which it contained, however, concerned the anonymous letter which Sir Sidney had mentioned in his first interview with the Duke of Kent and the entirely false accusation that William Austin was, in fact, the illegitimate child of the Princess of Wales.

It is abundantly clear that Lady Douglas's statement was made at the request of the Prince, probably as a result of information which he had received from the Duke of Sussex who had heard some of the rumours which Charlotte Douglas had been studiously spreading around. He sent for the Douglases, listened to what they had to say with evident relish, and asked them to put it all on paper and "not to spare the horses."

His Royal Highness [the statement begins], having judged proper to order me to detail to him, as heir apparent, the whole circumstances of my acquaintance with Her Royal Highness the Princess of Wales from the day I first spoke with her to the present time, I felt it my duty, as a subject, to comply without hesitation with His Royal Highness's commands: and I did so because I conceived, even putting aside the rights of an heir-apparent, he was justified in informing himself as to the actions of his wife who, from all the information he had collected, seemed so likely to disturb the tranquillity of the country; and it appeared to me that in so doing His Royal Highness evinced his earnest regard for the real interest of the country in endeavouring to prevent such a person from, perhaps, one day placing a spurious heir upon the English throne and which His Royal Highness had a right to fear and communicate to the Sovereign, as the Princess of Wales told me, if she were discovered in bringing her son into the world she would give the Prince of Wales the credit of it, for she had slept two nights in the year she was pregnant in Carlton House. As an English woman, educated in the highest respectful attachment to the royal family; as a daughter of an English officer, who has all his life received the most gracious marks of approbation and protection from His Majesty and from His Royal Highness the Prince of Wales; and as the wife of an officer whom our beloved King had honoured with a public mark of his approbation and who is bound to the Royal family by ties of respectful regard and attachment which nothing can ever brake [*sic*], I feel it my duty to make known the Princess of Wales's sentiments and conduct, now and whenever I may be called upon.

Seldom can such hypocrisy have been put on paper as in the introduction to this statement. Hell knows no fury like a woman scorned and Charlotte Douglas must have derived as much pleasure from writing it as the Prince must have enjoyed reading it. Necessity is said to be the mother of invention but malice can be an even more powerful incentive and in Lady Douglas's statement nothing was left to the imagination. Everything which the Princess said to this woman or in her presence was given a different meaning and twisted in such a way or given out of its context so as to create the impression that she was basically coarse, vulgar, unscrupulous, and completely lacking in morals.

The first intimation she had from the Princess, Lady Douglas wrote, was just after she had been at Montague House at Caroline's request. One evening the Princess arrived at the Douglases' house in great agitation. "I must tell you something," she said to Lady Douglas, "but I am sure you know all the while. I thought you had completely found me out and therefore I came to you . . . I am with child and the child came to life when I was breakfasting with Lady Willoughby. The milk flowed up into my breast so fast that it came through my muslin gown and I was obliged to pretend that I had spilt something and go upstairs to wipe my gown with a napkin."

Lady Douglas said that she hoped the Princess was mistaken as how could she possibly carry such an affair through? No, said Caroline, she was sure of it and these sort of things only require a good courage. "You will be surprised to see how well I manage it and I am determined to suckle the child myself."

It was because she was pregnant, the Princess later explained to Lady Douglas as set out in the signed statement, that she began her charitable work of providing for destitute children whose parents, through poverty, were unable to look after them properly. This was being done as a cover-plan. "When you hear of my having taken children in baskets from poor people," she said, "take no notice: that is the way I mean to manage. I shall take any that offer, and the one I will have will be presented in the same way, which, as I have taken others, will never be thought anything about."

Lady Douglas then asked her how would she be able to conceal the fact of her pregnancy from the outside world and particularly from other members of the royal family, whom she could not avoid meeting from time to time. "That," said Caroline, "would not be difficult." She knew how to manage her dress, and by continually increasing large cushions behind, no one would notice her condition.

A few weeks later, on 13th October, the Douglases received a note from the Princess asking that neither they nor Sir Sidney Smith should visit Montague House for the time being as it was feared that some of the children there had developed measles. From then until her return from Gloucestershire where she had been spending Christmas Lady Douglas never saw the Princess, but on her next visit there was a baby in Caroline's bedroom "asleep on a sofa with a piece of scarlet cloth thrown over her." Here, at last, was the evidence that this evil woman wanted to support what she had been telling everyone for some months past. It is, nevertheless, strange that she could really have believed that her plan to ruin the Princess could succeed. Everyone knew, including all the staff at Montague House, of Caroline's interest in babies and young children as Herr Campe had done. Nor had there been any concealment of the adoption of the Austin baby, it was known to all who were in any way connected with the Princess's household.

Shortly after Lady Douglas's first sight of William Austin she and her husband went to live in Devonshire and it was after their unexpected return to Blackheath, which the Princess had never expected to happen, that the anonymous letter incident arose. Lady Douglas, in her statement, described it in these words:

I now received by twopenny post a long anonymous letter written by this restless, mischievous person, the Princess of Wales, in which, in language which anyone who had ever heard her speak would have known to be hers, she called me all kinds of names . . . such is the spirit of this foreigner, which would have disgraced a house-maid to have written, and it enclosed a fabricated anonymous letter which she pretends to have received and upon which she builds her doubts and disapprobation of me as it advises her not to trust me, for that I am indiscrete and tell everybody that the child she took from Deptford was her own. The whole construction of both these epistles, from beginning to end, are evidently that of a foreigner, and a very ignorant one and the vulgarity of it is altogether quite shocking.

Lady Douglas showed the letter to her husband and he showed it to Sir Sidney Smith and both of them, according to Lady Douglas, were certain that the Princess had written it, but she had not, apparently, yet done her worst:

Her fury became so unbounded that she sought what she would do most atrociously wicked, and inhuman ... she made two drawings with a pen and ink and sent them to us by the twopenny post; representing me as having disgraced myself with my husbands' old friend, Sir Sidney Smith. They are of the most indecent nature, drawn with her own hand, and words upon them in her own handwriting. Sir John, Sir Sidney and myself can all swear point blank without a moment's hesitation, and if Her Royal Highness is a subject amenable to the laws of this country (and I conceive her to be so) she ought to be tried and judged by the laws for doing thus, to throw firebrands into the bosom of a quiet family.

Sir John put the drawings into his pocket and went at once to his old friend Sir Sidney who was as much astonished as Sir John was. He swore that the suggestion was a "wicked calomny" and that the handwriting was, indeed, that of the Princess of Wales.

They demanded an immediate interview with Her Royal Highness but received no acknowledgement, whereupon Lady Douglas wrote as follows to the Princess:

Madam,

I received your former anonymous letter safe; also your two last, with drawings.

I am, Madam,
Your obedient servant,
Charlotte Douglas

Lady Douglas ended her statement by declaring that she and her husband were prepared to confirm all the allegations made in it "if this should be required for His Majesty's further information."

THREE

The Delicate Investigation

ᏩᎦᎦᏤᎦᏤᎦᏤᎦᏤᎦᏤᎦᏤᎦᏤᎦᏤᎦᏤᎦᏤᎦᏤᎦᏤᎦᏤᎦᏤᎦᏤᎦᏤᎦᏤᎦᏤ

WHEN the Prince of Wales decided to leave Caroline and return to Mrs. Fitzherbert he had no intention of letting sleeping dogs lie. His feeling towards the Princess was not merely one of dislike but of hatred and revulsion, and he was determined if possible to humiliate and hurt her. As he read Lady Douglas's statement his hopes must have been raised and he showed it to Lord Thurlow, a former Lord Chancellor, and Sir Samuel Romilly, who advised him to inform the King and to make further inquiries as to whether the allegations made by Lady Douglas were supported by any independent evidence. Other statements were obtained from members of the staff at Montague House and, after studying them and consulting Thurlow, the King appointed a Commission under his Royal Warrant "to inquire into the truth of the allegations accusing the Princess of Wales of guilty intercourse with Sir Thomas Lawrence, Sir Sidney Smith, Captain Manby and others and to report thereon." The proceedings of the Delicate Investigation then began.

Robert Huish, in his *Memoirs of George the Fourth*, wrote this about it:

It is impossible to look back upon the intrigues described, and the character of the actors who played their parts therein, and not form some decided opinion in regard to the number of agents who lent themselves to "this most foul and damnable conspiracy". Men and women of the highest rank; lawyers of eminence; hireling understrappers; even clergymen of honest repute, and the whole of the Prince's Court, without exception, from Lord Moira (who in this business lost "the fame of a thousand years") down to the doorkeeper and the scullery wench, combined to destroy one lone woman, while her husband, rioting in wantonness and voluptuousness, openly or sinisterly encouraged the attacks which had for their end her death on a scaffold. Even the cradle in which her infancy was reared was ransacked for nursery tales, her infancy was slandered, and her puberty corrupted by the inventions of her enemies. By what course of tortuous policy was such a woman selected for the arms of the Prince of Wales? Who advised the connection or what must that man have been who consented to accept it?

The Commission, which for some unexplicable reason held its sittings at 10 Downing Street, opened its proceedings on 1st June 1806 by hearing the evidence of Lady Douglas, when she confirmed in every detail the statement which she had originally made at the request of the Prince of Wales. The first intimation which the Princess received that an official inquiry into her conduct was taking place was when two attorneys arrived at Montague House on the morning of the 7th June with a warrant summoning a number of her household staff to appear before the Commission for examination as witness. They included Frances Lloyd, Mary Ann Wilson, Samuel Roberts, Thomas Stileman, Charlotte Sander and John Sicard. In addition to these witnesses two other members of the household gave evidence, Robert Bidgood and William Cole; the Princess's doctors were also called, and a questionnaire by Lady Willoughby was admitted in evidence.

Bidgood and Cole gave some evidence of having seen Sir Sidney Smith alone with the Princess on a number of occasions quite late at night and Cole said that the Princess had appeared to him to be "too familiar" with the Admiral, but none of the other members of her domestic staff corroborated this evidence in the slightest degree. Sir Sidney was a striking personality and a great conversationalist and the graphic accounts of his campaigns must have brightened up the unfortunate Princess's enforced loneliness. From what has been said of him the gallant Admiral's exploits would have lost none of their glamour in the telling, but once he had opened his mouth it is unlikely that he would have stopped to do anything more sinister.[1]

With regard to the gravest allegation brought against Caroline, namely that she had given birth to a son in Montague House and that William Austin was the child in question, there was not a scintilla of evidence to support what Lady Douglas had told the Commission during her examination.

Bidgood and Cole, whose evidence regarding Sidney Smith was slightly compromising, both stated that they had no reason whatsoever to believe that the Princess was ever in a state of pregnancy. Mary Ann Wilson, who was housemaid to the ladies who attended the Princess, stated that the Princess could not have been "with child" without her knowing it, and the Princess's personal maid, Charlotte Sander, confirmed from her own knowledge that the child, William Austin, was the son of Samuel and Sophia Austin who lived in Deptford and that the baby was brought by the mother to Montague House when he was four months old. The mother identified "Willikins" as her own son and the Registrar of Births produced the entry in the register. The main allegations in Lady Douglas's statement, as repeated in her evidence, were conclusively proved to be a tissue of lies.

Finally the questionnaire which at Lord Spencer's request was put to Lady Willoughby was admitted in evidence. The questions put to her and her replies were as follows:

[1] *Knight of the Sword* by the author, page 115.

Question 1 Does Lady Willoughby remember seeing the Princess of Wales at breakfast or dinner at her house, either at Whitehall or Bechenham on or about the months of May or June 1802?

Answer In the course of the last ten years the Princess of Wales has frequently done me the honour to breakfast and dine at Whitehall and Langley, in Kent. Her Royal Highness may have been at my house in the months of May or June 1802 but at the periods at which I have had the honour of receiving her I have no precise recollection.

Question 2 Has her Ladyship any recollection of the circumstances of Her Royal Highness having retired from the company of such breakfast or dinner on account or under the pretence of having spilt anything over her handkerchief? And if so, did Lady Willoughby attend her Royal Highness on that occasion and what then passed between them relative to the circumstances?

Answer I do not remember Her Royal Highness having at any time retired from the company either at Whitehall, or at Langley, under the pretence of having spilt anything over her handkerchief.

Question 3 Had Lady Willoughby frequent opportunities in the course of that year to see Her Royal Highness, the Princess of Wales and at what periods, and did she at any time during the year observe any appearance which led her to suspect that the Princess was pregnant?

Answer To the best of my remembrance I had few opportunities of seeing the Princess of Wales in the year 1802 and I do not recollect having observed any particular circumstances relative to Her Royal Highness's appearance.

Question 4 Is Lady Willoughby acquainted with any other circumstances leading to the same conclusion, or tending to establish the fact of a criminal intercourse or improper familiarity between Her Royal Highness and any other person whatever, and if so what are they?

Answer During the ten years I have had the honour of knowing the Princess of Wales I do not bear in mind a single instance of Her Royal Highness's conduct in society towards any individual tending to establish the fact of a criminal intercourse or improper familiarity.

In their report to the King the members of the Commission stated that they were happy to declare their perfect conviction that there was no foundation whatever for believing that the child which was then living with the Princess was the child of Her Royal Highness or that she was delivered of a child in the year 1802, nor had anything appeared which could warrant their belief that she was pregnant in that year or at any other period within the scope of their inquiries.

The identity of the child, its parentage, the place and date of its birth, the time and circumstances of its being taken under Her Royal Highness's protection were so established by such a concurrence both of direct and circumstantial evidence as to leave no question of doubt. The child, the report stated, was beyond all doubt born in the Brownlow Street Hospital, on 11th July 1802 of the body of Sophia Austin and was first brought to the Princess's house in the following November. There was no doubt whatsoever about the Princess not having been in a state of pregnancy and the evidence of Lady Douglas on that count was "not entitled to the smallest credit".

With regard to the question of whether the evidence given by four of the witnesses who appeared before the Commission regarding any conduct of Her Royal Highness which, having regard to her exalted rank and station must necessarily give occasion to unfavourable interpretations, should be believed, the report stated that it was not for the members of the Commission to decide, "This was left to His Majesty's wisdom."

The Commission's report, therefore, triumphantly cleared the Princess of all the serious allegations which had been made against her, and in respect of the other suggestions made it placed the ball fairly and squarely at the King's feet.

During the proceedings conducted by the Commission the Princess had, most unfairly, been given no opportunity of giving evidence on her own behalf, and it was only after the report had been submitted to the King that she first learned of the allegations which had been made against her, when a copy of the report was delivered at Montague House by Lord Erskine's footman. Next day she wrote a letter to His Majesty.

In it she politely, but with good reason, complained that the Lord's Commissioners made their report without her being given an opportunity to "exculpate herself". She emphatically protested her innocence and stated that the "scandalous stories of Bidgood and Cole" were as false as the evidence of Sir John and Lady Douglas had proved to be. She reminded His Majesty that the whole of the evidence had been given behind her back without her having any opportunity to contradict or explain anything.

In a second letter, which she wrote five days later after taking the advice of Mr. Perceval who first read the evidence and the Commission's report, she made the following requests to the King which, she hoped he would think, were "reasonable and just to grant".

That she should be given copies of the declarations made by Sir John and Lady Douglas. As they were the basis of the whole proceedings of the Commission and as His Majesty had instructed the Lord Chancellor to send her a copy of the report she felt that she was entitled to "the foundation on which it rested".

That she should be informed "how many accusers" she had, and who they were.

That she should be informed of the date or dates on which the declarations were made.

That she should be entitled to receive "that redress which the laws of your Kingdom (administering, under your Majesty's just dispensation, equal protection and justice to every description of your Majesty's subjects) are prepared to afford to those who are so deeply injured as I have been".

These requests were granted and on 2nd September all the relevant papers were in Caroline's hands. Exactly a month later, to the very day, she sent a letter to the King, over 35,000 words in length, containing a masterly analysis of the so-called evidence given before the Commission which could have left no doubt whatsoever in the mind of any unprejudiced person of its complete unreliability. She emphasized to His Majesty the seriousness of the main allegation preferred against her by Lady Douglas, which amounted to nothing less than an imputation of high treason. With regard to that charge, she wrote, the extravagance of her accuser's malice defeated its own ends, for the Commission completely cleared her of it and specifically stated that Lady Douglas's evidence was not entitled to any credibility whatsoever.

The Princess also protested, with good reason it may be thought, that, having so emphatically cleared her of the allegation that she had given birth to an illegitimate child, the Commission should have listened to what really amounted to little more than malicious gossip and left it to "His Majesty's wisdom" to decide what conclusions should be drawn from it. What the Princess objected to more than anything else, and she made it abundantly clear in this letter, was not the principal charge that was made against her, because the Commission found that it was not supported by any evidence, but what were described in the report as "instances of great impropriety and indecency of behaviour which must occasion the most unfavourable interpretation." "From this opinion," Caroline wrote, "I can have no appeal. For as they constitute no legal crimes they cannot be the subject of any legal trial. I can call for no trial. I can, therefore, have no appeal. I can look for no acquittal. Yet this opinion on this judgement from which I can have no appeal has been pronounced against me upon mere *ex parte* investigation."

The Princess then proceeded to deal with the evidence of Bidgood and Cole in great detail and asked "if there ever could exist a case in which the credit of the witness ought to have been more severely sifted and tried." As she pointed out, they had both lived with the Prince of Wales before he married and were appointed by him to serve with the Princess after the separation. It was surely not beyond the bounds of possibility that these two servants did not consider that they owed the Princess that undivided loyalty which servants of her own choice might have done. There was every reason to believe that they were appointed to the Princess's household for the purpose of spying on her. The Prince was certainly not above doing this.

Had she not, the Princess asked His Majesty, not as Princess of Wales but as an accused person, a right to be thought and presumed innocent until she was proved guilty? In the happier days of her life, she wrote, before her spirit had been lowered by her misfortunes, she would have met such a charge with the contempt which it deserved. She would have defied her enemies to the utmost and have scorned to answer any accusation except a legal charge before a competent tribunal. Nevertheless she now confidently appealed to His Majesty's sense of justice and hoped to be restored to the blessing of his gracious presence. She trusted that he would confirm to her by his own gracious words his "satisfactory conviction of her innocence".

It is difficult to find words strong enough to criticize the members of the Royal Commission for not having reported at once to the King, after they had examined the servants, that the evidence of Lady Douglas was completely unreliable, and the fact that had they done so it would have greatly displeased the Prince of Wales cannot excuse them. Lord Thurlow, whose advice the King took before deciding to appoint a Commission, had warned him that the charges could never be substantiated. It must have been most distasteful to Lord Erskine, who was an upright man, to preside over the Commission, but the only way in which he could have avoided so doing was by resigning. He had only quite recently succeeded Lord Eldon on the Woolsack and he was, moreover, a friend of the Prince of Wales. Nevertheless, it serves to illustrate the difficulty in which a Lord Chancellor may sometimes find himself, being, at one and the same time, head of the Judiciary and a member of the Cabinet.

Having conclusively acquitted the Princess of the allegations made by Lady Douglas it was not in the best tradition of British justice to say that the slanderous suggestions of Bidgood and Cole regarding Sir Sidney Smith and Captain Manby "must be credited until they shall receive some decisive contradiction and if true are justly entitled to the most serious consideration." The Commissioners knew perfectly well that the only way in which these statements could have been satisfactorily contradicted would have been by allowing the Princess to be represented before the Commission, in which event her counsel could have cross-examined the witnesses and she could then have given evidence on her own behalf.

Having regard to the justifiable grounds for complaint which the Princess submitted in her letter to the King it was not unreasonable that she should expect to receive a quick reply. Nine weeks having passed without even a word of acknowledgement she wrote again to the King expressing her surprise at his silence. "Nine weeks of daily expectation and suspense have now passed," she wrote, "and they have brought me nothing but disappointment. I have remained in total ignorance of what has been done, what is doing or what is intended upon this subject." The complete silence was not only torturing her by the suspense, she continued, but her character was sinking in the opinion of the public, who were aware that a report had been made to His Majesty, which though it acquitted her of committing any crime nevertheless made grave imputations against her honour. It was also public knowledge that a copy of the report had been sent to her, that she had endeavoured to answer it and that she was still, after nine weeks, in receipt of no reply. The world, therefore, in total ignorance of the real state of the facts, would soon begin to infer her guilt. The Princess also stated that she understood that a copy of her reply to the allegations had been sent to the Commissioners and she implored His Majesty to urge them to advise him upon it without further delay.

Six weeks later she received a message from His Majesty through the Lord Chancellor. It is more than probable that the King would have liked to dismiss the whole affair as having been a storm in a tea cup but he appears to have felt that had he done so it might have left his profligate son open to still more criticism and the Prince of Wales was, after all, heir to the throne. In his reply to the Princess's long and fervent appeal, while stating unequivocally that the allegations about her pregnancy had been proved to be without foundation, the King stated that there had appeared circumstances of conduct which he never could regard but with serious concern. "The elevated rank which the Princess holds in this country," he wrote, "and the relation in which she stands to His Majesty and the royal family must always deeply involve both the interests of the State, and the personal feelings of the King, in the propriety and correctness of her conduct." He went on to express his desire and expectation that "such conduct might in future be observed by the Princess as would fully justify the marks of paternal regard and affection which the King always wishes to show every part of his royal family."

But what pleased Caroline more than anything else was the paragraph in which the King stated that it would no longer be necessary for him to "decline receiving her into his royal presence." She replied immediately and suggested that she should come and visit him on the following Monday. No such meeting took place and ten days later the Princess received a great shock when a letter arrived from the King stating that the Prince of Wales, after receiving all the documents relative to the Delicate Investigation, which had been sent to him at the King's request, had informed his father that he intended to consult his lawyers and

asked him not to meet the Princess until the Prince had decided
what other action to take.

The Princess was justifiably annoyed and immediately wrote
another letter to the King which was followed a few days later by
a lengthy document pointing out once again how shockingly she
had been treated and expressing the hope that her just requests be
granted without further delay otherwise she would have no
alternative but to disclose to the world, however painful it might
be, and regardless of the consequences, "the circumstances of that
injustice and those unmerited sufferings which these proceedings
and the manner in which they have been conducted have brought
upon me."

Meanwhile Mr. Perceval and Lord Eldon, the former Lord
Chancellor, had taken up the cudgels on poor Caroline's behalf
and made arrangements for what subsequently became known as
"The Book" to be printed privately. "The Book" was to be a full
and detailed account of the Delicate Investigation and was to
include all the depositions and the arguments in the Princess's
defence. Although Perceval and Eldon were Caroline's friends
their motives were not entirely altruistic for they both hoped that
one of the results of its publication would be the fall of the
present Government.

When they heard of the King's sudden change of plans they
took steps to expedite publication, and after waiting three weeks
for a reply to be sent by the King to Caroline's latest letter she
wrote on the 5th March 1807 warning His Majesty that the
publication of "The Book" would not be withheld beyond
Monday next. For the consequences which might follow its
publication, unpleasant and hurtful though they might be to her
own feelings, she would be content to take all responsibility; but
she was convinced that they could not be more unpleasant than
if she were to remain silent. As regards any consequences which
might well be unpleasant to the feelings and interests of others her

conscience would be clear. She felt that she had been extremely patient and had not acted precipitately and had done everything in her power to avoid taking this painful step, but she was not prepared any longer to leave her character or her reputation to the tender mercies of others. A copy of this letter was sent by the Princess to the Lord Chancellor so that both the King and his Government were left in no doubt as to what might happen.

Had "The Book" been published it is impossible to say what the results would have been, but it is not improbable that the persecution of the Princess by the Prince and his friends would have been finally circumvented and the disgraceful episode of the Bill of Pains and Penalties would never have taken place.

The whole situation was changed, however, by the fall of the Ministry of All The Talents when a bill for Catholic emancipation was introduced in the House of Commons. The Duke of Portland then became First Lord of the Treasury, Spencer Perceval was made Chancellor of the Exchequer and Lord Eldon returned to the Woolsack. Caroline's friends were now in power and the Whigs never held office again during George III's lifetime.

So after all "The Book" was never published, except in a limited private edition, because there was no need for it, and the King once more received his daughter-in-law at Court and often visited her at Montague House. This led to frequent protests by the Prince but all his remonstrances on the subject were in vain.

After coming to power the Princess's friends in the new Government, to their great credit, did not forget her and leave matters where they stood, as they might well have done, and on 22nd April a Minute of Council was signed by the Lord Chancellor, the Lord President of the Council (Lord Camden), the Lord Privy Seal (Lord Westmoreland) and seven others, including George Canning who had been a friend of Caroline for some years.

It stated that after the most deliberate consideration of the evidence which had been brought before the Commissioners and of the previous examinations, as well as the answers and observations which had been submitted by the Princess to the King, the Council felt it necessary to declare their decided concurrence in the clear and unanimous opinion of the Commissioners ... that the two main charges alleged against Her Royal Highness the Princess of Wales of pregnancy and delivery had been completely disproved. The Council further submitted to His Majesty their unanimous opinion that all other particulars of conduct to which the character of criminality could be ascribed had also been satisfactorily contradicted, or rested upon evidence of such a nature, and which was given under such circumstances, as to render it in the Council's judgement undeserving of credit. The Council also informed the King that in their opinion there was no longer any necessity for him to decline receiving the Princess into the royal presence and that she should be admitted with as little delay as possible and received in a manner due to her rank and station. The Council even went a step further and suggested that Caroline should be allotted some apartments in one of the royal palaces.

The Princess's triumph was, therefore, complete and the announcement, soon made, that she was to be given apartments in Kensington was received with general acclamation. The public were entirely on her side and all her troubles might well have been over had the King's mental condition not taken a turn for the worse after the death of his youngest daughter the Princess Amelia in 1810.

This so affected him that a bill was introduced in the House of Commons by Perceval, who was now First Lord of the Treasury, proposing that the Prince of Wales should become Prince Regent. The Regency Act was finally passed on 5th February 1811 but the Regent's powers were limited for twelve months in case the King should recover and be able to resume government of the country. The King, however, showed no signs of recovering, and on 18th

February 1812 the restrictions on the Regency came to an end.

In May, however, Caroline's friend, Mr. Perceval, was shot in the lobby of the House of Commons by a man named Bellingham. The latter had formerly been a Liverpool merchant whose principal trade was with Russia, in which country he had been imprisoned for debt. He had appealed to the British Ambassador for assistance but nothing could be done for him as it had been ascertained that he had been lawfully convicted under Russian law. He refused, however, to recognize the legality of his trial and brooded over his imaginary grievance so long that it eventually affected his mind. One afternoon he obtained entrance to the House of Commons and shot the Prime Minister through the heart as he was walking through one of the lobbies. And so, unfortunately for Princess Caroline, Perceval was no longer alive to take her side when further trouble overtook her later.

On 4th October 1812 Caroline went to Windsor to see her daughter. When she arrived at Augusta Lodge, where her daughter was living, the Princess of Wales was denied admittance. She immediately asked to see the Queen which she did but without satisfaction. She was extremely annoyed at her treatment and wrote an indignant letter to her husband.

It was with great reluctance, she wrote, that she found it necessary to interrupt "the more weighty occupations" of the Prince Regent or cause him any uneasiness on a private matter, but it concerned not only her alone but her daughter, who would one day be Queen of England. She felt, however, that the restrictions which only allowed her to see her daughter once a week could only be interpreted as a slur on her own reputation. "There is a point beyond which a guiltless woman cannot with safety carry her forbearance. If her honour is invaded the defence of her reputation is no longer a matter of choice and it signifies not whether the attack is made openly, manfully and directly, or by secret insinuation and by holding such conduct towards her as

Caroline of Brunswick, the unhappy queen

George IV as Prince Regent

"When George IV from earth descended
Thank God the Reign of Georges ended"
—*Landor*

countenances all the suspicions that malice can suggest." She asked the Prince to remove these restrictions and to give her the opportunity of visiting her daughter more frequently.

It was more than a month before Caroline received any acknowledgement of this letter and it was extremely curt and unsatisfactory. She was merely informed that her letter had been read to His Royal Highness who "was not pleased to signify any command upon it."

The Princess was now determined to carry the war into the open and sent a copy of the letter to the *Morning Chronicle* which published the full text. The Prince Regent's reply to this was to suspend for the time being all communication between his daughter and her mother. Before doing so, however, he took the precaution of obtaining the support of the Privy Council to such action and this was conveyed to the Prince in a report signed by twenty-one Privy Councillors who stated that they were of the opinion that under the circumstances "the intercourse between Her Royal Highness the Princess of Wales and her Royal Highness the Princess Charlotte should continue to be subject to regulation and restraint."

That Lord Ellenborough was one of the signatories need occasion no surprise for he was one of the Lords Commissioners who conducted the Delicate Investigation. That Lord Eldon also signed it requires some explanation. What reason had he to change his mind since he put his name to a Minute of the Privy Council in 1807 which not only completely cleared Caroline of the allegations made by Lady Douglas but stated that the rest of the evidence given at the Delicate Investigation was of such a nature as to render it undeserving of credit?

Such a complete volte-face on the part of Eldon can only be attributed to political expediency. In 1807 George III was King not only in name but in fact. By 1813, however, he was *non compos mentis* and his son was Prince Regent. Lord Eldon's eye was, doubtless, looking to the future, and it is not without interest to remember that on the death of George III in January 1820 Eldon handed over the seals to George IV but they were immediately returned to him. Political opportunism, like virtue, sometimes has its own reward. Later when the Bill of Pains and Penalties was introduced in the House of Lords and Queen Caroline appeared at the Bar of the House to answer grave charges Eldon, as Lord Chancellor, presided over the proceedings of the House, but, to give him his due, he carried out this duty with dignity and impartiality, and it has never been suggested, even by his most consistent critics, that he enjoyed the task.

The Princess of Wales, however, refused to be daunted by this latest rebuff and decided to bring the whole matter to the notice of the House of Commons. By this time she had given up her apartments in Kensington Palace and had returned to Montague House, and it was from this address that she wrote her letter to the Speaker.

On 2nd March 1813 the Speaker rose in the House of Commons and stated that he had received a letter from the Princess of Wales which he proposed, with the permission of the house, to read.

In it the Princess informed Mr. Speaker that she had received from Lord Sidmouth a copy of a report made to the Prince Regent by certain members of the Privy Council to whom, it appeared, his Royal Highness had been advised to refer for their consideration certain evidence respecting her character and conduct. This report was of such a nature that the Princess felt certain that no one could read it without considering that it cast most unjust aspersions against her and she thought it would be wrong of her "to acquiesce for a moment in any imputation affecting her honour."

She went on to say that she had no means of knowing upon what evidence the members of the Privy Council based their report, nor had she ever had any opportunity to be heard in her own defence. She felt compelled, therefore, to throw herself upon the House and upon the justice of Parliament and to require that the fullest investigation be instituted into the whole of her conduct during her residence in this country. She had nothing to fear from any such inquiry, however searching it might be, provided that she was tried by impartial judges and "in a fair and open manner such as the law of the land required." Her only desire was that she should either be declared innocent or proved guilty.

After the debate which followed, although nearly all the speakers reaffirmed the complete innocence of Caroline, no positive action was taken.

All this, however, made no difference to the Prince Regent's attitude towards the access he allowed Caroline to their daughter and he still persisted in his refusal to allow them to meet under any circumstances except with his permission.

He never left a stone unturned to poison his daughter's mind about her mother, as is well illustrated by a letter which he wrote on 16th May 1813 in reply to one from Charlotte asking whether she might be given permission to visit her mother on the occasion of Caroline's birthday.

"I cannot express to you," he wrote, "how much delighted I am with your most kind and affectionate letter. I shall not object to your visiting your mother on her birthday but I confide so much in your own discretion and sense of propriety and what you must feel in the delicacy of both our situations at the present moment that you will see how desirable it is to make this merely a morning visit and not to extend it to that hour of the day when you might be subjected to Society which I might not approve of and which consequently I have every reason to rest satisfied that you would not wish to meet . . . ."

What Charlotte thought of this hypocritical warning and advice from her worthless father, whose only interest in his daughter was to insult and injure his wife, we do not know, but she cannot have been totally unaware of his real character: a man whose friends were dissolute and whose morals were unspeakable, a man who was not unjustly described by Justin McCarthy in these words, "the malignant enemy of his unhappy father, the treacherous lover, the perjured friend, a heartless fop, a soulless sot, the most ungentlemanly First Gentleman in Europe whose memory baffles the efforts of the sycophant and paralyses the anger of the satirist." A man about whom Praed wrote the following epitaph:

> A noble nasty course he ran,
> Superbly filthy and fastidious,
> He was the world's first gentleman
> And made the appellation hideous.

What his father really thought of the Prince, although in public for the sake of the rest of the family he did his best to gloss over his son's behaviour, can be seen from a letter which he wrote shortly before the Prince left Caroline to return to Mrs. Fitzherbert:

The professions you have lately made in your letters of your particular regard to me are so contradictory to your actions that I cannot suffer myself to be imposed upon them. You know very well you did not give the least intimation to me or to the Queen that the Princess was with child till within a month of the birth of the young Princess. You removed the Princess twice, in the week immediately preceding the day of her delivery, from the place of my residence, in expectation (as you voluntarily declared) of her labour; and both times, upon your return, you industriously concealed from the knowledge of me and the Queen every circumstance relating to this important affair, and you at last, without giving notice to me or to the Queen, precipitately hurried the Princess from Hampton Court in a condition not to be named. After having thus, in execution of your own determined measures, exposed both the Princess and her child to the greatest perils, you now plead surprise and tenderness for the Princess as the only motives that occasioned these repeated indignities to me and to the Queen your mother.

This extravagant and ungrateful behaviour in so essential a point as the birth of an heir to my crown, is such evidence of your premeditated defiance of me, and such contempt of my authority, and of the natural right belonging to your parents, as cannot be excused by the pretended innocence of your intentions, nor palliated or disguised by specious words only; but the whole tenour of your conduct for a considerable time has been so entirely void of all real duty to me, that I have long had reason to be highly offended with you, and until you withdraw your regard and confidence from those by whose instigation and advice you are aided and encouraged in your unwarrantable behaviour to me and to the Queen, and until your return to your duty, you shall not reside in my palace which I will not suffer to be made the resort of them who, under the appearance of an attachment to you, foment the division which you have made in my family and thereby weakened the common interest of the whole.

In this situation I will receive no reply; but, when your actions manifest a just sense of your duty and submission, that may induce me to pardon what at present I most justly resent. In the mean time it is my pleasure that you leave St. James's with all your family when it can be done without prejudice or inconvenience to the Princess and the care of my granddaughter, until a proper time calls upon me to consider of her education.

G.R.

In addition to preventing Caroline from seeing her daughter and from attending Court receptions the Regent did his best to prevent any distinguished foreigners who visited London from seeing his wife. She was now living at Connaught House, on the north side of Hyde Park, having been evicted by the Prince from her apartments in Kensington Palace on the excuse that he needed them for another purpose. Even some of her close relatives were tactfully persuaded not to call on her.

This petty persecution was resented by nearly everyone, and the Princess's popularity increased at the expense of the Prince who was hissed and booed wherever he went.

The treatment of the Princess has excited almost universal disgust and I am told she was last night received at Covent Garden with unusual applause and "three cheers for an injured woman". The Regent is getting very unpopular again. He passed us yesterday in a very hasty style in the park, going in state with the Life Guards galloping after him, but not a symptom of applause.[1]

It is shameful [Lady Charlotte Bury wrote in her diary] how our Regent is kicking the dust in the poor Princess of Wales's face. There are moments when her wrongs make all her errors forgotten. There is that little vile Prince of Würtemberg, her own nephew, who has never been to see her. White's Club is to give a great ball and fête, and they have given tickets to the Regent that he may invite the royal family and this on purpose to avoid asking the Princess. Was there anything so shameful?

A few days later Lady Charlotte accompanied the Princess to the opera and on her arrival everyone in the pit and stalls turned to the Princess's box and applauded her.

We entreated her to rise and make a curtsey [Lady Charlotte wrote], but she sat immovable and at last, turning around she said to Lady —— "my dear, Punch's wife is nobody when Punch is present". We all laughed but still thought her wrong not to acknowledge the compliment paid to her but she was right, as the sequel proved. "I know my business better than to take the morsel out of my husband's mouth, I am not to seem to know that the applause is for me till they call my name." The Prince seemed to verify her words for he got up and bowed to the audience. . . . In fact the Prince took the applause to himself and his friends—or rather his toadies—for they do not deserve the name of friends, to save him from the imputation of this ridiculous vanity, chose to say that he did the most beautiful and elegant thing and bowed to his wife! When the opera was finished the Prince and his supporters were applauded but not enthusiastically, and scarcely had H.H. left the box, when the

[1] *The Jerningham Letters*, edited by Egerton Castle, 1869.

people called for the Princess and gave her a very warm applause. She then went forward, made three curtseys and hastily withdrew.

On the way home there were demonstrations of the people's goodwill and sympathy for Caroline. When her carriage was passing Carlton House the mob surrounded it and having found out that the Princess was in it they cheered her most enthusiastically. Some of the bystanders opened the carriage doors, insisted on shaking hands with her and asked if they should burn Carlton House. "No my good people," she said, "be quiet—let me pass and go home to your beds." They would not go away and followed the carriage for some distance shouting, "Long live the Princess of Wales, long live the innocent."

It was not only from the ordinary people that the Princess received sympathy and encouragement at this time. The Lord Mayor, Alderman and Livery of the City of London voted an address to H.R.H. the Princess of Wales in which they expressed indignation and abhorrence at "the foul and detestable conspiracy which by purged and suborned traducers, had been carried on against the Princess's honour and life".

Many meetings were held in the principal cities and large towns in the provinces expressing horror at the nefarious treatment of Her Royal Highness and wishing her happiness "at her complete triumph over her enemies".

These widespread demonstrations of public sympathy and goodwill were, doubtless, of great comfort to Caroline, and she must have regarded them as a triumph of truth and justice and a complete vindication of her reputation. As far as the Prince Regent was concerned, the only effect it had was to make him more determined than ever to continue the persecution of his wife. It was clear to Caroline herself that he would never let her live in peace and would not hesitate to use his daughter as a pawn in the game.

This realization, and events which happened during the year 1814, finally led to Caroline's decision to go abroad, contrary to the advice of Henry Brougham, whom the Princess had been in the habit of consulting from time to time since the end of 1810 with regard to her difficulties with the Prince and particularly in respect of her daughter Charlotte. Although, on occasions, Brougham gave Caroline sound advice and his conduct of her defence during the second reading of the Bill of Pains and Penalties in the House of Lords was masterly, there is an abundance of evidence that he was playing a double game. The account given in his own autobiography is hardly borne out by the correspondence on the same subject published in the Creevey Papers which clearly shows that the politicians were determined "to keep the game alive" and to exploit the unhappiness of mother and daughter to their party's advantage.

The first occasion on which Caroline had consulted Brougham was on behalf of her daughter and at her request. Charlotte wished to know where she stood *vis-à-vis* her father; was she entirely subject to his pleasure and control? It was important for her to know this as she was anxious to have her own home and establishment when, in a few years' time, she would be eighteen years of age. Brougham informed Caroline that the Crown had absolute power over all members of the royal family and, particularly, the reigning Sovereign had the exclusive right to direct their education, residence, and guardianship while under age.

During the whole of 1813 the battle over Charlotte went on, and Caroline wrote letters to the Regent and to the Queen her mother-in-law, some of them against the advice of Brougham. None of them made the situation any easier. Charlotte herself, although she was fond of her mother, naturally had no desire, for obvious reasons, to widen the breach between herself and her father, and she was anxious that nothing should be done by her mother which might have that effect. Hearing that Caroline was intending to write yet again to the Prince, Charlotte wrote to Brougham expressing her apprehension. On this occasion, although he had not always felt happy about some of the former letters, he did not think that it would raise any new difficulties in respect of Caroline's access to her daughter. It was in fact quite harmless and contained nothing more than a polite request to be allowed to see Charlotte once a fortnight. He wrote, therefore, direct to Caroline to that effect.

He also took the opportunity, however, to impress upon her the fact that nothing should be done to give her enemies the slightest pretext for throwing the blame on her, and everything should be avoided which could be construed by the Prince Regent's advisers as a disregard of his authority, however painful it might be. In any event it would not be for ever, as in about four years' time Charlotte would be of age and would then become her own mistress.

But there was another matter of even greater importance upon which Princess Charlotte was shortly to ask Brougham's advice, namely her father's wish to have her married. She was convinced, when it was suggested that she should become engaged to a drunken nit-wit, the Prince of Orange, and there can be no doubt that she was right, that the whole object of the plan was that she should live abroad after her marriage and cease to be a political issue.

Her father was bent upon a match and this formed the subject of a lengthy correspondence between Charlotte and Brougham, through her mother, as to what could be done to prevent it happening.

Caroline was also dead against such a marriage taking place, which is not surprising in view of her own experience, but she did nothing to influence her daughter, although she fully supported Charlotte's attitude.

Charlotte was, however, eventually persuaded to become engaged, but she continued to insist that there must be a proviso in the marriage treaty that she should have the right to revisit England "at her own pleasure".

During the summer of 1814, however, the Prince of Orange came over to England to finalize the preliminary arrangements before the marriage could take place, and he soon discovered that all was not well. Lady Charlotte Lindsay, who throughout the negotiations between Princess Charlotte and her father had been the channel through which the Prince's wishes had been conveyed to Brougham, wrote him an urgent letter in July informing him of the latest developments. She had just returned from Warwick House where Charlotte was then living. "The Princess," she wrote, "had been very anxious to see me having become very suspicious that as no arrangements had so far been made for her to have any place of residence in England after her marriage she felt convinced that 'they' intended to play a trick on her and get her out of England once the marriage had taken place." Charlotte had also told Lady Lindsay that she found the Prince of Orange's attitude towards her mother had greatly changed and that he appeared to be on the side of the Regent. Nevertheless, Charlotte was determined to support her mother and felt that they should both remain in England and protect each other.

While this interview was going on in Warwick House the Prince of Orange suddenly arrived, and Charlotte told him then and there that she would not leave England now and would avail herself of the discretionary power which she had been promised would be inserted in her marriage contract.

When Charlotte's ultimatum reached her father's ears he went immediately to Warwick House and told her that she must leave at once and go into residence at Cranbourne Lodge, Windsor, with a new staff of ladies-in-waiting which he had appointed after dismissing her present household. Charlotte received her father's instructions without making a scene and he left for Carlton House delighted with the day's work. He had hardly left the house, however, before Charlotte drove off to Connaught House where she expected to find her mother. On arrival there she was told that the Princess of Wales was at Blackheath.

What happened then has been described by Brougham in the second volume of his autobiography:

> I was in the midst of dinner when a message came to me that I was wanted at Connaught Place. . . . When I got there to my astonishment I found both my hands seized by the Princess Charlotte. . . . I asked by what extraordinary accident I had the honour and pleasure of seeing Her Royal Highness there. She said, "Oh, it is too long to tell you now for I have ordered dinner and I hope it will come up soon." She only added that she had come out of Warwick House alone, and had got into the first hackney coach she could see and had sent to Blackheath for her mother, who arrived sometime after with Lady Charlotte Lindsay. We sat down to dinner and she was in high spirits, seeming to enjoy herself like a bird set loose from its cage.

Brougham, knowing that the Duke of Sussex was dining in the neighbourhood, wrote a note begging him to come along and an hour later he arrived. During dinner several others came to Connaught Place, having been sent there by the Regent, including Lords Eldon and Ellenborough. The Duke of Sussex, not having been sent by the Regent, was allowed to come upstairs but the others were not. "Old Bags" (the name by which Eldon was often called), Charlotte said, "can wait in his carriage".

After dinner Brougham asked Charlotte to tell him exactly what had caused her to leave Warwick House. She told him that she could no longer bear the treatment she met with of changing her Ladies without her consent and of interrupting her intercourse with her mother and she was determined in future to live entirely with Princess Caroline.

Brougham advised her to return immediately to her own home, which upset her very much and she asked him why he refused to stand by her. He said that he was expressing no opinion about her proposed marriage except that she must follow her own inclination entirely but insisted that it was absolutely essential that she should return home and in this her mother, the Duke of Sussex, Miss Mercer (her great friend) and Lady Charlotte Lindsay, for whom she had a great respect and regard, were all agreed. Eventually she consented to go back to Warwick House and the Duke of York, her uncle, who had just arrived, accompanied her home.

Caroline, even before this incident, had already decided to leave England. She could see no end to her husband's senseless persecution and she thought that if she were out of the way it would eventually make it easier for her daughter. Brougham, however, tried hard to persuade her not to go. The advice was, doubtless, good, but it can hardly have been altruistic, for with the Princess away his principal instrument for annoying the Prince Regent would be gone.

George Canning, however, whom she consulted before making the decision, thought it was a wise one and said so. Being himself a Tory it is very probable that he warned her that the Whigs were exploiting her unhappy position for political ends and there was, undoubtedly, some truth in this. There is no reason to suppose that the motives of one of her most constant supporters, Samuel Whitbread, were not genuine. Before she left she wrote and thanked him profusely for all he had done and had tried to do but she said that she had made the decision because it was pitiable to see a child rendered on all occasions a source of dispute between her parents.

Charlotte, on the other hand, thought that her mother's conduct in going abroad at a time when her presence was most needed was "really heartless". Her feelings were understandable but Caroline can surely be forgiven for thinking that with her out of the way the Regent's treatment of his daughter might possibly improve. That it did not, that he shamefully neglected her, is not sufficient reason for blaming her mother, and it is most unlikely that had

Caroline remained in England Charlotte would have been any happier.

As soon as Charlotte heard of her mother's decision to go abroad she asked Brougham to do his utmost to make her change her mind. There was no need for this, for both Brougham and Whitbread were dead against Caroline leaving the country as both regarded the step as being full of danger. Brougham wrote her a letter solemnly warning her of the risks that she ran. He said that as long as she and her daughter remained in England, surrounded by their friends, he would answer for their safety with his head, but it would be quite different if she went, as she intended, to Italy.

As she still seemed quite determined to carry out her plan Brougham decided to make one last attempt to dissuade her and wrote a second letter ten days before she sailed from Lancing. His reason for writing again was that he still hoped that she would listen to his advice and thereby prevent incalculable mischief both to her and her daughter. He reminded her that he had, all along, been strongly against her leaving, but even if she were determined to ignore his advice he implored her not to do anything which might make it appear that she intended to remain abroad for any length of time. There would be no harm in a short tour on the continent of Europe but reports were already being circulated by her enemies that she was intending to take up permanent residence abroad and nothing should be done to encourage such rumours. Brougham assured her once again that as long as she remained in England he would answer for it that no plot could succeed against her, but if she went to live abroad, surrounded by spies, as she would be, ready to invent and swear as they might be instructed, who could say what might happen. Furthermore, the longer she stayed away the less friends she would have.

Brougham seems to have foreseen clearly what might and, in fact, did happen during her absence and, particularly, the damage that would ensue if she were still abroad when the Prince Regent succeeded his father and she became the legal Queen. She would be foolish, Brougham wrote, if she imagined that it would be time enough to return when she saw steps being taken against her. He hoped that what he had presumed to tell her would not cause offence, though he appeared to think that it might, for when he sent a copy of his letter to Lord Grey on the following day he said that it was "a strong dose but necessary" but that "after making her absolutely furious for some time it will do her good".

But Caroline was not offended and Lady Lindsay wrote to Brougham and told him so. "It seems to have struck her very much," Lady Lindsay wrote, "and although it may not make her change her determination of going abroad next Monday it may induce her to hold herself in readiness to return upon any indication of inimical designs from hence. She has written to Canning to desire him to tell Lord Liverpool that if she hears any alarming reports from England her return shall be immediate."

On 9th August she set sail in H.M. Frigate *Jason*. Having arrived at the Stein Hotel in Worthing about 4 p.m., she had then driven with Lady Charlotte Lindsay and William Austin, the boy whose adoption by Caroline in 1806 had created all the scandal that led up to the Delicate Investigation, to Lancing, two miles along the Brighton road, apparently wishing to avoid the large crowd of people who were waiting at Worthing to see her embark. She was not to see England again until almost six years later when she sailed into Dover Harbour on the *Prince Leopold*.

FOUR

The Years of Exile

ᘒᘒᘒᘒᘒᘒᘒᘒᘒᘒᘒᘒᘒᘒᘒᘒᘒᘒᘒᘒᘒᘒᘒᘒᘒᘒᘒᘒᘒ

CAROLINE could not have been more mistaken in imagining that her sojourn abroad would bring her husband's evil machinations to an end. Brougham's prophecy that she would be surrounded by the Regent's spies wherever she went proved to be only too true, and there is reason to believe that she was even being watched from the moment she boarded H.M. Frigate *Jason*. The Duke of Clarence was alleged to have written to *Jason's* captain suggesting to him that his amorous approaches to Caroline would not be unacceptable to her and would be forgiven by the Prince Regent.

It was the captain alone who would be forgiven, for the Prince would not have condoned adultery on Caroline's part. Brougham had warned her, "Depend upon it, Madam, there are now many persons who are waiting for a chance of divorcing you from the Prince." She, herself, was well aware of the dangers ahead, and any indiscretions on her part during her absence abroad were committed deliberately but they were of such a kind that, while they might annoy the Regent if they came to his ears, they could not give him any ground for divorce.

When told by a friend that everything she did was known at

Carlton House she said, "I know it and, therefore, do I speak and act as you hear and see. The wasp leaves his sting in the wound and so do I. The Regent will hear it, you say: I hope he will, I love to mortify him."

Her first stop was at Brunswick where she spent two months staying with her brother, after which she left for Milan, spending a few days in Switzerland *en route*. In 1815 she decided to go and live in Naples. There, shortly after her arrival, something happened which, when it was reported to the King of Naples, was regarded by him as highly suspicious, and he immediately reported it to the Princess as he was not prepared to have such a distinguished visitor spied upon while she was a guest in his country.

One day in December, while Count Macirone was walking through the city in company with a retired British general, Montague Matthew, they met an Englishman who was unknown to the Count but was later identified as a Mr. Quentin, a brother of the colonel of the 10th Hussars, and who was believed to hold some appointment in the Regent's household. General Matthew was later introduced to Quentin and asked him what he was doing in Naples. Quentin told the general, with apparent embarrassment, that he had been sent there by the Regent to buy some horses.

It was considered highly improbable that an Englishman would come to Naples, of all places, for that purpose, and the presence of Mr. Quentin and the reason he had given for being there were immediately reported to the Princess of Wales, but she refused to regard the incident as in any way suspicious.

Meanwhile, however, Count Macirone had reported the matter to the King, who instructed the Chief of Police to keep an eye on Mr. Quentin's movements and this was done. When it was discovered that Mr. Quentin was not the least interested in the purchase of horses the King told Macirone to inform Caroline that should the presence of Mr. Quentin, "or any other possible agent of her persecutors", occasion her the least umbrage or displeasure

The Countess of Jersey, mistress of George IV

Mrs. Fitzherbert, the morganatic wife of George IV

"The Marriage of Mrs. Fitzherbert and George IV": Charles James Fox is holding Mrs. Fitzherbert's left hand and Colonel Hangar's head can be seen between them. Lord North is sitting fast asleep he would at once take steps to have the offender escorted to the frontier and asked to leave. This message was delivered to Caroline by her physician, Doctor Holland. On receipt of it she informed the King that she was completely indifferent to the activities of any persons who, as she was well aware, might be sent from England to spy upon her, as her conduct was such that "it could never with impunity be misrepresented". Mr. Quentin, shortly after this, left Naples horseless and returned to London.

Count Macirone, during Caroline's stay in Naples, got to know her quite well and was often a guest in her house. "No Princess," he once said, "ever existed who so well combined affability and condescension with the reserve and dignity fitting to her station."

It was while she was living in Milan that she first met Baron Pergami who became the Chamberlain of her household. It was he who was later described in the Bill of Pains and Penalties as Pergami alias Bergami, and throughout Queen Caroline's trial he was always referred to, except by the Italian witnesses, by the latter name, doubtless to convey the impression that he was a dubious character. In fact he came from a highly respectable family but when the Princess met him he had lost all his money. He was one of the Knights of Malta and had served on the staff of Lieutenant-General Count Pino in the campaigns of 1812, 1813 and 1814.

About this time Caroline received some very bad news. Samuel Whitbread, who had regularly corresponded with her since her departure, had died and, on hearing of his death, she said, "I have lost one of my best and most zealous friends."

Meanwhile, she had taken a villa on Lake Como and it was while she was there that the first rumours of her misconduct began to reach London. A Mr. Burrell had been staying with her, one of whose servants was named White. When Burrell and his domestic staff left Lake Como to stay in Brussels, White met some servants of the Duke of Cumberland who were in the Belgian capital on their way to England. The servants started gossiping and White told them wild and untruthful stories about what went on in Caroline's villa. When these stories reached the Prince Regent, as they were bound to do, he arranged for the Hanoverian Minister, Count Munster, to organize a network of spies to watch Caroline's movements. Munster did this and put in charge of it Baron Ompteda, who was then the Hanoverian envoy to the Vatican, and no one better could have been chosen, for Caroline knew his family well and the thought that he could be spying on her never crossed her mind. When she arrived in Rome early in 1815 one of the first people she invited to dine with her was Ompteda and while she remained there he was a constant guest in her house, a snake in the grass if ever there was one. It was not difficult, therefore, for the Baron to obey the instructions which he had been given by Munster, "to locate himself as close as possible to the Princess with the object of accumulating such evidence of her doings as can be brought up against her in court." Ompteda wasted no time and within a fortnight of Caroline's arrival in Rome he was sending back to London scandalous fictitious reports based on material supplied by persons whom he had introduced into the Princess's domestic staff. Pergami was chosen to be the villain of the piece and was described by Ompteda in one of his earliest reports as "a sort of Apollo, of a superb and commanding appearance more than six feet tall: his physical beauty attracts all eyes".

Caroline knew perfectly well by then that she was surrounded by spies. In February 1815 she sent a letter from Naples to Lady Charlotte Bury by the hand of someone who she described in a postscript as "a person who never tells the truth: he is a spy of the Cabal". The letter was written in French. "I have been living here", she continued, "since last November and the place is full of spies. They are a wretched lot."

But there was something which Caroline presumably did not know about Ompteda otherwise she would have suspected his bona fides from the beginning. He had disgraced himself in the eyes of his family and of his country when he accepted the appointment as Ambassador of Jerome Napoleon to the Viennese Court when Jerome became King of Westphalia. Ompteda did all he could to corrupt members of Caroline's domestic staff by means of bribes and other promises, but only one of them yielded to the temptation, a German named Maurice Crede. He undertook to arrange for Ompteda to obtain entrance to the Princess of Wales's apartments by supplying him with a set of false keys, but the plan was discovered and she was informed of it. She took the opportunity of dismissing Crede, giving as an excuse an amorous intrigue which had, apparently, been going on for some time between him and Annette, who was one of Caroline's personal maids.

In the hope of being reinstated, Crede wrote to Chevalier Tommassia who was one of the Princess's gentlemen-in-waiting:

I was yesterday dismissed from the service of Her Royal Highness for having intrigued with her waiting-woman Annette. This event, which has thrown me into the utmost consternation, has awakened in my heart a remorse which had agitated me for some time and which I feel a necessity of imparting to you in the hope that you may interest yourself for me and get me to be received again into her Royal Highness's service.

I must then confess that I merit my disgrace since I suffered myself to be seduced by a certain Baron Ompteda to betray the best of mistresses and the most generous of Princesses. It is about a year ago or about a month before the departure of the Princess that the Baron was to take all possible steps to discover where my mistress slept and to endeavour to precure false keys to her apartment. I persisted for some time in refusing to have any concern in this plot but at length the Baron's threats, who told me I was a ruined man if I did not listen to him, together with the money he offered me from time to time, corrupted me and I was weak enough to accept the commission, although fully persuaded that there was no foundation whatever for the Baron's infamous suspicions.

I must say, however, with the utmost sincerity that the guilt of my conduct went no further than answering the questions put to me by Ompteda in the conferences I had with him in which he interrogated me closely upon the situation of the different apartments in the palace as well as concerning the persons who were about the Princess.

Crede ended his letter with a plea that the Princess should be asked to forgive him.

The letter had been written in Como on 3rd November 1816, and with this definite evidence in her possession Caroline informed the Governor, who immediately took steps to banish Ompteda from the Empire. Lieutenant Hownam, who was Caroline's private secretary, challenged Ompteda to a dual, but it never took place, Ompteda accepted the challenge but left Italy the next day. Nevertheless, he still remained in the pay of the Regent until he died in Rome shortly afterwards.

All these efforts to obtain evidence against the Princess which would give the Regent grounds for divorce, however, produced nothing of any substance. In 1818, therefore, the Prince asked the Lord Chancellor to appoint a Commission to set up an office in Milan and to go through Italy with a fine tooth comb for more satisfactory evidence. The task of setting up the Commission was entrusted to Sir John Leach, an ambitious lawyer who had his eye on the Woolsack. He appointed as investigators Mr. Cooke, K.C., Allan Powell, a solicitor, and Colonel Browne, a former cavalry officer. The Commission cost the tax payer more than £30,000, in those days a considerable amount of money, but it produced virtually nothing of any value.

In any event that is what the Cabinet thought, and the Lord Chancellor was given the unenviable task of informing the Prince Regent when the Commission reported in 1819, of their considered opinion.

Meanwhile Princess Charlotte had died in 1817, after giving

birth to a still-born child. When Caroline heard the tragic news she regretted the distance and the circumstances which had prevented her from seeing her daughter after the marriage to Prince Leopold. She was much criticized at the time for her absence, and perhaps she regretted her decision three years earlier to leave England, although it had only been made because she thought that with her away Charlotte's life would be less unhappy.

During the years of Caroline's sojourn abroad her daughter had remained in close friendship with her mother and it had not been thought advisable by the Prince Regent to renew a quarrel which had proved more injurious to him than to his daughter. It was when she was no longer there to take her mother's part that the Commission had been sent to Milan. Brougham, who during Caroline's absence abroad had been continually in correspondence with some of her friends on whom he felt he could entirely depend, was convinced that after Charlotte's death her mother no longer had any desire to return to England and would be quite happy if some arrangement could be made which would ensure her being free from further trouble and vexation. Her wish, Brougham thought, was to be allowed to assume some royal title in the family and, with an adequate income secured, to be in future officially recognized by the British Ambassador in any country in which she might choose to live.

He therefore wrote a letter to Lord Hutchinson, who was a political as well as a personal friend, and was also on intimate terms with the Prince Regent. The contents of the letter Brougham asked Hutchinson to convey to the Prince. Being certain that Caroline would adopt the plan outlined in his letter Brougham purposely avoided any communication with her so as not to commit her definitely and to make it possible for him to stress that i t was only a proposition which he was prepared to put to the P rincess and, at the same time, advise her to give it serious consideration.

Whether or not, had the proposal been at once accepted by the Regent and his advisers, Caroline would also have accepted it cannot be said with any certainty, but the whole position was shortly to be changed by the King's death in January 1820, when Caroline became Queen and the question of recognizing her position as such became much more difficult than if she had still been the Princess of Wales.

It is only fair to say, and Brougham himself readily admitted it, that the Regent was placed in a position of some embarrassment by certain members of the opposition in Parliament calling for an inquiry into the reports which were circulating about Caroline's conduct and declaring that without such an inquiry they would not feel disposed to vote for the suggested increased allowance for her lifetime.

As soon as the news of the King's death reached her, however, Caroline determined to lose no time in returning home so as to reach London before the coronation and assume her rightful station as Queen.

George IV's first reaction on the death of his father was to ask his Ministers to begin divorce proceedings on his behalf, but Lord Liverpool doubted very much whether there was enough evidence to justify such a course of action and warned the King that the Queen would certainly defend such proceedings and would bring counter charges, *which would be supported by ample evidence* and would bring great discredit not only on His Majesty but on the monarchy itself. He suggested a settlement based on Brougham's proposal to Hutchinson that the Queen should be voted a substantial annuity for life on condition that she lived abroad.

After a great deal of opposition the King saw the red light and, withdrawing his threat to change his Ministers or, alternatively, retire to Hanover, gave way. But it was too late, for the ball was now definitely in the Queen's court and it was most unlikely she would let it go. No one doubted for a moment that Brougham's advice to her would be guided by political or personal considerations, perhaps by both. It would probably bring down the present government if he persuaded the Queen to return and claim her just rights.[1]

For a time Brougham was in two minds what to do but he eventually decided to try and sell the Queen's interest for a silk gown. This was refused by the Lord Chancellor, Lord Eldon, who hated him. Lord Liverpool had asked him to inform the Queen about the offer of an annuity but he did not do so until much later and then he advised her to reject it.

The Queen now decided to go to St. Omer, near Calais, and sent word to Brougham asking him to meet her there.

Meanwhile another of Caroline's most consistent supporters had decided to step into the ring, Alderman Sir Matthew Wood, who had been Lord Mayor of London from 1815-16 and then became a Member of Parliament for the City of London. Like Brougham he was a Whig and had supported Caroline from the beginning of her troubles, but in his case the reasons for so doing were entirely altruistic. He had always believed in her innocence of the charges brought against her and despised her husband for the way in which he had treated her.

He now wrote to Caroline and said that he would come to France and meet her in St. Omer, having heard of her intention to go there from his son who later, as Lord Hatherley, was to become Lord Chancellor in the Gladstone Government of 1868. Young Wood had met Caroline while she was living temporarily in Geneva and had joined her household.

So when Caroline arrived at Villeneuve on her way to St. Omer she found Sir Matthew was already there waiting for her. She at once told him of her determination to return to England, assert her rights as Queen and confront her enemies.

While at Villeneuve she wrote three important letters. The first,

[1] See E. L. Woodward, *op. cit.*

addressed to the Earl of Liverpool, asked that a palace should forth-with be prepared for her reception as she intended to leave for London at the earliest opportunity. The second letter was to Lord Melville, who was First Lord of the Admiralty, asking that a royal yacht be sent to Calais to receive her on board. The third was for the Duke of York repeating the two requests made in the other letters and protesting against the way in which she had been treated. The messenger to whom these letters were handed was instructed to return to France as soon as possible and to join the Queen in St. Omer. When she reached St. Omer the messenger had just arrived with news that Brougham hoped to be with the Queen in two days' time. No replies, however, had yet been received from either Lord Liverpool or Lord Melville.

Two days later, as promised, Brougham arrived at St. Omer with his brother James, and Lord Hutchinson. After the Queen had received them Lord Hutchinson told her that he had a proposition from the King to submit to her. She told him, how-ever, that whatever the proposal was she had no intention of giving any answer to it until after her return home and, in any event, she wished to see it in writing.

This placed Hutchinson in a difficult position and he immediately wrote a letter to Brougham explaining that he did not have any proposition in a specific form of words which he could place before the Queen, but he set out in detail for her information the gist of the conversations which he had had with the Prime Minister before leaving for France. These were in substance the same as he was to tell the Queen next morning when he saw her for the second time. He thought it right, however, to warn Brougham that if Caroline were so ill-advised as to return to England that would mean an end to all negotiation and com-promise.

As soon as this letter was handed to Brougham he showed it to the Queen, who was most indignant and asked for his advice.

While admitting that she could not possibly accept the conditions set out in Hutchinson's letter he begged her to consider what conditions would be acceptable. She replied without hesitation, "I shall set out for England. It is in London and London alone that I shall consider any proposals by the King of England."

On the following morning Lord Hutchinson saw the Queen again and repeated the terms of the offer. He also warned her that unless she agreed to those terms and conditions the moment she set foot in Great Britain proceedings would, in all probability, be taken against her.

Caroline listened with mounting indignation and, when Hutchinson had finished speaking, she left the room without saying a word. Shortly afterwards, accompanied by Sir Matthew Wood and her retinue, she left for Calais and about 10.30 p.m. embarked on the packet steamer *Prince Leopold*, her request for a royal yacht having been completely ignored.

Lord Hutchinson was not very pleased with the Queen's reaction to the offer conveyed from her husband and that evening after she had left for Calais he wrote the following letter to Sir Benjamin Bloomfield:

> We arrived here about 3 o'clock yesterday. I saw the Queen for about an hour . . . drank tea with her and left a little after 8. She then appeared calm and collected and I entertained a distant hope that she might be induced to listen to reason. . . . It is impossible for me to print the insolence, the violence and the precipitation of this woman's conduct. . . . I never saw anything so outrageous, so un-dignified as a Queen or so unamiable as a woman. . . . She has set the King's authority at defiance and it is now time for her to feel his vengeance and his power. Patience, forbearance and moderation have had no effect on her. . . . The Queen has thrown down the gauntlet of defiance. The King must take it up.

Strong words indeed, though it is difficult to understand how, bearing in mind the fact that Lord Hutchinson knew all the past

history, he can have been surprised that the Queen appeared outraged when the King's proposal was put to her. Furthermore, it
would have been interesting to ask Lord Hutchinson on what
occasion had Caroline's husband ever treated her with "patience,
forbearance or moderation!"

In any event it was the King and his Ministers who were trying
to bribe Caroline not to return home. There might have been
some justification for Hutchinson's unrestrained tirade against her
had it been she who was blackmailing the King for an annuity of
£50,000 in return for a promise to remain abroad for the rest of
her life.

FIVE

The Queen Comes Home

BEFORE the white cliffs hove in sight news reached Dover that the *Prince Leopold*, with the Queen on board, was already on her way across the channel, news which created some confusion, especially among the military authorities, as to how she should be received. After some consideration, but obviously on his own responsibility, as in those days it was not possible to get in touch with the War Office for orders so quickly, the Garrison Commander, Colonel Monroe, decided to welcome Her Majesty with a royal salute. There was really no other decision that he could properly make, for she was, without doubt, the Queen Consort, and his standing orders were to fire a royal salute whenever a royal personage landed at Dover.

His decision was, at any rate, popular with the local inhabitants, who had heard the news of the Queen's impending arrival and were already thronging the quayside to welcome her. The *Prince Leopold* arrived off the harbour just before 1 o'clock, but owing to the tide was unable to enter. The Queen, therefore, decided to come alongside in a small boat in spite of a heavy swell, and as she approached the beach she was greeted with loud cheers from the thousands who were waiting for her.

The following description of what then happened is taken from a newspaper account of her landing which appeared next morning:

At 1 o'clock Her Majesty put her foot on British ground: the royal salute began to fire and a universal shout of congratulation welcomed her arrival. For a few moments her countenance and manner bespoke considerable agitation: she was visibly affected by the cordial symptoms of regard which welcomed her home, but she soon recovered herself and with a firm step, a composed manner, and a smiling but steady countenance walked slowly along the crowded ranks of the principal inhabitants. Well dressed females, young and old, saluted her as she passed with exclamations of "God Bless Her: She has a noble spirit: She must be innocent". The Queen returned the salutations with the warmest marks of affectionate pleasure and repeatedly thanked the ladies for their expressions of cordial attachment. She appeared in good health, her blue eyes shining with particular lustre, but her cheeks had the appearance of a long intimacy with care and anxiety. She is not so much *en bon point* as formerly and her manner and figure altogether seemed perfectly befitting her exalted station. She was dressed with great elegance. As she moved along, the crowd gathered so fast and pressed so closely around her that she was compelled to take refuge in the York Hotel.

Mr. Wright of the Ship Hotel, seeing that it would be impossible for Her Majesty to reach his house on foot, immediately despatched a handsome open carriage to the York. Her Majesty, Lady Hamilton, and Alderman Wood ascended the carriage: the populace removed the horses and drew it themselves. A band of music preceded Her Majesty and two large flags bearing the inscription of "God Save Queen Caroline" were carried by some of the principal tradesmen. A guard of honour was placed at the door of the hotel, but the people did not seem to relish their appearance, and the Queen observing to Alderman Wood that their presence appeared rather to produce an unpleasant and angry feeling, the worthy alderman suggested the propriety of their going away. After playing "God Save the King" the soldiers retired and the populace seemed highly delighted. Her Majesty observed that although she appreciated, as it deserved, the attentions of the commandment, yet she wanted no guard of soldiers: her firm reliance was on the just principles and cordial attachment of her people. Her Majesty then went to the principal window of the hotel and bowed several times with great grace and sweetness of manner to the happy assemblage.

Next day, before she continued her journey to London, a deputation of the inhabitants of Dover asked for an audience so that they could present her with an address of welcome. The request was granted and the address duly presented. In it the people of Dover offered their heartiest congratulations on Her Majesty's safe arrival, expressed "the highest and most profound veneration and respect" for her, and assured her of "their full participation in every happiness which her return might bring to her."

The same evening the Queen left by carriage for Canterbury and was again loudly cheered by the thousands who had come to line the streets and wish her God-speed. By the time she reached Canterbury it was nearly dark but the news of her coming had spread all over the city and on the outskirts she was greeted by a hundred men carrying lighted torches. Here, also, the streets were lined with thousands of people who cheered her all the way shouting: "Long live Queen Caroline."

After staying the night in Canterbury Caroline began the last stage of her journey to London early next morning, Tuesday 6th June, and it was like a triumphal procession all the way. From Canterbury she was escorted by a number of cavalry officers who were stationed there, until she reached Sittingbourne, and in every village through which she passed the same enthusiasm prevailed. All the shops were closed, everyone left their offices, people streamed out of their houses, all to see the cavalcade pass and to cheer their Queen on her way.

It was expected that she would arrive in London some time during the evening and from three o'clock onwards the crowds began to gather. Through Dartford and Greenwich the procession made its way through cheering throngs, many of whom had been waiting since early morning in the pouring rain. As the cavalcade drove down Shooter's Hill the sun came through the clouds, the carriage was thrown open and a roar of welcome greeted Her Majesty. She was obviously delighted with her reception but, as she later told Lady Anne Hamilton who rode in the same carriage together with Alderman Wood, she had expected no less. She had been of the opinion for a long time that the mass of people were sympathetic to her and rightly resented the treatment she had received from the King during the past twenty-three years. As she drove through the streets of London itself she was greeted everywhere with deafening cheers: none were louder than when she passed Carlton House where the sentries on duty presented arms. When, at last, she arrived at Alderman Wood's house she appeared several times on the balcony and bowed her thanks to the jubilant crowd, which immediately dispersed as soon as she disappeared inside for the last time.

What the King's feelings were while all this was going on is not difficult to imagine. Although Greville, in his *Memoirs*, wrote that His Majesty was in excellent spirits and his Ministers affected the greatest unconcern and talked of the time it would take to pass the bills "to settle her business", he added, "Her business, as they called it, will in all probability raise such a tempest as they will find beyond all their powers to appease; and for all His Majesty's unconcern, the day of her arrival in England may be such an anniversary as he will have no cause to celebrate with much rejoicing."

Brougham knew well that no time would be lost after the Queen's arrival before the battle was on again. He managed to return to London before the Queen got there and said to Denman, "now we are for it". And so they were.

On 6th June, the day after the Queen set foot on English soil, Lord Liverpool in the House of Lords and Lord Castlereagh in the

House of Commons laid on the table the famous "Green Bag" containing copies of the depositions made before the Milan Commission together with a recommendation from the King that they should receive the "immediate and serious attention of Parliament".

After reading the King's message to the House of Lords Lord Liverpool proposed that it should be considered on the following day, when he would move that an address be sent by their Lordships to His Majesty pledging themselves to do no more than adopt that course of proceeding which the justice of the case and the honour and dignity of the Crown would appear to require. He would then move that the contents of the "Green Bag" should be referred to a secret Committee "having for its object to inquire whether any and what course of proceeding should be adopted".

When the King's message was brought to the House of Commons, however, an interesting debate took place. Lord Castlereagh, having made a similar statement to that which had been made in the Lords by Lord Liverpool, and the vote of thanks to His Majesty for his gracious message having been carried, Mr. G. Bennet rose and asked whether a letter which had appeared that morning in one of the London newspapers and which purported to have been written by Lord Hutchinson to the Queen's legal adviser was genuine. If so, Mr. Bennet wanted to know whether Lord Hutchinson had received instructions from the Ministers of the Crown to call upon the Queen of England to lay down her right and title—a right held by the same constitutional securities as that of the King himself—for a bribe of £50,000 a year.

Mr. Bennet would not be convinced of the genuineness of that letter until he had heard it admitted by Lord Castlereagh. Until there had been such an admission he could not believe that any British Minister, without the authority and consent of Parliament, could have dared to call upon the Queen to divest herself of her rightful title for such a bribe, not a bribe to be paid by the King himself, but to be taken out of the pockets of the people of England, who were labouring under the severest distresses, and to be given to a person who, if the statements circulated against her were true, was not only unworthy of being the Queen of England, but of being allowed to place her foot upon its shore.

Lord Castlereagh could only get out of this by saying that in the circumstances he did not feel disposed to answer the honourable member's question but that if he wished he could put down a question the following day when an opportunity would occur for its discussion.

This evasive action by Castlereagh only produced further protests from the opposition. Mr. Beaumont thought that the question asked by his honourable friend was very fair and reasonable and he could only assume from the noble lord's decision not to answer it that the letter referred to was genuine and that His Majesty's Ministers were ashamed to own it.

But that was not the end of it by any means. Mr. Bennet was supported by a number of other speakers and, in particular, by Mr. Creevey, who objected most strongly to the action which His Majesty was asking Parliament to take. Had Mr. Bennet not asked the question which Lord Castlereagh had declined to answer he, Mr. Creevey, had intended to move for the production of the papers connected with the recent negotiation at St. Omer. The Queen of England was to be prosecuted for what? For having dared to set her foot in England? His Majesty, Mr. Creevey said, had the same objection to be in the same country with his Queen which he once had to be in the same drawing-room with her. There was now to be a prosecution founded on the result of an unsuccessful menace and an unaccepted bribe, a bribe offered to the Queen of England to renounce her title.

When His Majesty called upon the House to consider the evidence in the "Green Bag" he was, in fact, asking them to become parties in a private prosecution in which the same person was the accuser, a party, the prosecutor, the procurer of evidence, and might eventually, in the event of a Bill of Attainder, be the judge. Since the time of Henry VIII the House of Commons had not been in the habit of interfering with the Queens of England. They should beware before they now ventured on such a course. They should not, said Mr. Creevey, participate with a Cabinet whose fifteen members had on another occasion forsaken their duty to fight against a single woman. Who was she? The daughter of the Duke of Brunswick, the niece of the late King, the cousin and wife of His Majesty and the mother of the lamented Princess Charlotte. Would anyone believe that had Princess Charlotte lived the House would ever have heard of these proceedings? No one would believe it! Mr. Creevey asked the House to pause and think carefully before they put themselves in such a position in which every future step would involve them in greater difficulties.

Before the debate ended and the House adjourned until Wednesday the 7th, when an address thanking His Majesty for his gracious message was moved by Lord Castlereagh, there was a speech by Denman who eventually represented the Queen in the House of Lords during the passage of the Bill of Pains and Penalties. He made it clear at the outset that he had no intention of discussing the King's message, but he felt that before they adjourned Lord Castlereagh should make one thing clear in justice to the Queen, whose arrival in England had brought about the debate. The accusation against her was at present based on documents and not upon witnesses and was to be referred not to the ordinary tribunals of the country but to a secret Committee. He therefore called upon Lord Castlereagh to tell the House when they met next day *distinctly and unequivocally* what was the nature of the proceedings which it was intended to institute against the Queen.

Denman was followed by Brougham who also had no wish or intention to enter into the merits of the case but, he said, unhappily for everybody, for the parties concerned, for Parliament itself, and for the country, a decision appeared to have been taken by the

Government which rendered silence on the subject no longer possible. The time had now arrived when everyone would be called upon to make up their minds upon this most important question. At this moment, however, he would only say this, that in his opinion H.M.G. would not only have to succeed in proving a strong case against the Queen but would also have to convince Parliament and the country that there was no longer any possibility left of postponing or suppressing the discussion of this question. It must be shown that the mere fact of the Queen's landing in this country rendered all further forbearance quite impossible.

It was then agreed upon a motion of Lord Castlereagh that the "Green Bag" should be kept in the custody of the Clerk of the House until the following day when the House would meet again.

So far things had not gone too badly for the Queen. Her return to England and her journey to London had been a triumph, and in the House of Commons the debate had gone strongly in her favour. Lord Hutchinson in a letter to Sir Benjamin Bloomfield admitted that up to the present time the Queen's tactics had been successful and, he wrote, "We have been entirely out-generalled, the violence and the determination of this woman have made her succeed in all her plans."

On Wednesday 7th June both Houses of Parliament sat again to continue the discussion on the King's message. Lord Liverpool immediately moved that a secret Committee should be appointed to examine the papers relating to the conduct of the Queen. The motion was then agreed to and the House adjourned.

Meanwhile, the Queen had not lost any time in addressing a message to the House of Commons answering what the King had asked the House to do. She informed them that what determined her to return to England was the campaign against her honour which had been carried on for so long by secret agents abroad and latterly by the Government at home on the King's instructions. She was determined to have the opportunity of defending her character and maintaining the rights which had devolved on her by the death of the late King.

She was surprised to discover on her arrival that His Majesty had sent a message to parliament asking it to study the contents of the "Green Bag" and she had since learned with still greater astonishment that it was the intention of Parliament to refer these documents to a secret Committee. It was exactly fourteen years to the day since the first charges were brought against her. She had always shown the utmost readinesss to face her accusers and had pressed for a full inquiry into her conduct. All she now wanted was a public investigation at which she could see both the charges and the evidence brought against her, "a privilege not denied to the meanest subjects of the Realm."

She solemnly protested to the Sovereign, to Parliament and to the country, against the formation of a secret tribunal to examine documents which had been privately prepared by her adversaries. This was a procedure unknown to the law of the land and a flagrant violation of all the principles of justice and she relied on the House of Commons to defeat such a proposal.

The Queen's message was read to the House by Mr. Speaker in profound silence, but there were cheers from both sides of the House in support of her demand for a public inquiry.

Lord Castlereagh then moved that the King's message be taken into consideration. The question for the House to consider was what was most likely to satisfy the ends of justice. It would be for the House to decide, after the Committee had reported, whether the case should be brought before the High Court of Parliament or before the Legislature in the form of a bill. He insisted that H.M.G. had been most anxious to avert this painful issue but could do so no longer.

Castlereagh was followed by Brougham, who said that he regretted the whole business as much as the Leader of the House had done. Nevertheless he was glad that the time had come when this question could be fully and fairly met. The Queen, whose cause he was advocating, had not appealed to the mob. Her appeal was confidentially made to Parliament and to the nation and it was now left to him to ask the House to act with justice. He implored them, above all, to believe Her Majesty to be innocent until the contrary was proved.

And what, he asked, was the so-called evidence which was contained in the "Green Bag". Brougham gave his opinion of it and of the means by which it was obtained and he did not mince his words:

> Letters and papers, with or without names, I know not which, forwarded from beyond the Alps, the result of a Commission sent by God knows who. . . . They were the results of a ten months residence in Milan. A man of high rank and learning who stands high in the profession to which I belong and who, till then, was esteemed by all who knew him, procured this evidence. This expectant Master of Chancery had obtained the contents of the Bag.
>
> That individual, who so far lowered himself to engage in such a transaction, went about prying into all corners and mixing in the lowest conversations to pick up idle and malicious gossip. He had mixed with bargemen on the lakes and ferrymen on the rivers and with the company of cellar men and wine servants. He had taken the evidence of cast-off menials. He had gone to the impure source of every pollution and by such means had the Green Bag been filled.

Brougham then asked Lord Castlereagh and his colleagues how they would like to have their conduct similarly examined and made the subject of a Committee. How would they like to be examined in privacy and darkness on documents procured by the same means as the contents of the "Green Bag", and what, he warned them, could wash out the blemish of such a report. How ridiculous it was to liken the Committee to a grand jury, as the Lord Chancellor had done in the House of Lords. The object of setting-up this Committee was to get confirmed the result of a previous inquiry on which Ministers had already expressed their opinion. Let them act on that opinion without going to a Committee. Let them act on their own responsibility without seeking to shelter behind names more respectable than their own. The procedure, Brougham said, was gross, glaring, and unpardonable and after the experience they had had of "Green Bags" and secret Committees they had little reason to be fond of them.

The Queen had commanded him to call for a full, fair, public investigation. The sooner it started and the more thorough it was, the better she would be pleased. She did not care, however, what the inquiry was called, whether it was a grand jury, a secret committee, a select committee, a private tribunal, or even an inquisition. What's in a name? But she did insist that the body called upon to pronounce an opinion on her conduct must give her the opportunity to hear the evidence against her, see the witnesses who gave it, and confront them by every means in her power.

George Canning, who was then still in the Cabinet although he left it six months later, followed Brougham and replied on behalf of the Government to Brougham's indictment. Canning had been a friend of Caroline ever since the days of Montague House and it was partly due to his advice that she had decided in 1814 to go and live abroad. He had not so advised her because he believed in her guilt "but rather to use his own words, 'faction had marked her for its own', and Canning had declared that in similar circumstances he would give the same advice to his nearest relative."[1]

In the opinion of Brougham Canning, in his reply, acted most honourably "and bore such testimony to the virtues and high bearing of the Princess whose honour was assailed by a husband whose whole life and conduct in the marriage statute had been a barefaced violation of his vows," that the Ministers were forced

[1] See *The Life of George Canning*, by Sir Charles Petrie, 1932, page 138.

to give way and an adjournment was agreed to without a division. It was due to the speech of Mr. Wilberforce, however, that a motion that the House should adjourn until the 9th of June was later carried without a division. He was convinced that there was no member of the House who was not anxious to prevent the investigation proceeding further, if it were possible, for the simple reason that once the step now recommended by H.M.G. was taken there could be no turning back.

The debate was now, therefore, adjourned until the evening of the 9th, but just before it began a communication from the Queen was delivered to the Prime Minister by Mr. Denman, in which she stated that, on the advice of her counsel and several other members of the House of Commons, she thought it proper to inform Lord Liverpool that she was ready to receive any proposition consistent with her honour which he might feel disposed to make on behalf of H.M.G.

She made it clear, however, that she was only taking this step after a great deal of persuasion on the part of her many friends and supporters that it would be in her own interest so to do. Her firm determination, from which she had never wavered, was to challenge her accusers to prove their allegations and to continue to demand the full and unqualified acknowledgement of all her rights as Queen.

Upon receipt of this message just before the debate was to be resumed there was nothing left for Lord Castlereagh to do but to move the further adjournment of the House until Monday the 12th, and this he did. He told the House that he felt it his duty to take this course in consequence of a communication from the Queen which had only just been received by the Prime Minister and the nature of which he did not, at that stage, intend to divulge.

Meanwhile, in the House of Lords a last attempt was being made to avoid taking any action which was certain to lead to trouble in

Parliament and in the country and also to do considerable injury to the monarchy itself.

Lord Liverpool had just moved the Order of the Day calling for the appointment of a secret committee when Lord Kenyon rose to address the House. He wondered whether there might not be, even at this late hour, if not a hope at least a possibility of conciliation, which would avoid the disastrous consequences which would inevitably follow an investigation of the contents of the "Green Bag". He suggested that the House should follow the example set by the Commons and postpone the division until Monday.

This received considerable support but the Prime Minister tried his best to persuade the House to divide without further discussion. He even went so far as to say that nothing had been communicated to him nor had he any information which led him to hold out any prospect of conciliation.

Having regard to the fact that it was to the Prime Minister himself that the Queen had just written to say that she was ready to receive any proposition consistent with her honour, Lord Liverpool was hardly being honest, even by political standards, in failing to disclose the fact that he had received a message from the Queen, although he might have been justified in refusing to give any details as Lord Castlereagh had declined to do in the Commons.

The Prime Minister, was, however, prepared to make one minor concession in order to obtain an immediate division, namely to propose that the Committee should not meet until Tuesday 13th "in order that an opportunity may be given for the possibility of conciliation".

This proposal that the House should proceed at once to appoint the secret committee and then postpone its meeting for one day was hardly a suggestion he can have imagined that the House could take seriously, unless he had a very low opinion of noble lords' intelligence, for, as Lord Carnarvon pointed out, it would have the same effect as the motion which Lord Kenyon was proposing. If the House waited until Monday before dividing, the Committee could still meet on the Tuesday. Nevertheless, the Prime Minister's motion was eventually carried by a large majority.

On the following morning, Saturday 10th June, Brougham and Denman had a consultation with the Queen which lasted for about an hour. Immediately afterwards Brougham received a reply from Lord Liverpool to the message which the Queen had sent to him the previous day. It stated that the Prime Minister had handed a memorandum to Mr. Brougham on 15th April which contained the offer which Lord Liverpool had been instructed by the King to communicate through Brougham to Caroline. Although no reply had yet been received, the letter continued, H. M. Ministers were still prepared to consider any suggestion which the Queen or her advisers might have to offer.

This memorandum had never, in fact, been handed to the Queen, and Lord Hutchinson had gone so far as to tell her in St. Omer that he had no proposals in writing. Nevertheless, the offer made verbally to the Queen by Hutchinson was, to all intents and purposes, the same as that contained in the memorandum, namely that His Majesty was willing to ask Parliament to settle an annuity of £50,000 on the Queen for the term of her natural life, provided she would agree not to set foot *in any part of the King's Dominions* and to assume some other name or title than that of Queen and not exercise any of the rights and privileges appertaining thereto. Should she violate any of these undertakings the annuity would cease forthwith. If she consented to agree to these conditions Brougham was to obtain a signed declaration from her together with full authority for him to conclude a formal agreement on her behalf.

The Prime Minister was informed that the memorandum

referred to in his letter had never previously been shown to the Queen and he wrote next day to express his surprise that this should not have been done.

After an exchange of one or two further useless letters over the week-end a meeting took place between the Duke of Wellington and Lord Castlereagh, representing the King, and Brougham and Denman, on behalf of the Queen, who had suggested that she was willing to leave everything to the decision "of any person or persons of high station and character" agreeable to both the parties concerned with authority to decide the important questions of "residence, patronage and income," subject, of course, to ratification by Parliament.

The Prime Minister's reply to this suggestion was typical of H.M.G.'s attitude to the whole question from the very beginning. After stating that "the King's confidential servants", who ever they might be, could not think it consistent with their constitutional responsibility to advise the King to submit to any arbitration, a matter so deeply connected with the honour and dignity of the Crown, Lord Liverpool went on to say that they were, nevertheless, fully sensible of the advantages which might be derived from a frank personal discussion and were, therefore, prepared to advise the King to appoint two representatives who, in conjunction with a like number to be named by the Queen, could "frame an arrangement to be submitted to His Majesty for settling upon a basis of Lord Liverpool's note of the 11th instant, the necessary particulars of Her Majesty's future situation."

A lot of time and ink would have been saved had this letter never been written. Everybody must have known that it would lead to nothing and was not intended to lead to anything.

During the meetings which took place between the Queen's representatives and the Duke of Wellington and Lord Castlereagh, representing the Government, Brougham and Denman made it clear that the Queen had no insuperable objection to living abroad, and if this were deemed to be indispensable to the completion of an agreement she might be prevailed upon to acquiesce. Nevertheless, in that event, steps would have to be taken to ensure that no inference unfavourable to the Queen's honour and dignity should be drawn from such compliance. One of these steps, Brougham suggested, should be the restoration of her name in the liturgy, to which Castlereagh replied, "You might as well try and move Carlton House!"

The liturgy question put an end to the negotiations and on the following day the House of Commons met in order to be informed of this final breakdown. This was done by Lord Castlereagh, who then moved that the House should adjourn until the 21st so that it could have an opportunity of studying a full report of the negotiations, which would be printed immediately and sent to all M.P.'s

Brougham agreed with what Castlereagh had said about the failure of the negotiations, which he regretted as much as anyone else, but he went on to say that he thought that the whole House would agree, when they had read the report, that there was no reason to blame the Queen for what had happened.

The House having met again on the 21st adjourned once more without doing any business until the next day, when Mr. Wilberforce moved a resolution which was so prolix that he had to explain to the House what it meant, for its real meaning was hidden in a mass of verbiage. The only difference still remaining between the King's representatives and the Queen's legal advisers, he said, were in regard to Her Majesty being publicly acknowledged as the Queen of England in foreign Courts and the restoration of her name in the liturgy. His motion called upon her to waive both these claims and, he asked, would the Queen not go forth without any stigma on her character if she yielded to the wishes and authority of Parliament and after doing so and receiving the gratitude of Parliament would not all imputations against her be removed ? He believed that the dignity of the monarchy would always be greater in proportion to the degree in which they conformed to the wishes and feelings of Parliament.

After the motion had been seconded by Mr. Stuart Wortley an important debate took place. Although a large number of members spoke against it, including Brougham, Denman and Sir Francis Burdett, the resolution was carried by a substantial majority.

Dealing with the unfortunate failure of the recent negotiations, Brougham said that the Queen had, nevertheless, gained something, for the only basis on which she had consented to negotiate at all was that she be fully acknowledged in her rank and title. This had now been conceded on behalf of the King. The only other question which admitted of no alternative was an unqualified recognition of her rights and privileges as Queen. The way in which she was now treated and addressed had greatly altered since her arrival in England. Four months ago, Brougham said, there was no possibility of getting the gentlemen opposite even to mention the name of the Queen. They always took evasive action by using such terms as "illustrious personage", "a person of high consideration", "a great lady", or "a lady of great distinction". That was now changed and one heard nothing but "The Queen", "Her Majesty's dignity", "Her Majesty's honour", and "Her Majesty's rights and privileges".

From Calais to Dover she had to sail on an ordinary packet boat and she travelled from Dover to London in a hired carriage. Now she was to have yachts for the channel, and frigates for the Mediterranean and could travel to and fro as she pleased. Those were improvements in her situation but they were not of tremendous importance. The question of restoring her name to the liturgy, however, was *vital* and it did not become less so even if she decided to live abroad, which it was possible she might wish to do. Her leaving England, however, could be misconstrued while charges still remained hanging over her head without being rebutted.

Both Brougham and Denman considered that were her name restored to the liturgy it would prevent any such misconstruction and that is why they had insisted at the negotiations that this should be done. By placing her name in the liturgy every obstacle would be surmounted and it would be easier to restore it than it was to omit it. It had not only been impolitic to remove it but it was also illegal as there was no law in the country which gave the King power to alter the liturgy by an Order in Council. According to the law, in all prayers relating to the Royal family the names had to be changed from time to time to suit the occasion. When one Sovereign died the name of his successor was substituted, and instead of Queen Charlotte the words Queen Caroline should have taken their place.

The specious arguments used by some of those who spoke in support of Mr. Wilberforce's motion that there was no need for the Queen's name to be inserted as she was "prayed for along with other members of the royal family" were not worthy of those who used them. As Denman rightly said, "If Her Majesty was included in any general supplication it was in the prayer for all those that are desolate and oppressed".

More than anything else Brougham disliked the way in which these preliminary discussions in Parliament were dragging on interminably and he hoped that this would be the last time that they would be discussed. It was high time that it came to an end.

Brougham was supported by Denman who reminded the House of the abominable way Her Majesty had been treated almost from the very moment when in 1795 she set foot in this country for the first time. When George III died while she was in Italy she had not even been informed of his death. This was not due to the fact that the Queen was not easily accessible, for the Milan Committee had been there practically on her doorstep and in regular communication with the Prince Regent and the Cabinet. Her Majesty had been pre-judged and on no occasion had she ever been confronted with the witnesses who made the accusations against her. Not to restore her name in the liturgy would be the final insult.

Sir Francis Burdett, who also opposed Wilberforce's motion, was most scathing in his condemnation of the Government's attitude towards the Queen and left the House in little or no doubt as to who was behind it all. "He who held a threat in one hand and a bribe in the other—what was to be thought of him? The threat was conditional but she rejected the conditions with contempt. Lord Castlereagh had denied that a bribe had been offered." This reminded Sir Francis of a character in a play who was asked by a girl whether taking money was not a bribe, she said, "If you take money first it is a bribe, but if you take it afterwards it is only remuneration." His Majesty's Ministers had acted on this principle but Her Majesty had rejected their remuneration. Then they came down with their "Green Bag". Mr. Wilberforce had said that this Bag contained such abominable disclosures of filth that it must stifle all morality. Sir Francis thought that this was a strange way of keeping up the dignity of the Crown and he believed that the Bag was "as false as it was filthy." "This Pandora's box without hope at the bottom, whether it contained truth or not, should never be opened. An honest Minister would, if he felt a repugnance to any act which his master wished him to perform, say candidly I cannot do it."

At the close of the debate when the Speaker put the question to the House it was carried by a majority of 267 and the House appointed the proposer and seconder of the motion, together with two other members, to "Wait upon Her Majesty and present to her the resolution of the House".

It soon became known all over London that the deputation of the House of Commons would present the resolution to Her

Majesty at one o'clock on Saturday, 24th June. Caroline was still staying at Alderman Wood's house in Portman Street and by midday an enormous crowd had assembled. The whole of Portman Street from the Square to Oxford Street was packed with people, nearly all of whom, with hardly an exception, were openly on the Queen's side and anxious to hear what reply she would give. As the deputation arrived at Alderman Wood's house at about 11.5, Wilberforce and Stuart Wortley, who were riding in the first carriage, were greeted with hisses, boos and groans.

Brougham and Denman, who were already with the Queen when the deputation arrived, had decided what attitude they would adopt. They were resolved to give no advice whatsoever and to leave it entirely to her as to whether she would agree or refuse. They both thought it essential that they should take this course because, if she had acted on their advice, it would, in their opinion, have completely destroyed the effect of her determination, and they also felt certain that if they had advised her to comply with the desire of the Commons and leave the country, some of her "violent and secret advisers", as Brougham described them in his autobiography, would have said that although she wished to remain in England and meet the grave charges which were brought against her, her official legal advisers Brougham, Denman, and Lushington were the cause of her going. Brougham doubted very much whether, if they gave such advice and the Queen followed it, they would escape the fury of the multitude. The Queen tried hard to persuade them to advise her but they resolutely declined, saying that the decision was for her to make and not for them: they were merely her legal advisers.

Brougham was most anxious that she should say "Yes" and accept the proposition contained in the Commons's resolution, for that would have saved him from "a most laborious and irksome duty". He also did not want her to have to face the consequences of an inquiry, although he was fairly confident that she had no reason to be apprehensive so far as the result was concerned. What he was afraid of was that she would be persecuted even more than before if she emerged from any inquiry or investigation completely vindicated.

The Queen's advisers withdrew, after the deputation had presented her with the resolution, so that she could come to a decision without them. Later they were called in and told that she would refuse although she would have liked to have their opinion.

When the Queen's refusal was handed to the House of Commons' deputation they expressed their regret and immediately left for Westminster, as the House had decided, for once, to sit on a Saturday so that they could receive Her Majesty's reply.

When the news of her refusal was announced to the waiting crowd outside it was greeted with loud cheers and shouts of approval. As the deputation left the House to enter their carriages there was much booing and hissing and they only narrowly escaped violence.

After the four M.P.s had driven away and Brougham and Denman, who were well received by the crowd, had followed them, there were calls for the Queen, who appeared on the balcony to acknowledge the cheering, which lasted for several minutes.

The text of Caroline's message was as follows:

I am bound to receive with gratitude every attempt on the part of the House of Commons to interpose its high mediation for the purpose of healing those unhappy differences in the royal family which no person has so much reason to deplore as myself. And with perfect truth I can declare that an entire reconcilement of those differences, effected by the authority of Parliament on principles consistent with the honour and dignity of all parties is still the object next to my heart. I cannot refrain from expressing my deep sense of the affectionate language of these resolutions. It shows the House of

Commons to be the faithful representative of that generous people to whom I owe a debt of gratitude that can never be repaid. I am sensible, too, that I expose myself to the risk of displeasing those who may soon be the judges of my conduct. But I trust to their candour and their sense of honour confident that they will enter into the feelings which alone influence my determination. It would ill become me to question the power of Parliament or the mode in which it may be exercised. But however strongly I may feel the necessity of submitting to its authority, the question whether I will make myself a party to any measure proposed must be decided by my own feelings and conscience and by them alone. As a subject of the State I shall bow with deference and, if possible, without murmur to every act of the sovereign authority. But, as an accused, an injured Queen, I owe it to the King, to myself, and to all my fellow subjects, not to consent to the sacrifice of any essential privilege or withdraw my appeal to those principles of public justice which are alike the safeguard of the highest and the humblest individual.

The disappointment of the Government at the Queen's refusal was profound and genuine, unlike the King's, for he was bent only upon some action which would expel his consort from England never to return. All he wanted was his Bill of Pains and Penalties, including a divorce clause. H.M.G., however, and Canning more than any of them, had only one desire—to see the whole business ended once and for all.

The Queen's rejection of the advice of Parliament had definitely closed the door to further negotiations and the Government could no longer delay proceeding with the investigation by the secret committee which the House of Lords had already appointed.

Realizing that there was no time to lose, the Queen's next move was to send a petition to the Lords appealing strongly against the measures to be taken against her and demanding that she be heard by counsel at the Bar of the House.

The petition informed the House that she was perfectly ready,

George Canning

Charles James Fox

The interior of the House of Lords during the trial of Queen Caroline, 1820

as she had always been, to meet every charge affecting her honour and she called for a complete investigation of her conduct, but not a secret inquiry. She could not suppose, however, that the House of Lords would commit such a travesty of justice as to authorize a secret examination of her conduct, in the absence of herself and her counsel, while her defence must rest on evidence abroad which for some weeks could not be available in this country. When such evidence arrived the Queen would ask the House to proceed in any way they might think consistent with the ends of justice. Meanwhile, and before the first step was taken, she desired to be heard by her counsel at the Bar of the House of Lords immediately.

As soon as the petition from her had been read by the Clerk at the table of the House Lord Dacre, who had presented it, moved that counsel should be called in. The question being put by the Lord Chancellor and agreed to without opposition, Mr. Brougham, Mr. Denman and Mr. John Williams appeared at the Bar and Brougham addressed the House on the Queen's behalf and explained his position. The application being made, he told their Lordships, must not be understood to be, in the vulgar sense of the word, an application for delay of the prosecution or of the judgment, but the Queen was entitled to expect and to request that she would receive a fair and equitable investigation at their Lordships' hands. Her Majesty and her counsel had a right to know what proceedings were about to be instituted in both or either of the Houses of Parliament. The Bags laid before both Houses were said to contain evidence to support charges against the Queen's conduct whilst resident abroad. What was not known, however, was the nature of the evidence or how it had been "raked together" except that a great deal of it had been procured beyond the Alps and the Appenines and it would, therefore, be physically impossible to produce the necessary evidence for her Majesty's defence within at least six weeks. The more innocent the Queen was, Brougham said, the more abominable, base and treacherous the witnesses to testify against her were, the more essentially necessary did it become that she should have available those witnesses and documents which she was quite confident she could get to overwhelm her opponents with confusion.

There was another factor, Brougham said, which made her defence more difficult. Practically every one of the witnesses who would be called to support whatever charges might be brought against her were foreigners with whom the obligation of an oath might be diminished by their belief in the efficacy of subsequent confession. Counsel did not hesitate to say that it was his firm belief that not one of their Lordships would fail to tremble with apprehension if his wife or daughter were to be exposed to the testimony of such a cloud of witnesses. Furthermore, Her Majesty was not in a position to compel the attendance of those who could speak in her favour: they could not be subpoenaed. They could refuse to attend and she had no power to force them.

All he asked, Brougham said, was that the House would not proceed to hear the case in a manner which must inevitably lead to the condemnation of any individual however innocent. Her Majesty must be given time to bring forward her witnesses. Brougham was followed by Denman, and the Earl of Liverpool then moved that the petition should be considered next day in order that they might have twenty-four hours to deliberate on the powerful arguments which had been submitted by counsel.

The House met again, therefore, on the Tuesday evening, when Earl Grey made a last effort to stay the proceedings of the secret committee by moving that the order already made for its appointment be discharged. After a long debate, however, his motion was defeated by a majority of fifty-five.

The proceedings of the House of Lords on these two fateful days had been closely followed all over the country and a series of meetings was held throughout the length and breadth of the land for the purpose of presenting addresses of sympathy and support for the Queen. But the die was now cast, and only seven days were to elapse before the Bill of Pains and Penalties was introduced in the House of Lords by the Prime Minister.

SIX

Pains and Penalties

ᐤᐤᐤᐤᐤᐤᐤᐤᐤᐤᐤᐤᐤᐤᐤᐤᐤᐤᐤᐤᐤᐤᐤᐤᐤᐤᐤᐤᐤᐤᐤᐤᐤᐤ

ON WEDNESDAY 15th July the House of Lords met, the main business on the Order Paper being the first reading of the bill which was presented to the House by the Prime Minister.

He said that even were it possible for him to retrace the steps he had so far taken he did not know of any other course he could have adopted than that which had finally been decided upon. Although the Bill could not be considered a bill of divorce in the ordinary sense of the word, its effect would be the same. When it had been read to the House by the Reading Clerk a copy would be sent to the King and to the Queen and the first question then to be considered would be whether to fix a date for the second reading immediately or to postpone such decision for two or three days in order to ascertain the wishes of their Majesties.

The whole subject was of the utmost importance, the Prime Minister went on, and called for a dispassionate inquiry. It was satisfactory to reflect that no similar case had arisen during a period of two hundred years, except in the instance of one individual who never came over to this country. There had not been a Queen during that time against whom even a whisper of shame had been raised to affect her character or sully her reputation. The question now was, if the allegations were proved to be true, whether impunity should be extended to guilt or justice be allowed to triumph.

It was most improper of the Prime Minister to say this at that stage of the proceedings unless he was also prepared to say that it was a long time since there had been such a profligate and debauched King as the present one, and that there had, perhaps, never been a King of England more worthless.

The preamble of the Bill which was then read by the clerk was as follows:

BILL TO DEPRIVE HER MAJESTY CAROLINE AMELIA ELIZABETH OF THE TITLE, PREROGATIVE, RIGHTS, PRIVILEGES, AND PRETENSIONS OF QUEEN CONSORT OF THIS REALM, AND TO DISSOLVE THE MARRIAGE BETWEEN HIS MAJESTY AND THE SAID QUEEN.

The Bill alleged that the Queen had conducted herself both in public and in private with indecent and offensive familiarities with Bartolomo Pergami who was engaged in her service and had carried on with him a disgraceful, licentious and adulterous intercourse to the great scandal of the royal family, and that she should, therefore, be wholly deprived of the style and title of Queen Consort and that the marriage between His Majesty and the Queen should be dissolved and annulled.

Lord Grey objected to the way in which the Bill had been drafted. Instead of making general accusations without any specifications of time and place, these should have been clearly stated to enable the Queen to meet the charges. He wished to know whether any more particular details of the offences would be laid before the House and was it intended to supply Her Majesty with a list of the witnesses by whom she was accused?

To this the Prime Minister replied that after the close of the case for the prosecution time would be given to Her Majesty to enable her to rebut the evidence adduced against her.

Next day about noon Sir Thomas Tyrwhitt, who held the office of Black Rod in the House of Lords, and who had been commanded by the House to deliver a copy of the Bill to Her Majesty, waited upon her. She entered the room where he was and received the Bill graciously. "I am sorry that it comes so late," she told him, "for twenty-five years ago it might have been of some use to His Majesty. But as we shall not meet again in this world I hope we shall in the next," and then she paused for a moment, "Where justice will be rendered me."

She then asked Black Rod to convey these sentiments to the King if ever he got the opportunity. Sir Thomas had not seen Caroline since the time when she and the King were still living together and he said, later, that he would never forget what she said to him until his dying day.

He had scarcely left the Queen's presence when a deputation arrived from Westminster headed by Sir Francis Burdett, who had made such a moving speech in the House of Commons during the debate on the Queen's message. The deputation brought with them a loyal address from the citizens of the City of Westminster, for which she was most grateful and handed them a long reply. The address would long be treasured in her memory, it stated, as a lasting proof of their regard. The last occasion on which she had received the sympathy and understanding of the people of Westminster was at the time of the Delicate Investigation, which they truly described as "a nefarious conspiracy against her honour".

The people of England almost universally on that occasion considered the outcome of the investigation as a triumph of rectitude and innocence over perfidy and falsehood. Now new and even more appalling efforts were being made to destroy her character, but she was delighted to find that those same people felt that she was entitled to have her reputation unsullied until she had been proved guilty.

On Monday 17th July the House of Lords met again, when

Lord Liverpool moved that the Bill should be read a second time on 17th August. There was no opposition to this, although Lord Grey said that he thought that the Queen should be given sufficient time to prepare her defence.

Lord Holland told the House that he could think of no reason why the names of the witnesses should not be disclosed and, if possible, copies should be made available of the precise evidence that would be offered. The ends of justice could not properly be met unless the necessary information was given to the Queen's legal advisers and sufficient time allowed for them to examine the evidence.

Even Lord Erskine, the former Lord Chancellor, who had presided over the Committee of the House which had carried out the Delicate Investigation agreed that Her Majesty ought to have the advantage of knowing who the witnesses were so that their character and antecedents could be inquired into. That appeared to him to be essential in the interest of justice. The motion, however, was carried without a division.

The Prime Minister was obviously determined that there should be a maximum attendance when the House was to reassemble on 17th August, for he moved a resolution, which was passed without a division, that no peer should absent himself on that day or any other day during the passage of the Bill without leave of the House, "On pain of incurring a fine of £100 for each day's absence, unless he was over seventy years of age, sick, or had been abroad since the 20th of July and was still away, or was overseas on His Majesty's Service or on account of the death of a parent, wife, or child." The Lord Chancellor was ordered to write to every Peer acquainting him of this resolution. The Government certainly meant business.

Between the day on which the Bill had its first reading and the date fixed for the second reading Caroline received numerous addresses and messages of good will and encouragement from nearly every part of the country. From Poole, Newbury, Shaftesbury, Newcastle, Bedford, City of London, Rochester, Morpeth, Wakefield, Ilchester, Sunderland, Lewes, Berwick, Canterbury, Norwich, Kirkcudbright, most of the London boroughs and one signed by 7,800 women from the town of Nottingham. All of these, without exception, assured Caroline of their sympathy and their thoughts for her during the trying days which lay ahead. The women of Nottingham wrote, "All in whom the spirit of the days of chivalry is not utterly extinct, all who would not immolate the best impulses of their nature on the altar of modern policy will rally around their Queen and save her alike from foreign enemies and spies and domestic persecutors."

On Thursday 17th August the House of Lords in its legislative and quasi-judicial capacity met to resume their proceedings on the Bill of Pains and Penalties, better known as the Trial of Queen Caroline.[1]

At 8.30 a.m. the Lord Chancellor, Lord Eldon, arrived and took his seat on the Woolsack and at 10 a.m. the roll of peers was read and several were excused on various grounds. The three Roman Catholic peers, the Duke of Norfolk, the Earl of Shrewsbury and Lord Petre, were excused on account of their religion. The Duke of Sussex, to his credit, obtained leave of absence because of the ties of consanguinity which existed between him and the parties so intimately connected with the Bill. The Duke of York, his brother, however, said that if anyone had stronger claims than another to ask for leave of absence he was that person, but he did not intend to allow any private feelings to deter him from doing his duty, however painful it might be. He had obviously received the family Whip!

[1] Although the proceedings in the House of Lords were not a trial in any legal sense and no criminal charges were, in fact, preferred against the Queen, in the account of the proceedings which follows they will frequently be referred to, as a matter of convenience, as "the trial".

As the names were being called the shouting of the crowd waiting outside in Palace Yard announced the Queen's arrival. Since the early hours of the morning thousands of people of every kind had been assembling in the streets leading to the Houses of Parliament. Shortly before ten o'clock the sound of cheering from the direction of Charing Cross gave the crowds waiting outside the Houses of Parliament warning of the Queen's approach. Along the whole of the route from her house to Parliament Square she was greeted with tumultuous cheers and they were never louder than when she passed Carlton House, where the sentries on duty spontaneously and, in all probability contrary to orders, presented arms and were loudly cheered by the crowd for the compliment. The sentries outside the Admiralty and the Horse Guards did the same, only the guard outside the Treasury took no notice of her.

At the entrance to the House the Queen was received by Black Rod and Brougham, who escorted her to the waiting-room which had been provided for her. As she entered the Chamber by the passage leading from the robing-room the peers rose to receive her. When she was seated the Earl of Liverpool moved that the Order of the Day for the second reading of the Bill be now read, and the Duke of Leinster, who had previously given notice, moved that the same order be rescinded, but on a division his motion was defeated by 206 votes to forty-one.

When the Prime Minister rose a second time to propose that counsel should be called and heard in support of the Preamble of the Bill there was a lively debate during which the "inexpediency and mischievous nature of the Bill" was argued by a number of peers, one of whom stated that the House of Commons shared this view as they had declared that whatever the result of the proceedings they would be "injurious to the best interests of the Empire."

As many peers expressed a doubt whether, as the alleged

adulterous intercourse had been committed abroad with a foreigner, it exempted the Queen from the consequences of the statute of Edward III relating to high treason, the judges present were asked to decide "whether, if a foreigner owing no allegiance to the Crown violates the wife of a King of England in a foreign country and she consents to such violation, she thereby commits high treason within the meaning and true construction of the statute of Edward III."

The judges retired and returned after an absence of twenty minutes, whereupon the Lord Chief Justice gave the House their unanimous opinion that "such an individual, under such circumstances *does not* commit high treason within the meaning of that Act".

Counsel were then called upon to appear at the Bar and Brougham addressed their lordships and advised them against proceeding any further with the Bill. His first reason for objecting was on the grounds that the Bill was private law introduced in a particular case for the punishment of an individual. It was a mode of procedure known unhappily in the jurisprudence of all countries but never resorted to without producing a deep sense of its hateful consequences and its utter repugnance to every sound principle of jurisprudence and he gave the House several historical illustrations. In this case Her Majesty was gravely prejudiced by this form of procedure. Had impeachment been resorted to in this instance she would have been furnished with some specification of the charges, or at least they would have been set out in greater detail as to the various points of the accusation. Perhaps also a list of witnesses could not then have been withheld and the Queen would have had all the advantages of a real judicial proceeding.

In this case, however, the charge was not any illegal act and the whole proceeding was legislative and not judicial. For this reason Brougham felt bound to discuss the expediency, as well as the justice, of this prosecution. What was the impelling and overruling necessity (he did not say motive for that might be guessed) which alone could justify this measure? The question at issue was not between man and wife but between King and Queen, and the promoters of this Bill delayed until they thought that at least she was deprived of one protection. If she had been brought before the House when Princess of Wales, and charged with offences alleged to have been committed in that capacity, no one could deny that a bill of divorce from her royal husband would have been the remedy and that divorce could only have been obtained on the usual terms. All the preliminary forms would have had to be observed, the party claiming the bill would have had to come to the House by petition, and he would have come in vain if he had not done so *with clean hands*. But here the promoters of this Bill waited until the Queen had lost her status as Princess of Wales and then said "we will proceed against her for offences alleged to have been committed while she was, in fact, Princess of Wales"; thus taking special care not to take any action while she still possessed those rights against her husband which every ordinary wife enjoys.

Counsel then dealt with the question of why it was argued by the Government that the passage of this Bill was a matter of public necessity because the Queen had been guilty of "improper familiarity". She was charged with licentious and adulterous conduct which, the Government stated, made it absolutely necessary for Parliament to intervene. Brougham appealed to the many Bishops present and asked them a direct question. Is adultery considered a crime only when it is committed by a woman? And he then proceeded to ask them another question, whether the Crown could be dishonoured, the fame of the country tarnished and the morals of the nation put in jeopardy if an adulterous intercourse is proved against a lady when that which he (Brougham) ventured to call adultery, because the exalted person himself had confessed it to be so, has actually been committed by a Prince. Counsel said that he regretted having to say this but he was forced to do so because it was, in truth, an answer to this case.

Whatever Parliament might think of it Counsel was sure that the good sense of the nation could not be deceived. "He is a man," the people will say, "who wishes to get rid of his wife. He talks of the honour and safety of the country, yet its dearest interests, its peace, its morals and its happiness are to be sacrificed to gratify his desires." The only way to judge the sincerity of what men professed was to look at their conduct. Who had encouraged the Queen to go abroad? Who had opposed the advice given to her by her friends, including counsel himself, that they would answer with their heads for her safety while in England but that when abroad she would be surrounded by spies and informers? The persons who had encouraged her were those who were now lined up against her, with a Green Bag of documentary evidence in one hand and this bill of degradation in the other, and they had done everything they could to encourage the Queen to stay abroad. She was warned not to come back and, in case that was not enough to deter her from returning home, she was to be bribed to stay away.

As Brougham sardonically put it, she was to be given a large income to enable her to be wicked on a large scale. All levity, all indiscretion, even adulterous intercourse was to be pardoned or condoned on one condition, namely that she would never come back. *Bearing all that in mind how could any sensible man believe that H.M. Ministers in their heart of hearts really supported the Bill?* It would never have seen the light of day if the Queen had turned back from St. Omer after the meeting with Lord Hutchinson, and it was only after she landed at Dover that anyone began to think of "national degradation".

Before he sat down Brougham told their Lordships that the fact that the secret Committee had reported in favour of this action being taken did not bind the House from taking a different view. "He is the greatest of all fools," Brougham said, "who consults his apparent consistency at the expense of his absolute ruin. The sooner you retrace the step into which you may have been led in an unwary moment the greater will be the service you render to your country. If you decide that the Bill ought not to proceed you will be the saviours of the State and, indeed, promote the substantial welfare of the kingdom and the trust and honour of the Crown".

The House then adjourned until the following day, when Denman was also heard in support of the Queen. He ended a powerful speech by telling the House that the Queen had demanded a proper trial with the opportunity of herself denying the charges. The Bill was no alternative and was calculated only to bewilder and betray. The public viewed it with the gravest suspicion.

Before the House adjourned until Saturday the 19th, both the Attorney-General and the Solicitor-General spoke on behalf of the Crown. Theirs was not an easy task and their speeches made little impression on the House. When the Solicitor-General sat down Brougham was given an opportunity of being heard a second time. He maintained, once again, that there were no public grounds for these proceedings. There had been no public inquiry until their Lordships decided to act on the recommendation of the King's Ministers and the whole proceedings had for their foundation nothing but rumour. He said that he did not wish to enter into the realms of recrimination but he felt some relief in knowing that in so doing he had only acted in the discharge of his professional duty.

Lord King then moved a resolution to be debated when the House reassembled on the following day: "That it is the opinion of this House that it is not necessary to the public safety, nor the security of the Government to pass this Bill".

When the House met next day, the third day of the trial, Lord

King's motion and a similar one by Earl Grey, both of which advised the House not to proceed further with the Bill, were defeated by substantial majorities. The Attorney-General then outlined the evidence to be given in support of the charges set out in the Bill.

The Attorney-General said that the adulterous intercourse was alleged to have been committed by the Queen with Pergami, his real name, but which the Attorney-General insisted throughout the entire proceedings was Bergami for reasons which have already been suggested.

Bergami, he told the house, at the time he entered Her Majesty's service was without employment but she appointed him as her courier. Three weeks later the Princess of Wales, as she was then, left Rome and went to live in Naples. With her was the boy whom she had adopted, named William Austin, who, Lady Douglas had told the Committee which conducted the Delicate Investigation, was her own illegitimate child.

Having regard to the fact that the Delicate Investigation Committee had found that there was no truth in Lady Douglas's accusation whatever, it was extremely dishonourable for him to have mentioned the allegation without making it clear to the House that it had been dismissed as a palpable lie in the report which the Delicate Investigation Committee had submitted to George III. The fact that he did so shows to what extent the Government and their legal advisers were prepared to go.

The Attorney-General then told the House that, until the move to Naples, Willikins, as Caroline used to call him, had been in the habit of sleeping in her bedroom. On the first night spent in her new home the same arrangement continued and Bergami was allotted a bedroom at the other end of the house where all the domestic staff had their quarters. Next morning, however, they learned with some surprise that in future Bergami was to sleep in another room, from which there was a communicating passage leading to the Princess's room, and Willikins was, in future, to have a bedroom of his own. She explained that this was because he had now reached an age when it was no longer becoming for him to sleep in her room.

On the following evening the Princess returned home late, having been to the Opera House, and went straight to her room where her maid, Louisa Demont, was waiting for her. Louisa was given strict orders that Austin was not to be admitted to her room that night, and she then saw the Princess go in the direction of the room assigned to Bergami and, as she did so, she told the maid that she could go as she would not be needed any longer. This young woman thought that her mistress's behaviour was rather extraordinary and became highly suspicious, for on entering the Princess's bedroom it was evident that the bed had not been slept in. It was equally apparent that two persons had been sleeping in Bergami's bed.

From then onwards the servants noted a marked change in his attitude to the other members of the staff. He became "more haughty and assumed an air of great importance". They were also struck by the fact that the Princess and Bergami always rose at the same time each morning and had breakfast together in a room which was "completely secluded from the rest of the family", and the Princess was frequently seen walking arm in arm with him on the terrace in front of the house.

Shortly afterwards a servant was engaged to wait on Bergami, and this man, who slept in a room close to that which was occupied by his master, had stated on a number of occasions that he saw the Princess, after the other servants had retired for the night, walking stealthily and with great caution from her own to Bergami's room, which she entered and in which she remained for a considerable time. On one occasion while the Princess was in Bergami's room, his servant heard noises which convinced him that the Princess and "her lover" were kissing each other.

During the whole period during which the Princess was living in Naples, which was from November 1814 to March 1815, this intimacy continued and evidence would be called, the Attorney-General said, to prove it. It would also be proved that at that time Bergami was still a married man and this aggravated the charge now made against Her Majesty. It was not merely adultery but double adultery.

From Milan, the Princess moved to Venice and by this time only one member of her entourage was of English nationality, Mr. Burrell, and after he left, a month later, the Princess became more familiar with all her servants and she frequently played cards with them.

It must have seemed strange that the Attorney-General should mention this and he appears to have realized it for he hastened to add that he was not suggesting that this amounted to an offence but that it was a "circumstance arising out of her infatuated and licentious attachment". This clearly showed how little the Attorney-General really knew about the Queen, who was always extremely sociable and courteous and a very kind and considerate mistress. It also demonstrated, beyond doubt, how slender was the case against the Queen and how the prosecution had to clutch at every straw.

On leaving Venice, the Attorney-General told the House, the Princess returned to Milan and while she was there paid a visit to Mont St. Gothard, and Bergami went with her. *En route* they stopped for lunch at an inn in Vannes where the couple spent the afternoon, according to one witness, in one of the bedrooms. As this happened in the daytime the Attorney-General suggested that there could only be one reason for this.

The following night the Princess's party slept in Borromeo, which she had visited on a previous occasion, when she was, not unnaturally, given the best bedroom that the hotel could offer. It was only reasonable to expect that on her second visit there she

Count Pergami, alias Bergami

Henry Brougham in 1810

Queen Caroline returning from the House of Lords, 1821

would occupy the same room and it was, in fact, the Attorney-General said, offered to her but she did not take it. It did not, however, have any means of communication with any other room and the Princess, on this occasion, chose another much smaller room which happened to have a door adjoining the room in which Bergami spent the night. Their Lordships, the Attorney-General said, would presumably draw their own conclusions from that. Was it not obvious that she took care on that occasion that his room should be near hers for no other reason but to afford the means of carrying on that intercourse which, according to the evidence already mentioned, had been going on for some time? The Attorney-General continued to give many more instances of this kind until the House adjourned, when he said he would finish his opening speech on the following day.

When the House met on the fourth day of the trial the Attorney-General continued his summary of the evidence which he would be calling later. On 8th April 1816, at Salma, an incident happened which the Attorney-General was satisfied would remove from their Lordships' minds any doubts, if any still remained, about the adulterous intercourse between Bergami and his mistress. A large bed was provided in an inner room in the hotel for the Princess, while in an outer adjoining room which was assigned to Bergami there was no bed. It would be proved in evidence that on the morning after she had slept there her bed had the appearance of having been slept in by two persons. The only way into the Princess's bedroom was through Bergami's. In any ordinary case, in a court of law, the Attorney-General said, this would be sufficient proof to a jury that the "crime of adultery" had been committed that night.

For at least another hour more incidents of this kind were submitted by counsel as evidence to support the most serious charge set out in the Bill's preamble, but before he sat down he dealt with the comments by his learned friends (Brougham and

Denman) about the unsatisfactory way in which the evidence had been obtained and the doubtful reputation of the witnesses who had supplied it. It was the fault of Her Majesty if the facts could not be proved except by Italian witnesses. Her conduct, and the nature of the case made such evidence inevitable. It would be for the House to assess its value.

The Attorney-General announced that he would now call his witnesses. Before he could do so, however, Lord King wanted to know whether they would be liable, if it appeared that any of them had committed perjury, and could they be brought to trial; to which the Lord Chancellor replied that although the present proceedings were a little unusual (a typical British understatement if ever there was one) it was his opinion that this could be done.

Before the first witness was called to the Bar the Queen, who had not been present during the Attorney-General's opening speech, entered the House accompanied by Lady Anne Hamilton and took her seat in a chair within a few feet of the Bar in such a position as to enable her to confront the witnesses.

The Solicitor-General then called the first witness, Theodore Majocchi, and as soon as the Queen saw him take his place before the Bar she exclaimed in a piercing voice, according to the reports which appeared next morning in all the daily papers, "Theodore, Theodore!" Many peers and spectators who also heard her, however, were under the impression that what she called out was, "*Tradidore, tradidore!*" (Traitor, traitor!)

Whether she said Theodore or *tradidore* is of some consequence because of the use that was subsequently made of the incident by the prosecution to suggest that the Queen's reaction on seeing Majocchi enter as the first witness was a sign of her guilt. It is more reasonable to infer, however, and more consistent with the evidence given by this witness in the course of his cross-examination, that his treachery and ingratitude to a kind and indulgent mistress so mortified her as to provoke her into calling him a traitor.

One commentator on the trial compared the Queen's reaction to that of Julius Ceasar when he saw his old friend Brutus among his assassins, and quoted the famous lines from Mark Antony's funeral oration:

> For when the noble Caesar saw him stab,
> Ingratitude, more strong than traitor's arms,
> Quite vanquished him: then burst his mighty heart. . . .

The Solicitor-General then asked permission for the Marchese Nicolas Spinetto to be sworn in as an interpreter. He was then asked who had appointed him and replied that he had received his instructions from Mr. Planta of the Foreign Office and Mr. Maule, solicitor to the Treasury. Brougham told their Lordships that those were two sufficient reasons for his asking for a second interpreter to be sworn and this application was agreed to and Binetto Cohen was sworn in as interpreter on behalf of the Queen.

The Solicitor-General surprised everyone, when he began his examination of Majocchi by calling Pergami by his proper name instead of using the name Bergami as the Attorney-General had done throughout his opening speech. This was, presumably, because otherwise none of the witnesses would have known to whom he was referring.

Majocchi told the House that he first met Pergami in 1814 in the house of the Princess of Wales when he entered her service as a "livery servant or lackey". At that time Pergami used to have his meals at the table of the upper servants with Mr. Sicard, and the room in which he slept was close to the Princess's bedroom and was connected with it by a small corridor leading through a tiny closet. This was the same Sicard who had been in Caroline's service at Montague House and had given evidence in the Delicate Investigation.

Shortly after Majocchi began his employment on the Staff of the Princess, he said, Pergami was kicked by a horse and was confined to bed for a few days, during which time the witness slept in the closet at the far end of the corridor. On two occasions while he was sleeping there the witness saw Her Royal Highness pass through the corridor leading to Pergami's room during the night. She did so very quietly and as she passed the witness's bed she stopped to see whether he was awake or asleep and then proceeded to enter Pergami's room where she remained for about a quarter of an hour during which time he could hear them whispering.

This sounded most unlikely and a murmer of disbelief was heard throughout the House. At this stage an argument took place between the Solicitor-General and Brougham as to whether other witnesses should be allowed to remain in the House during the examination of a witness before they had themselves given evidence. Exclusion of witnesses was the general practice in all courts of justice and Brougham had no doubt that it would be adopted by their Lordships. The Lord Chancellor agreed that it should be done.

When the Solicitor-General said, in reply, that he hoped that Brougham would take equal care to ensure that his witnesses would also be excluded Brougham retaliated by saying that if all the Crown's witnesses were only going to give the kind of evidence which he had so far heard from Majocchi the defence would not bother to call any witnesses, at which there was much laughter.

Majocchi then described the sleeping accommodation at the hotel in Venice, but all he was able to say was that the bedrooms in which the Princess and Pergami slept were at opposite ends of a large drawing-room and that while they stayed in the hotel the Princess dined with him at the same table. When they moved from Milan to a villa on the shores of Lake Como the witness used to make Pergami's bed each morning and on some occasions it did not appear to have been slept in.

This evidence was exactly the opposite of what the Attorney-General had stated in his opening speech would be proved by his witnesses, namely that it was the Princess's bed which had not been slept in whereas there were signs that two persons had slept in Pergami's bed.

The examination of this witness continued until the end of the day's proceedings when the House adjourned until 10 a.m. the following day, but it was all extremely trivial and unconvincing. During his evidence the Queen spent most of her time in her waiting-room but when she left in her carriage and drove through St. James's Park and Hyde Park she was again greeted with loud cheers from the crowds who were waiting to see her pass.

The fifth day of the trial opened with the further examination of Majocchi, but nothing of any importance was elicited from him. He was supposed to be the Crown's chief witness, the mainbrace of its case, but his evidence had been very disappointing and in some particulars it had fallen far short of what the Attorney-General had predicted the evidence would be. If Majocchi were not believed that was an end of the case.

Now it was the Queen's turn and it did not take Brougham very long to demolish this witness entirely. He began with a preliminary skirmish, being guided chiefly by the first answers he received and by Majocchi's demeanour as a witness. After this had revealed weak spots in the enemy's defence, and there were plenty of them, the attack could begin.

As Brougham wrote in his autobiography,

I went to work as cautiously as possible, and after dealing with other topics I remembered an expression he had dropped in the former part of my cross-examination. It seemed to give me an opening and I went back and got an answer which made me quite secure. I indicated my sense of the advantage I had got by some gesture, which alarmed Denman who whispered words of caution; but I felt secure and then poured question after question into him and got him to repeat his *"non mi ricordo"* as often as I chose. The story among us was that my rising taller at the first opening the man gave me, put them in mind of the Duke of Wellington at Salamanca when he discovered that Marmont had left an opening in his line; and certainly the defeat of the Bill turned very much upon Majocchi's cross-examination. I mean the defeat as regards the opinion of our case by the Lords; for our strength against the Bill lay in the general demurrer which all men . . . made, namely that, admit everything true which is alleged against the Queen, after the treatment she has received ever since she came to England her husband had no right to the relief prayed by him and the punishment he sought against her.

Quite early in his cross-examination Majocchi began to give the answer "I don't remember" to almost every question. Brougham went through all the evidence the witness had given about the juxtaposition of the bedrooms, but whenever he tried to get a few more details they were very rarely forthcoming.

In the Princess's house in Naples where did William Austin sleep?—I do not remember.

Will you swear that he did not sleep in the next room to Her Royal Highness?—This I cannot remember.

What was the room next to the room in which Her Royal Highness slept?—I have seen no other [room].

Where did Doctor Holland, Her Royal Highness's physician sleep?—I do not remember.

Where did Hieronimus sleep?—I do not remember.

Where did Sir William Gell's servants sleep?—I do not remember.

Where did Louisa Demont, the maid, sleep?—I do not know.

Where did the other maids sleep?—I do not know.

Did you ever see Her Royal Highness go into Sir William Gell's room when he was ill?—I do not remember.

Or into Hieronimus's room?—I do not remember.

This was the same witness who remembered every detail about

the Princess and Pergami; where their bedrooms were, who slept in which bed, what arrangements were made at the various hotels where they stayed so that their rooms could be close together, how and when they breakfasted together and in what state of dress or undress. All these details which were, doubtless, contained in the Green Bag documents, had obviously been studied and learned by heart.

As the cross-examination proceeded the position became so farcical that after a series of *"non mi recordo"* the interpreter said that he found it most difficult to make himself understood. "The witness," he said, "is so confused."

At five o'clock the House adjourned with Majocchi still under cross-examination. He had had a gruelling time and when he left the witness stand he must have known that no one was prepared to believe him any longer.

On the sixth day of the trial, the Lord Chancellor having taken his seat on the Woolsack, Brougham renewed his cross-examination, during which twenty-nine questions were asked of the witness, of which fifteen were answered in the following words: "I do not know; I do not remember; I cannot recollect; I am not sure."

After a short argument between a number of peers, the Lord Chancellor and the interpreter about the correct translation of *"non mi recordo"*, Brougham was told that he could continue. He told their Lordships that he did not intend to question the witness further. "In this case," he said, "I have certainly no reason to ask him a single further question."

Very soon after the Solicitor-General had begun his re-examination of Majocchi the Queen, accompanied as usual by Lady Anne Hamilton, entered the Chamber. The peers rose and her Majesty bowed in return. She was noticed to be looking remarkably well. She took her seat near the Bar and followed the proceedings closely.

The re-examination did not take very long and it accomplished nothing. It was impossible to rehabilitate this witness in the eyes of the House and it might have been better if the Solicitor-General had declined to re-examine. He took great care, however, to ask questions which he felt quite certain Majocchi would not be likely to answer with the parrot cry of *"non mi recordo"*.

The Lord Chancellor then asked whether there was any noble Lord who had any questions to ask of the witness at the Bar. Several peers did ask questions and some of them were awkward and very much to the point. They certainly indicated that the majority of peers had already dismissed the evidence of the Crown's chief witness as unreliable.

At the close of the proceedings on the sixth day of the trial the Government and their Law Officers must have been more than somewhat depressed. With the exception of Louisa Demont, who was still to come, Majocchi was intended to be the most damaging witness against Caroline, but Brougham's cross-examination had destroyed his credibility and there was nothing the prosecution could do about it.

What the King felt that evening nobody knows, but he also had put complete faith in Majocchi as a witness and had actually received him at Carlton House on the very day of his father's funeral, so anxious was he to meet the man who was to rid him of Caroline.

Thomas Creevey, who attended the proceedings regularly, wrote daily about it to a friend and these letters provide an interesting running commentary of the scene. "Nothing," he wrote, "can be more triumphant for the Queen than this day. The truth is the Law Officers of the Crown are damnably overweighted by Brougham and Denman."

The effect on the general public of Majocchi's failure was also tremendous. From then on the King's witnesses, whose expenses must have cost the country many thousands of pounds, were called by everybody *"Non mi recordos"*.

On the seventh day of the trial only two witnesses were called but their evidence carried the case no further. One of them was Vincenzo Garguilo, who was master and owner of the *Palacca* in which Caroline had made her cruise around the eastern Mediterranean, when she was supposed to have allowed Pergami to take a bath in her cabin although not in her presence. The other was Francisco Birollo, who had been a cook in the Princess's household for about two years.

Immediately after Garguilo had finished his evidence and before Birollo began his, an application was made by Brougham to have Majocchi recalled immediately. Counsel said that he was making the application in consequence of a letter which he had just received. This had been written by a Mr. John Marsh of Gloucester to his friend Mr. Watts who lived in London. On receipt of the letter Mr. Watts had taken it to Alderman Wood who at once sent it to Brougham. The letter read as follows:

Gloucester, 23 August.
I know you to be a well-wisher of the Queen. The first witness called against her, I have every reason to believe, is a man who lived with Mr. Adam Hyatt, who brought him over from Italy. He always spoke in the highest terms of Her Majesty and said he had been offered a considerable sum of money and a place for life if he would appear against her. I can find very creditable people in Gloucester to whom he told this. I request you will make known these circumstances to Alderman Wood and some person may be sent from London to make the necessary inquiries here.

John Marsh

Brougham told the House that he wished to cross-examine Majocchi on this one subject only and the first question he wished to put was whether the witness had been in Bristol in the course of the last twelve to fourteen months. After a short argument the

Lord Chancellor advised their Lordships to allow the Queen's Attorney-General to cross-examine Majocchi, who was then called to the Bar. Although in the second half of this renewed cross-examination there were more than a few *"non mi recordos"* the answers to some of the questions were quite illuminating, and the first part of the cross-examination is, therefore, set out in full.

Were you or were you not at Bristol last year or in the course of this year?—I do not know this Bristol.

Were you at Gloucester?—Gloucester I know very well.

Were you in the service of a gentleman of the name of Hyatt?—Yes.

Did you ever declare to any person that the Princess of Wales was an excellent woman?—Yes, that the Princess was a good woman.

Did you ever declare that the conduct of the Princess was highly becoming?—Of her conduct I always said that she was a good woman but was surrounded by bad people.

Did you ever say that she was a prudent person and that you had never observed anything improper in her conduct?—*Non mi recordo.*

Did you ever say that the Princess of Wales behaved with propriety?—This I have never said.

Did you ever represent the Princess of Wales to any person in a stage coach as a much injured woman?—This I remember no more no than yes.

Majocchi consistently refused to admit, however, that he had ever told anyone that he had been asked to give evidence against the Queen and offered money and a permanent situation if he would do so. "I will lay down my life," he told Brougham, "if this be true." It is not surprising that he drew the line there, for he must have realized that the consequences of such an admission might be very serious.

25th August, the eighth day of the trial, was no better for the Government's supporters of the Bill than the sixth day had been. Captain Pechell and Captain Briggs, two British officers, were called and it was expected that their evidence would be most damaging to the Queen. The King's friends had for a long time been boasting about the evidence which Sir John Leach, who was in charge of the Milan Commission, had been collecting from various British officers.

Thomas Creevey, in one of his letters to Miss Ord, written after the House adjourned on the 25th, referred to the failure of these two officers to come up to the Crown's expectations:

> Our matters, so far in the day, stand much better than they did at the close of yesterday. The two Captains, Pechell and Briggs have been called and, so far from proving anything against the Queen, they have distinctly sworn there was not the slightest impropriety in the conduct of the Queen during the period she was on board their ships.
>
> The fact of Pergami having come the first time as servant and afterwards sitting at table on board one of those ships was, of course, proved; but everybody knew it before and it does not signify a damn. . . . The discovery of this day, viz that Captains Briggs and Pechell were to be the only English witnesses produced against the Queen, was most agreeable and unexpected to me because of a conversation which had passed between the Duke of Wellington and myself on the subject. The night after I made my speech in the House of Commons . . . I saw the Duke at the Argyle Rooms, who, with his usual frankness came to me and said: "Well Creevey, so you gave us a blast last night. Have you seen Leach since?"
>
> Then we talked about the approaching trial with the most perfect freedom, and upon my saying that foreign evidence would find very few believers in this country, he said, "Oh, but we have a great many English witnesses—officers."

The next witness called was Pietro Cuichi, who was supposed to prove, amongst other things, that when the Princess was staying at an inn in Trieste of which Cuichi was the landlord, her bedroom and that of Pergami were only separated by the dining-room into which both bedrooms led.

What Cuichi did not say, however, was that before Pergami could reach the dining-room he had to pass through another bedroom in which his sister, Contessa d'Oldi, slept. Nor was the Contessa called to say that during the night she had seen her brother pass through her room on the way to the Princess or vice versa.

The next witness called was Barbara Kress, who before her marriage had been a chambermaid at the Post Inn at Karlsruhe and remembered the Princess staying there and occupying a bedroom which had a communicating door to the dining-room. One evening, at about seven, Kress had to go to Pergami's room with some water. She entered the room, which was not locked, and saw Pergami in bed and the Princess sitting on the edge of the bed. Pergami had his arm round the Princess's neck. She noticed that it was white and she agreed with the suggestion that this could probably be explained by the fact that he was, at the time, wearing a shirt. The Princess, however, was fully dressed and when the chambermaid entered she jumped up.

At this stage of the evidence the interpreter explained that the literal translation of what the witness had just said was that the Princess "got up, or rose", which was not quite the same thing. This led to a long argument about the efficiency of the interpretation and it was suggested that the second interpreter should be sworn in to check the official interpreter. When questioned a second time Frau Kress repeated what she had said the first time and the interpreter translated the words used as "she got up".

The House then adjourned until the following day when the chambermaid gave further evidence to the effect that when she made Pergami's bed on another occasion she discovered that the sheets were stained. Again, however, there was some doubt about the interpretation of the word used by the witness and it was agreed that the correct translation should have been "soiled".

Although the Solicitor-General tried hard to get the witness to amplify this part of her evidence he failed dismally so Brougham, perhaps wisely, did not pursue the matter any further in his cross-examination.

This kind of evidence, this determination of the Crown to leave no stone unturned to blacken the Queen's character was having an effect quite different from what the supporters of the Bill hoped. As the trial proceeded the chances that the Bill would be passed by the House became more and more remote, unless, of course, their Lordships decided to vote on party lines.

When the House met again on 29th August Brougham asked permission for the Queen's counsel to be allowed to cross-examine witnesses after the examination-in-chief, to such an extent that they thought proper, with liberty to call back the witnesses later for such further cross-examination as they might desire.

Barbara Kress, therefore, was then recalled and further cross-examined by Brougham. The first part of the cross-examination appears to have been an attempt to suggest that she had been promised a large sum of money if she came to England to give this evidence. It achieved little success, however, for she would only admit that she was told she would receive due compensation. Remaining questions were no more successful and produced nothing of any value to either side. Frau Kress seems to have been an exceptionally stupid woman, but when she said that she did not understand a question it was not always because she did not know how to answer it.

On the following day, 30th August, after three or four more witnesses had been called by the Crown to give trivial evidence which carried the Crown's case no further, the great moment arrived and Louisa Demont was called to the Bar and was then examined by the Solicitor-General. She described how it was that Willikins ceased to sleep in the same room as his adopted mother and how Pergami was allotted a bedroom which had a communicating passage and a small closet between it and the Princess's room.

The witness then stated that during the time they were in Naples Pergami slept in his own room but she frequently saw him in the Princess's room when she was also in the room "assisting H.R.H. to make her toilette." On some of these occasions Willikins was also present. He was then about twelve years old.

She also said that on a number of occasions when she went to the Princess's bedroom to make up the large bed it appeared as though two people had slept in it, which was, of course, in complete contradiction to what Majocchi had said, namely, that the Princess's bed appeared not to have been slept in whereas there were signs that two persons had slept in his bed.

The more the evidence of these two witnesses is examined the more unreliable it becomes. Not only were the two stories diametrically opposed but Majocchi's story was self-contradictory. If the Princess left her room, entered Pergami's room, stayed there for only fifteen minutes and then went back to her room, where did she sleep the rest of the night, having regard to the fact that Majocchi next morning found that her bed had not been slept in? Even the Solicitor-General did not suggest that she had spent the remainder of the night on the bedroom floor.

This witness then went on to describe the sleeping arrangements when they were all living in Genoa. The Princess's room had two communicating rooms, one on either side. Pergami slept in one of them and Demont in the other. In the morning Her Royal Highness would call her maid into the room and, Demont swore, "More often than not the bed appeared not to have been slept in."

Having regard to the fact that Caroline knew from the moment she left England that she was being spied upon day and night and that she must have realized that some of her domestic staff were there for that purpose, it is difficult, if not impossible, to believe that she would have regularly spent the night in Pergami's bed with her own maid a stone's throw away, and in the morning called Kress into her bedroom without even bothering to ruffle the sheets.

Although the examination of this witness by the Solicitor-General lasted for almost a day and a half, most of the evidence given, apart from that already mentioned, was of a very trivial nature. She had seen the Princess and Pergami *sitting* on the sofa together; in a canoe on Lake Como; walking arm in arm with him in the garden at the Villa D'Este; drinking together, and a number of other harmless things. Demont also stated that although the Princess often called him "*mon cher ami*" and addressed him as "*tu*", he always called her Princess.

This was hardly the kind of evidence required to prove a charge of adulterous intercourse, and at the end of Demont's examination many of their Lordships must have been wondering whether the Queen had not been speaking the truth when she told someone that the only man with whom she had ever committed adultery was the husband of Mrs. Fitzherbert!

On Friday 1st September the cross-examination of Louisa Demont began and Brougham entrusted this very important task to Mr. T. Williams, one of Her Majesty's three junior counsel. No one could have done it better. By the end of the day, although her cross-examination was not quite finished, she left the witness stand greatly discredited.

Thomas Creevey, who was in the House all day, in a letter written to Miss Ord said:

The chienne Demont turns out everything one could wish in her cross-examination. Her letters have been produced written to her sister living still in the Queen's service. . . . They contain every kind of panegyric upon the Queen, and she often writes of a journal or diary she has kept of everything that has occurred during the whole of her service and travels with the Queen—the object of such journal being, as she said, to do the Queen justice and to show how she was received and applauded wherever she went.

Mr. Williams began by asking the witness whether it was not a fact that she had been living in England for the last thirteen months under the name of Colombier, to which she answered "Yes". She also admitted that after being in the Princess's service for just over three years she was dismissed in 1817 for saying something which she afterwards admitted to be false. After her dismissal she did not take up any further employment until after her arrival in England in July 1819.

From most of counsel's questions during the early part of her cross-examination she took evasive action. First she would answer, "I do not recollect having done so," and on being asked whether she would *swear* that she had not done so, her reply was always, "I will not swear but I do not recollect it".

The Solicitor-General must have begun to realize that his "storm troops" were not doing too well as he kept interrupting the Queen's counsel and complaining of the form in which a question had just been put. In no case were any of the questions put improperly, but as the Solicitor-General was allowed by the Lord Chancellor to get away with his objection every time, it was obviously worthwhile his continuing to interrupt whenever possible, as each time he did so, Demont, who was under great pressure from Mr. Williams, was given a little breathing space, which must have been a great relief to her.

The most vital part of her cross-examination, however, began when counsel suggested that she was very short of money before she came to England and that about six months after she was dismissed from the Princess's service someone approached her in order to find out what she had to say with respect to her former mistress. Demont fenced with counsel over these questions for several minutes, although she finally had to admit that she had been approached but rather later than counsel had suggested. The effect of her prevarication, however, cannot have been lost on anyone present.

When the House met on the following day, 2nd September, Mr. Williams said that with the permission of the House he proposed to read two letters which had been written by the witness Demont. The first was addressed to Mademoiselle Mariette Bron at Pesaro and dated, Colombier, 8th February 1818. The second was addressed to H.R.H. the Princess of Wales.

When the first letter was read out by counsel it was then seen to be the same letter about which the witness had been cross-examined earlier and of which she pretended that she could not remember any of the details—a letter which stated that while Demont was having some refreshment at her aunt Clara's an unknown man had brought her a letter. Counsel now asked if this was true and, after a lot more prevarication, for this witness seemed to be constitutionally incapable of telling the simple truth, she admitted that such a letter was delivered to her and she wished to explain it. This explanation, which was later proved to be palpably false, was put forward with the object of showing that the flattering things which the witness had said about her former mistress were not genuine and were written for an entirely different reason.

"I wrote to my sister several times," she told counsel, "and always in these letters I spoke much about Her Royal Highness because I knew they would be intercepted. At that time I had decided to leave Switzerland and go to England and I was afraid that the Princess would dismiss my sister. I knew that since I had left the service of Her Royal Highness she had always feared that I would speak against her and as I knew that she would read these letters I wanted to convince her that I would not speak against her even if I went to England and that even money would not tempt me. I did this in the hope that she would not dismiss my sister from her service."

After that nothing could really rehabilitate this witness, neither

her re-examination by the Solicitor-General nor her examination by a number of Tory peers who were strong supporters of the Bill for purely political reasons. A good deal of what she had told the House about the conduct of the Princess and Pergami may still have left some suspicion in the minds of some, but no reasonable person could be so certain of her truthfulness as to be prepared to act on it.

The House only sat for six more days before they adjourned for a little more than three weeks in order that the Queen's counsel might have time to prepare her defence. On the first four days further witnesses were called and the Solicitor-General summed-up in support of the Bill. Only one of the witnesses contributed anything new to the case and even his evidence covered mostly the same ground as that of Majocchi and Demont. That the Crown thought it necessary to call a baker to say that he was once in the kitchen at the Villa D'Este and saw Pergami take a spoonful of polenta, put half of it into the Princess's mouth and then the remainder in his own mouth, only shows how desperately short they were of evidence to support the charges.

Nor was the Solicitor-General's summing-up very impressive. He went through the evidence in considerable detail, but had to admit that Majocchi was a witness "unworthy of belief" and that the facts to which he had sworn were not directly confirmed by the witness Demont.

A strange point of which he made special mention was the evidence of Giuseppe Sacchi that during the whole of the Princess's journey through Germany and the Tyrol, Sacchi had stated, the greatest anxiety had been shown by Her Royal Highness to avoid the English upon every occasion; the first question asked on arrival at any inn or hotel was, "are there any English of rank here?" If the answer was yes, the party immediately went somewhere else. Which of all the allegations made against the Queen this was supposed to prove it is difficult to conceive, but whether guilty or innocent, it was more than understandable, after the treatment she had received ever since she first set foot in England, that the Queen might not want to be seen dead in the same ditch with any compatriots of her royal husband.

In the last few words of his speech the Solicitor-General laid bare the complete injustice of the procedure adopted by the Government at the bequest of their King in order to get rid of his wife. He hoped that in conclusion he might be allowed to say, and he said it from the bottom of his heart and with the utmost sincerity, that he devoutly wished that Her Royal Highness would establish to the satisfaction of their Lordships, and every individual in the country, her full and unsullied innocence. He apparently had forgotten that, if justice was to be done, it was for the Crown to establish her guilt, and not for her to establish her innocence.

At the close of this speech the House adjourned so that Brougham could decide whether or not they required an adjournment in order to prepare the defence. On Saturday 9th September, after hearing Brougham's wishes, the House adjourned until Tuesday 3rd October when the Bill would be further considered.

The Government was apparently quite determined not to let Brougham open his case at once, but when he was allowed an adjournment of more than three weeks the House of Lords were not at all pleased. As Creevey wrote, "You can form no conception of the rage of the Lords at Brougham fixing this time: it interferes with everything,—pheasant shooting, Newmarket etc.!"

During the proceedings of the House since the commencement of the second reading of the Bill the King must have been watching them with some uneasiness. Just before the House adjourned the Prime Minister wrote to give His Majesty a report of how everything was going. It was difficult to assess, he wrote, what the real effect of the evidence had been upon their Lordships. Parts of it had made a considerable impression in the minds of peers who were already ganged-up against the Queen but two of the most material witnesses had been badly shaken regarding their credit and character. Lord Liverpool was not prepared to prophesy about the result, particularly as he understood that the Queen had some important witnesses including Demont's sister, Mariette Bron, and two officers of the British Army.

The Prime Minister also warned the King that the opposition were determined to make a party question of the trial and would "strain every nerve and raise every doubt, however futile" to acquit the Queen. The main object of his letter, however, was to call attention to the last four lines of the Bill which dealt with divorce and, by inference, would enable the King to marry again. He told the King that he had been in constant touch with most of the peers, including the Bishops, and this had convinced him that there was little chance of that part of the Bill being passed in the House of Lords, and no possibility whatsoever that it would pass through the Commons. As far as the House of Lords was concerned this proved to be a wrong prediction because on 8th November the divorce clause was retained in the Bill by a majority of sixty-seven.

The Prime Minister also thought it necessary to remind the King that the proof required of adultery would be far stricter if a divorce were to follow than if the Bill was limited to the degradation of the Queen as unfit, because of her conduct, to share and enjoy the rights and privileges of Queen Consort. He therefore asked the King to give him authority to offer to give up the divorce clause before the defence commenced, should the King's Ministers think it desirable. Such an offer would, probably, conciliate the House and it would make it very difficult, if not impossible, for the defence then to bring up "the distressing subject of recrimination." He also thought it was preferable that His Majesty should make this concession rather than have it extorted from him, and it would also ensure considerable support from the public.

The King, in his reply, told the Prime Minister that this was not a decision he could make without serious consideration and this would take time. He would have to discuss the suggestion with Lord Liverpool personally before he could accept such a compromise.

Eventually, after a meeeting with some of his Ministers, the King regretfully agreed to the suggestion and wrote to tell him so. He expressed the hope, however, that the Prime Minister would protect the King's honour and not yield to political expediency.

On 3rd October the House reassembled to resume the second reading of the Bill and the proceedings began with Brougham's opening speech for the defence, a speech which did more than anything else to kill the Bill.

He began by expressing the hope that the Queen's innocence would be realized before the proceedings ended and that it would not be prejudiced by his unworthy handling of the case. There was, however, one thing in his favour. Public opinion had already decided on the case and he had nothing to fear but the consequences of perjury.

He then dealt with all the evidence which had been given by the witnesses of the Crown. Although there had been a great deal of mud slinging and some of the mud would certainly stick, it did not substantiate, beyond doubt, any of the charges contained in the Bill.

The witnesses Majocchi and Demont stood apart from the rest of the witnesses; they were the main witnesses on whom the whole case depended. All the others could do was corroborate these two witnesses in some material particular. Both of them, however, were gravely shaken under cross-examination and their credit virtually destroyed. The reason why Demont prevaricated so obstinately about her handwriting was that her evidence had been given in utter ignorance that her letters were still in existence and could be produced in evidence to contradict her. As Brougham said, had she known that those letters were available and that their contents were known to the King's advisers "their Lordships would never have heard of her and she would have been shipped off again as many other bribed witnesses had been who were even less worthy of credit than those who had been called."

Some of the disgusting evidence was also the most incredible, because it was impossible to believe that the Princess and Pergami, unless they were quite mad, would have dreamed of doing some of the things they were said to have been seen doing, in circumstances in which they were almost certain to be caught in the act.

Brougham's speech ended with the following peroration:

Such, my Lords, now before you, is the evidence in support of this measure; evidence inadequate to prove a debt, impotent to deprive of a right, ridiculous to convict of the lowest offence, scandalous if brought forward to support a charge of the highest nature which the law knows, monstrous to ruin the honour, to blast the name of an English Queen.

My Lords, I pray you to pause, I do earnestly beseech you to take heed. You are standing on the brink of a precipice, then beware! It will go forth as your judgement, if sentence shall go against the Queen; but it will be the only judgement you ever pronounced which instead of reaching its object, will return and bound back on those who gave it.

Save the country, my Lords, from the horrors of catastrophe. Save yourselves from this peril. Rescue that country, of which you are the ornaments, but in which you can flourish no longer, when severed from the people, than the blossom when cut off from the roots and the stem of the tree. Save that country that you may continue to adorn it. Save the Crown which is in jeopardy, the aristocracy which is shaken. Save the altar which must stagger with the blow that rends its kindred throne.

You have said, my Lords, you have willed, the Church and King have willed, that the Queen should be deprived of its solemn service. She has, instead of that solemnity, the heartfelt prayers of the people.

She needs no prayers of mine, but I do here pour forth my humble supplications at the throne of mercy that that mercy may be poured down upon the people in a larger measure than the merits of their rulers may deserve and that your hearts may be turned to justice.

Sir Fitzjames Stephen once said, "eloquence of the past resembles nothing so much as mouldy wedding cake," and the above peroration certainly sounds very flowery to modern ears. Nevertheless, it made a great impression on the House, and Lord Erskine, himself no mean orator, left the chamber in tears, during the short adjournment which followed, and many other noble Lords stood about in groups in the lobbies discussing it.

Brougham is supposed to have been in two minds whether or not to call any witnesses at all in defence of the Queen and, had this been a trial before a jury in an ordinary criminal court, that might have been the best course to have adopted. Instead of calling any evidence he would have merely submitted that there was no case to answer. Very different considerations, however, applied to this case. The House of Lords in no way resembled a jury, chosen haphazardly from a register of householders and all liable to be challenged for cause. Had the same principle been applicable to this jury of peers all those of the same political persuasion as the Government of the day would have been challengeable on the ground of prejudice, for the Bill which was before the House was a political measure. But apart from that consideration, if no witness had been called in the Queen's defence, the King, his Ministers and his friends would have claimed, without doubt, that the reason for not calling any witnesses was that the defence dare not risk it. In any event, the Queen herself was not willing to let the matter go by default and insisted that witnesses should be called.

That was, no doubt, why Brougham eventually decided that they should be called, and why he had dealt with it earlier in his speech and had told the House that the evidence which had been given against Her Majesty in support of the charges did not call upon him to make any rebuttal.

He also frightened the Government and its supporters by saying that although he did not at that stage of the proceedings intend to utter one whisper against the conduct of "Her Majesty's illustrious Consort" he would not hesitate to "resort to such a course and fearlessly perform his duty" should it become necessary.

The House knew perfectly well what he meant by that. The whole story of the King's unpleasant and disreputable amours and his marriage to Mrs. Fitzherbert would then have been blazoned all over the country and would have done irreparable harm, not only to the King but to the monarchy itself. It would, also, have been a defence to any legal claim for a divorce which was still part of the Bill.

After Mr. Williams, one of the Queens' junior counsel, had with their permission addressed their Lordships he called a number of highly respectable witnesses, all of whom had either been on the Princess's staff or had met her during her absence abroad. One of them, the Bishop of Pesaro, testified that, during the three years when she was living there, there had never been the slightest report or even rumour that could be injurious to her honour or reputation. He told the House that had there been any scandal connected with her household it certainly could not have remained concealed from his court. A large number of other witnesses holding important positions in various parts of Italy in which the Princess had been living gave similar evidence.

Lady Charlotte Lindsay, who was one of the Princess's Ladies of the Bedchamber when Her Royal Highness was living in Naples and Rome, swore that she had never seen any impropriety of conduct between the Princess and Pergami nor had she noticed anything to make her suspect that there was any such conduct. When cross-examined by the Solicitor-General she would not swear that she had never seen Pergami take the Princess's arm but if she did it was certainly not done in such a way as to give rise to any suspicion that there was undue intimacy.

Sir William Gell, who had been Chamberlain in the Princess's household from the time she went abroad until shortly before her cruise to the eastern Mediterranean, testified, and his evidence was not shaken in cross-examination, that Pergami's conduct was that of a gentleman and that he (Sir William) had never observed anything in Pergami's conduct towards the Princess different from the conduct of any English member of the staff, except, perhaps, that he was more attentive.

But the most important evidence was given by Sicard, who had been in Her Royal Highness's household for more than twenty years. It was important because it explained how it was that in Naples Pergami was allotted a room not far from that of the Princess. It was, in fact, Sicard who, on Gell's instructions, engaged Pergami as courier, on the recommendation of the Marchese Ghisiliari in whose service he had previously been. Two or three nights later Sicard moved Pergami to another room. The room was chosen principally because it had a glass door which led to the garden and was not safe, and, therefore, Sicard "thought it right that a male servant should sleep in it". Unlike Majocchi and Demont, Sicard was not shaken in cross-examination and throughout his evidence gave every appearance of being a thoroughly reliable witness.

During the next few days a number of other witnesses were called by the defence and dealt with various aspects of the evidence given by Majocchi and Demont. By the time they had finished the Crown's case was even further demolished.

On 13th October an application was made by Brougham to recall one of the Crown's witnesses, Rastelli. It had become clear by then that Rastelli had committed perjury, and as the Attorney-General had promised that any such witnesses would be prosecuted there was an uproar when he announced that Rastelli had, without the knowledge of the Law Officers, been sent to Milan with despatches. He had been ordered to return immediately. Brougham protested at this, because, he said, the nature of Rastelli's cross-examination was such as would lead any reasonable person to suspect that it would be contradicted.

Lord Holland also severely criticized the Crown for allowing this to happen and said that if their Lordships allowed themselves to be thus dragged through the mire they would place the country's institutions in the utmost jeopardy and danger. In his opinion a prima facie case had already been made out of the existence of a conspiracy to prevent the course of justice and the House would do well to get rid of the disgust and fatigue of this infamous proceeding.

These were strong words and they left the Prime Minister with no alternative but to get up and rebut the accusation. He admitted that someone was seriously to blame but neither he, the Attorney-General, nor the Solicitor-General knew anything about this. He was sure that whoever had been responsible for Rastelli's departure had acted from the highest motives.

Lord Liverpool had fallen back on the politician's age-long device of professing ignorance when to admit knowledge would be most embarrassing, but he was not allowed to get away with it too easily. Lord Lansdowne thought that their Lordships should always have the power to recall any witness whose evidence was suspect. He poured ridicule on the reason given by the Attorney-General for Rastelli's absence and said that it was incumbent on their Lordships to do all they could to repair the error.

The Lord Chancellor also did what he could to cover up for the Crown, professing, at the same time, his complete ignorance. He said that it was most unfortunate, but an error of judgment rather than "an error of intention".

But this did not stop several other peers joining in the protest. Lord Carnarvon maintained that these proceedings made the

House of Lords "an object of execration to every Englishman and of contempt to the rest of Europe". Lord Alvanley wanted to know the name of the person who had sent Rastelli to Milan and asked whether, by any chance, he was one of the Milan Commissioners, an awkward question to which, of course, he received no reply; and Lord Grey disagreed with the Lord Chancellor's excuse that it was merely an error of judgment. He thought it highly iniquitous.

Creevey, as usual, had some lively comment to make and wrote, "Here's a breeze of the first order! The last witness having ended Rastelli was called back when, behold, it turned out that he had been sent *out of the country* instead of staying and being indicted for perjury. . . . Liverpool admits it was scandalous to send him away but that it was unknown to the Government!"

Although the Prime Minister had not deigned to answer Lord Alvanley's pertinent question the mystery, if there were any, was cleared up by a witness who was called just before the House rose. His name was Powell and Lord Alvanley's suspicions had been well founded, for in answer to the first question put to him by Lord Grey the witness admitted that he had been employed under the Milan Commission and was then assisting agents in support of the Bill. He had suggested to the Foreign Office that Rastelli should be sent on this mission to Milan. He had, however, given Rastelli firm instructions to return on or before 3rd of October but had since heard that he was too ill to travel.

So the King's Ministers managed to evade personal responsibility by passing it on to a civil servant. It is not customary for a Minister to do this and it is not to Lord Liverpool's credit that he did not have the courage to shoulder the blame himself. The House, however, was not left with any illusions and there can have been few peers who were not convinced that Rastelli's illness was diplomatic. As Powell well knew that an indictment for perjury would later be made against Rastelli he must have realized that it was most unlikely that this Italian would return to face such a charge and that it would not be possible to extradite him.

As the proceedings of the House of Lords, since the second reading of the Bill began, had received wide coverage in *The Times* and in all the other newspapers, the whole of England had been avidly following the trial and its reaction had not been favourable to the King, to put it mildly. The King himself was incensed at the way the trial was going and dare not show his face outside Carlton House because of the public hostility. The crowds assembled outside kept shouting, "Nero's hotel, let's burn it down," and it was then that the first police force was formed. Robert Peel, watching the crowds moving along the streets in the vicinity of Carlton House and threatening to overthrow the monarchy, wondered whether, if the situation got out of hand, the army could be relied upon, for the troops were very much on the Queen's side. He suggested the formation of a regular police force directly under the Crown. His friends thought it an excellent idea and suggested that its members should be called Peelers, the name by which the police in London were known for some time.

The King, however, was not only furious at the way things were going. He was also frightened because he knew only too well what Brougham had meant when he alluded, in his opening speech, to the fact that unless there was later some reason which gave him no option, he intended to draw a veil over the period between the Queen's first arrival in England and her departure in 1814, but that he could not do so if he found later that this would prejudice the Queen's case. Should it become necessary he would not hesitate to make a personal attack on the King whatever the consequences might be.

The Queen's legal advisers had abundant evidence which would have proved a strong case against the King, but Brougham thought, at that stage, that it would never have induced His Majesty to give up the Bill. The King knew that everyone in society knew of his relationship with Lady Jersey and it would make no difference if it were to be proved at the Bar of the House.

Had it been necessary the real ground of defence which Brougham would have brought forward would have been nothing less than impeaching the King's title by proving that he had forfeited the Crown. He had married a Roman Catholic while heir-apparent and this was declared by the Act of Settlement to be a forfeiture of the Crown, "as if he were naturally dead". Brougham was not at that time in possesion of all the evidence to prove this, as he became later; but he was now confident that he had enough evidence to prove the fact. Mrs. Fitzherbert's uncle, Mr. Errington, who was present at the marriage, which took place in his house, was still alive, and although he would have had a right to refuse to reply to a question, an affirmative answer to which would have incriminated him, it was almost certain, in Brougham's opinion, that on Mrs. Fitzherbert's behalf he would have waived the protection and given his testimony to prove the marriage. Even his refusal to answer such a question would have left the conviction in everyone's mind that the marriage did take place.

There was, in fact, ample evidence in existence which would have enabled Brougham to prove that the marriage had taken place without involving Errington. Mrs. Fitzherbert had in her possession a will made by the Prince of Wales in her favour and signed in his own hand in which she was referred to as "his dear wife". Brougham had actually obtained a copy of this will from a Mrs. Dawson Damer, who was the adopted daughter and was only too pleased to help in any way in defending the reputation of her adoptive mother, of whom she was very fond.

How far Brougham could have gone in proving all this it is impossible to know, for it was many years before all the evidence was disclosed to the public. The mere suggestion of it, however, would have been quite enough to create a terrible scandal, if no more, and it would, surely, have been the end of the Bill. No wonder George was worried.

On 24th October Denman began his summing-up for the defence, which lasted for the best part of two days. It was extremely forceful and telling and completely demolished the Crown's evidence. It had only one blemish and that was an unfortunate gaffe which marred his peroration. He quoted Our Lord's words to the woman taken in adultery, "Go and sin no more". Having regard to the fact that the whole object of his speech had been to prove that the Queen had not sinned at all, nothing could have been more inept.

This was too good for London's lampooners to miss, and it was not long before the following verse was current in all the taverns:

> Gracious lady, we implore,
> Go away and sin no more,
> And if that effort be too great,
> Go away at any rate.

On 27th October, the forty-third day of the trial, the Attorney-General replied to the defence and was followed by the Solicitor-General. In *The Times* of the following day one of the leader writers stated that there had been a prevalent opinion that the failure of the charges against the Queen being now clear there would be no point in the Law Officers of the Crown being called upon to attempt to reply. It was thought that they would have been glad to be excused. What their feelings may have been it is impossible to say but the effect of their speeches was not great and did nothing to re-establish their case.

The so-called trial having now ended all that remained was for the House to vote on the second reading of the Bill, but before a division was called a number of peers spoke after the Lord Chancellor had first addressed them.

Notwithstanding all that had been heard, he said, the only

question for the House to judge was whether the Bill should or should not be read a second time. Suggestions had been made regarding certain amendments which would alter its nature (this referred to the divorce clause) but these had nothing to do with their Lordships' decision.

No one should vote for the second reading unless he thought that the substantial parts of the Preamble had been proved and especially that an adulterous intercourse had taken place. He did not intend to go into the evidence in any great detail as it was not part of his duty to sum-up like a judge in a court of law, but it was his duty to state his opinion and, in giving it, to refer to those parts of the evidence on which that opinion was founded.

He told them, however, that they must observe the great principles of British justice (which must have sounded strange in the Queen's ears), namely to consider the accused innocent until proved guilty and to pronounce the Queen innocent unless *"perfectly satisfied"* that she had been proved guilty.

One would have thought that no reasonable man could have been perfectly satisfied of her guilt after the evidence of witnesses like Majocchi and Demont, yet in the division on the second reading of the Bill which took place at the end of this debate 123 peers voted for it and it was carried by a majority of twenty-eight.

The question which the Lord Chancellor asked himself, before deciding how to vote, was "does the evidence which stands unsuspected in support of the Bill and uncontradicted by the defence evidence sustain the allegation of an adulterous intercourse or does it not?" Again, it is difficult to understand how Lord Eldon, experienced lawyer and judge, could have answered that question in the affirmative particularly as the standard of belief which he had already set himself, and the other peers, was that they should be "perfectly satisfied".

When, however, he came to deal with the evidence itself he was in some difficulty and he never even mentioned the evidence of Majocchi or Demont, although he said that it should not be thought that both these witnesses on many occasions had not told the truth.

When he sat down he was followed by Lord Erskine, a former Lord Chancellor, who, it will be remembered, had presided over the Delicate Investigation and had cleared the Princess of Wales, as she then was, of all the serious charges brought against her. He already knew the kind of persecution which the Princess had undergone, ever since her husband left her for Mrs. Fitzherbert after the birth of Charlotte, and he naturally viewed the Bill with some suspicion. He told the House that he felt bound to say that Lord Eldon had not exhibited the same impartiality which he had recommended to others.

Lord Erskine had always been of the opinion that when the Queen's name had been omitted from the liturgy, almost before the last breath had left the late King's body, she had been unjustly deprived of the prayers of the Church by the agency of the new King's Ministers. The Lord Chancellor, Lord Erskine said, would appear to have forgotten that incident, otherwise he could never have said that in England no one could be considered guilty until it had been proved and that no opinion ought to be expressed against an accused prior to the trial.

Before he could finish his speech, however, he was taken ill and fell "senseless on the table". It was not realized that his indisposition was serious and the House adjourned for a quarter of an hour to give him time to recover. He had not, however, recovered by that time and the debate had to go on without him. Now that poor Erskine was, at least temporarily, out of the way the Lord Chancellor rose to say that he could not let the debate go further without saying that Lord Erskine, whose absence and indisposition he regretted, had mistaken what he meant when he (Erskine) said that Lord Eldon had overlooked many of the points in the case.

What the Lord Chancellor meant to say was that in the points and cases upon which he had commented he saw enough for his own judgment.

It is always unfortunate to have to say in public that one did not mean what one said, although it is still done almost every day by politicians from Prime Ministers downwards. In this particular instance it was quite clear that what the Lord Chancellor had said could only have meant one thing to any reasonable person and that was exactly what Lord Erskine had taken it to mean. In his explanation Lord Eldon completely gave the game away by saying that the evidence that he had mentioned was enough for *his* judgment.

During the remainder of this last debate on the second reading there were more who spoke against the Bill than in favour of it although there was by then very little doubt that the Government would get a majority even though it might not be a large one.

In a letter dated 2nd November, the same day on which Erskine was taken ill, Creevey wrote:

> Eldon began this morning and it was expected he would have made a great masterly judicial summing-up; instead of which he spoke for an hour and a quarter only and a more feeble argument for his own vote I never heard in my life. . . . Erskine followed and had spoken for about three quarters of an hour when he fainted away and was carried out of the House, since when that villain Lauderdale has been speaking.

"That villain Lauderdale" came up to expectations for he made a very long speech and examined the whole of the evidence in great detail. Unlike Eldon, who was only able to rely on parts of it—enough to satisfy an easy conscience and vote for the Bill—Lauderdale swallowed it all hook, line and sinker, going so far as to say that in all its material parts the evidence of Majocchi and Demont was unimpeached. His final exhortation was a little too much even for some of his own colleagues, namely that they should vote for the second reading in order to protect the morals of their wives and children. Everyone knew, whatever their political colour, that the last thing the Bill was about was the protection of either public or private morals.

A number of peers who spoke later criticized Lauderdale's hypocritical speech, including Lord Grosvenor, who had some hard things to say about the Archbishop of Canterbury and the Lord Chancellor. It was generally understood that on his accession the King had asked the Archbishop to come and see him with the book of Common Prayer and had ordered the Primate to erase Caroline's name from the liturgy. Lord Grosvenor did not know whether those were the facts but in those circumstances, if he had been the Archbishop, he would have thrown the book in the face of a King who commanded him to do an act which was contrary to law, to humanity and to justice.

Similarly had Lord Grosvenor been the Lord Chancellor he would, sooner than set the seal of office to such a Command, have dashed the seal to pieces at his feet and thrown away the trammels of his office rather than remain any longer in the service of such a King.

His exhortation to the House was very different from that of Lauderdale. Rather than pass the Bill to protect the morals of their wives and children Lord Grosvenor thought that in respect of a woman who had been "so injured, so unquestionably persecuted and oppressed" they should not exhibit to their wives and daughters the "sad spectacle of oppression which the Queen would present were she to become the victim of this Bill". They should judge this measure as they themselves expected to be judged.

When the division was taken on 6th November, there voted contents 123, non-contents ninety-five, majority for the second reading twenty-eight; but this was no victory for the King or for his Government, for everyone knew that the Bill would never pass through the House of Commons, if ever it reached there.

The voting had little to do with the merits of the case, otherwise the Bill would have been defeated by quite a substantial majority. Many peers voted solely for political reasons and it must have been a relief to those whose political sympathies, on this occasion, coincided with the course of justice.

An analysis of twenty-eight peers who voted in support of the Bill and accounted for the majority is not without interest.

Princes of the blood holding high office at His Majesty's pleasure	2
Cabinet Ministers	9
Peers holding offices under the Crown	13
The Archbishop of Canterbury	1
Three Peers who were present during the presentation of the prosecution's case but not in attendance to hear the defence	3
	—
	28
	—

When the House met next morning the Prime Minister attempted to carry out the promise which he had made to some of the Bishops that he would get rid of the divorce clause in the Bill, and the House went into Committee.

Before proposing that this clause should no longer stand part of the Bill, he proposed one or two absurdly trivial amendments typical of the Government's attitude ever since the Bill had been introduced. Firstly it was proposed that the name Bartolomo Pergami should be altered to Bartolomo Bergami. The orignial spelling of his name in the Preamble of the Bill was, in fact, one of the few statements in it which could be substantiated for the simple reason that it was his real name. One or two other amendments equally trivial were also proposed and accepted.

But it was when the Chairman of the House in Committee came to the divorce clause that the Government got a shock. The opposition, who were out to destroy the Bill in any event, supported the retention of this clause, believing, and they were later proved to be right, that with the divorce clause still in the Bill the majority obtained by the Government on the second reading would be considerably reduced on the third reading.

Friday 10th November was to see the end of the Bill. It was the third reading, and after a fairly short debate it was passed by a majority of only nine. While the division was taking place Brougham was standing by Croker, who had taken a very active part in the affair. When the result of the division was announced Brougham said, "there is an end of your Bill!" "Why?" Croker asked. "Because," Brougham replied, "the majority is the number of Ministers and high officers in this House, and it will never do to pass such a Bill by their votes."

By this time, however, the Government had seen the red light and the Prime Minister rose at once and said that he could not be ignorant of the state of public feeling with regard to the Bill and the majority in favour of the third reading had not been more than nine. Had the Bill been passed by a larger majority the Government would have felt it their duty to proceed with it. What Lord Liverpool omitted to say, however, was how delighted they were not to do so.

In the present state of the country and having regard to the nearly balanced division of opinion in the House the Government had decided not to proceed further with the Bill and he would now move that the question that "this Bill do now pass" should be amended to read, "that this Bill be now read this day six months," which, in parliamentary language, meant that the Bill was withdrawn.

This announcement, which appears to have taken many peers by surprise, was received with loud cheers and Lord Grey rose to speak but was unable to do so for some time because of the general confusion. When, at last, he was able to make himself heard, he charged the Government with gross neglect of duty in listening only to *ex parte* evidence and giving willing credence to the most exaggerated and unfounded calumnies. The Government had betrayed their King, Lord Grey said, insulted their Queen and shocked the morals of society by promulgating such detestable and disgusting evidence. He also blamed the Milan Commissioners. He was followed by Lord Erskine who said how happy he was to have lived to see justice done to the Queen, tardy and reluctant though it was.

Creevey, who had left the House of Lords immediately after the Prime Minister's announcement and dashed off to Brook's to celebrate, wrote from the club: "The Bill is gone thank God to the devil. Their majority was brought down to nine, and then the dolorous Liverpool came forward and struck. He moved that his own bill be read this day six months. You may well suppose the state we are all in . . . the state of the town is beyond everything."

SEVEN

Peace at Last

ᘒᘒᘒᘒᘒᘒᘒᘒᘒᘒᘒᘒᘒᘒᘒᘒᘒᘒᘒᘒᘒᘒᘒᘒᘒᘒᘒᘒᘒᘒᘒ

THE WELCOME news first reached the public when someone threw open a window in the House of Lords and shouted, "The Bill is rejected," whereupon the crowd outside cheered like mad. By night time there were illuminations in Piccadilly, Bond Street and St. James's where there were celebrations in all the clubs. Crowds paraded through the streets carrying torches and shouting, "Long live Queen Caroline," and marched along keeping time with cries of "*Non mi ricordo, non mi ricordo.*"

On the following morning the Lord Mayor of London had a poster displayed in front of the Mansion House announcing that there would be illuminations in the City in honour of Her Majesty's triumph. Many houses were decorated with portraits of the Queen and Brougham and with posters proclaiming, among other things, that Caroline was still Regina.

Outside the auction rooms of Mr. Machin, which were brilliantly illuminated, there was a poster advertising that "In a few days will be submitted to public auction, if not previously disposed of, twenty-eight Elastic Consciences at all times devoted to their employer's wishes. For reference re character inquire at the office of the L — — d Chancellor. Further particulars may be had from the office of the secretary to the D——— of N—wc—stle. May the Queen be protected from her enemies and the King be preserved from his pretended friends."

During the week following the withdrawal of the Bill the Queen's Vice-Chamberlain was instructed by her to apply to the Prime Minister for a "Palace suitable as the residence of the Queen of England" to be placed at her disposal without further delay. She received a curt reply stating that the King was not prepared to assign any of the royal palaces for her residence. Until Parliament reassembled, however, "the allowance hitherto enjoyed by the Queen would continue to be paid until the amount of future provision for Her Majesty had been determined." The Queen quite properly sent a long reply to the Prime Minister's letter on 18th November. As Parliament, which should have reassembled to do business on 23rd November was further prorogued to 23rd January the Queen made the contents of her letter public.

Written on her command by Mr. Craven, her Vice-Chamberlain, it began by stating that Her Majesty could not for a moment understand the real purport of Lord Liverpool's letter.

The Queen perceives that the King's Ministers have resolved to prevent Parliament from assembling for the despatch of business at the time to which both Houses had adjourned. The justice and wisdom of the legislature would at that period beyond all doubt have restored her to the full enjoyment of those rights which the constitution has vested in the Queen-Consort. The Ministers plainly show that such is their belief and they are determined, for some purposes of their own, to delay the redress to which she is entitled.

The letter then went on to say that the Queen saw behind all this something more sinister, namely that the authors of the Bill were trying to think out a new scheme to degrade her. "Defeated in their first attempt, disgraced in the eyes of the people, consigned to the contempt of all Europe, deserted by the most rational and respected of their own adherents, they meditate a new attack on the honour of the Queen."

If the Government really thought that any new scheme would be likely to succeed, the Queen felt sure that they were banking on the possibility that the public would get tired of supporting her as they had so loyally done in the past and that, perhaps, she also would give up the long struggle. She owed it to the British nation, the letter stated, to declare that she still had the utmost confidence in their support so long as she continued to be the victim of oppression, and no ill-treatment by the King's Ministers would ever shake the duty which she owed to the generous people who continued to stand up for her.

To the offer of money which the Prime Minister had thought proper to make when informing her of the further prorogation of Parliament she had no answer to give other than a direct refusal. The late King had been dead for nearly ten months, but no parliamentary provision had yet been made for her.

That public support for her had not yet wavered was evident from the numerous loyal addresses that poured in from all over the country as they had done, six months before, after the return of the Queen from abroad.

Caroline decided that it would be appreciated by the people, though not by the King or the Government, if she were to give thanks in public for what had been referred to as her "providential deliverance from her enemies and persecutors." Arrangements were, therefore, made for a service of thanksgiving in St. Paul's on Wednesday 29th November. The streets were lined with crowds of sympathizers and she was received at Temple Bar, on her way to the cathedral, by the Corporation.

The King did everything he could to make things difficult, but he could not barricade the streets through which the procession was to have passed for no one would have enforced the order had one been given, nor could he close the doors of the cathedral against her. He did, however, succeed in arranging that there should be no sermon by persuading the Dean and Chapter, who should not have been so weak and feeble, to give instructions to that effect. Nor was that all. The Dean also refused to allow a carpet to be laid from the West door through the nave and the choir to where the Queen's seat was situated, a remarkable example of Christian magnanimity. The pulpit and the lectern were not even allowed to be used for reading the lessons or any other purpose.

When the House of Commons met again after the recess an attempt was made by motions put down by Lord Archibald Hamilton and Mr. Wetherell to reinstate Caroline's name in the liturgy. They were moved during the debate on the King's speech, at the commencement of which Castlereagh had assured the House that no further measures of a hostile nature were intended towards Her Majesty and that a proposal would be submitted to the House for suitable provision to be made for her.

The attempt failed, however, for Hamilton's motion was defeated by 101 votes, but when the House was about to go into Committee to discuss financial provision for Her Majesty Brougham rose and said that he had the Queen's command to present the following message:

The Queen having learned that the House of Commons has appointed this day for taking into consideration that part of the King's most gracious speech which relates to her, deems it necessary to declare that she is duly sensible of His Majesty's condescension in recommending an arrangement respecting her to the attention of Parliament. She is aware that this recommendation must be understood as referring to a provision for the support of her estate and dignity; and from what has lately passed, she is apprehensive that such a provision may be unaccompanied by the possession of her rights and privileges in ample measure wherein former Queen-

Consorts, her Royal Predecessors, have been wont in times past to enjoy.

It is far from the Queen's inclination needlessly to throw obstacles in the way of a settlement which she desires in common with the whole country and which she feels persuaded the best interests of all parties equally require; and being most anxious to avoid everything that might create irritation, she cautiously abstains from any observation upon the unexampled predicament in which she is placed, but she feels it due to the House and to herself respectfully to declare that she perseveres in the resolution of declining any arrangement while her name continues to be excluded from the Liturgy.

The reading out of the Queen's message was greeted by loud and continued cheering and a lively and, at times, acrimonious debate took place, at the end of which a resolution that she should receive £50,000 per annum was agreed to without a division. Eventually, as she had debts to pay and had to have some income to live on, Caroline agreed to accept the sum voted without consulting Brougham.

Outside Parliament, however, the battle still went on and everything possible was done by the King and his clique to make life unbearable for the Queen. Some of the things done were described by Brougham in his autobiography:

Carlton House now took the course of filling the press with libels to deter all ladies from visiting the Queen. Papers were established with the avowed purpose of attacking every woman of rank who accepted her invitations. At the same time Carlton House was thrown open to such as refused to visit the Queen, and I hesitate not to declare that this course was perfectly successful, not merely with the women but also with their male relations so as, to my certain knowledge, to influence their votes in both the houses. Both were unwilling to expose their wives and sisters to a slanderous press, and averse to losing for them the balls at Carlton House.

The Queen bore it all with great patience and even good humour.

She used to say, "Oh it is all in the common course. People go to different inns: one goes to the King's Head, another to the Angel."

Brougham considered, however, that she did not act with discretion and that, although it would have been difficult to avoid making any mistakes in her peculiarly difficult position, she often invited the wrong people to visit her, people who came "for no other purpose than to gossip and laugh at her".

Life was not very pleasant for the Queen during these few weeks, for her attention was constantly being drawn to scandalous reports which appeared in the newspapers and which were purposely brought to her notice in the hope that she would become weary of it all and go abroad, which was what the King wanted, and quickly, before the coronation, when he rightly anticipated that there would be more trouble.

Caroline, however, had no intention of leaving England before the coronation, which it had now been decided would soon take place. Her claim was made to be crowned as a right and it was referred to the Privy Council and heard before a very crowded meeting at which Lord Harrowby was in the chair. The Law Officers attended and also present to advise were the Lord Chancellor, the Lord Chief Justice, the Chief Baron, and all the other judges who were Privy Councillors.

Brougham thus describes the meeting:

Denman and I argued the case for the claim, and Gifford and Copley against it and the decision was that as the Queen was living separate from the King she had no right to be crowned. Thus it was left to the King to refuse it.

This was manifestly a political judgment, entirely influenced by what had taken place the year before; for we showed by the clearest proofs that there was no instance whatever of a Queen not being crowned, except one when she was abroad, and another where there was a difference of religion and she declined it; but none whatever of a Queen-Consort not being crowned when she was within the realm, of the same religion as the King, and willing to be crowned.

My own impression was that the lay-Lords, not being in office—and even Lord Harrowby though in office—were inclined to our case, but that the Law Lords, including the judges, were against us—those judges who had taken a very decided part against us in the Lords as assessors to the House, and done themselves as little credit as possible in their answers to the legal question put to them, the most important of which has been disapproved by all lawyers since, and declared to be erroneous by late statutes—so much so that "the rule in the Queen's case" has been a strong topic of ridicule in the profession.

The hearing of the Queen's case to be crowned was heard on 4th July, and it was on that very day that the news first arrived in England that Napoleon had died on St. Helena on 6th May. Announcing the glad tidings to the King, his equerry said, "Your greatest enemy is dead, Sir." "Is she," said the King, his eyes glinting with joy and satisfaction, but his expression changed immediately when he was informed that it was not the Queen who was dead, but Bonaparte.

Realizing that Caroline was determined to appear in Westminster Abbey on the day of the coronation her legal advisers urged her strongly that it would be a great mistake to make the attempt. But it was useless: she had made up her mind.

It was not the first time that Caroline had committed errors of judgment, some of which she had probably regretted when it was too late, but there was nothing impetuous about this decision. She must have realized only too well that her attempt would, in all probability, fail, but she was determined to have one final fling and, having regard to all she had suffered during the past twenty-five years, who can blame her? Meanwhile, the King, who was not looking forward to his coronation and the scandal which it was likely to cause, had taken every precaution to prevent the

Queen reaching the Abbey. He had, however reserved a prominent seat for his present mistress Elizabeth, Lady Conyngham, who was frequently referred to as the Vice-Queen, and Sir Charles Bagot stated that while the King was kneeling at the altar, even during the Communion service, he repeatedly kissed a ring which had been given to him by Lady Conyngham.

Early on the day of the coronation Caroline left her house accompanied by Lady Hood and Lady Anne Hamilton, both of whom rode in the same carriage with her. In the other carriage were Lord Hood and her Vice-Chamberlain, Craven. The cortège was allowed to pass through the barrier which had been erected near the west door of the Abbey and eventually, after some confusion, her carriage drew up by the entrance and she approached the west door, leaning on the arm of Lord Hood. As they reached it the door was shut in her face. Lord Hood, having demanded entrance, the door keepers asked to see their tickets and the following conversation is reported to have taken place:

> Lord Hood: "I present you your Queen, surely there is no need for her to have a ticket."
>
> Door keeper: "Our orders are to admit no person without a Peer's ticket."
>
> Lord Hood: "This is your Queen, she is entitled to admission without one."
>
> The Queen: "Yes, I am your Queen, will you not admit me?"
>
> Door keeper: "My orders are explicit and I must obey them."
>
> Lord Hood: "I have a ticket."
>
> Door keeper: "Then, my lord, we will let you pass if you will produce it."

Lord Hood then drew from his pocket a peer's ticket for one person, the original name had been erased and the name of Wellington had been substituted.

> Door keeper: "This allows for the admission of only one person."

Lord Hood: "Will your Majesty go in alone?"

The Queen indicated that she would, but hesitated.

Lord Hood: "Am I to understand that you refuse her Majesty admission?"

Door keeper: "We have our orders."

Lord Hood: "Then you refuse the Queen admission?"

The Queen then decided to return to her carriage and, as she left the porch, some of the spectators laughed and hurled insults at her. She then went to the north entrance to the Abbey and was again refused admission.

Public opinion is forever changing, and the fickleness of the mob is proverbial. It is a question of "here today and gone tomorrow". Perhaps, being British, the crowd thought that she was a bad loser and felt that she should now take the lampooners' advice and "Go away at any rate". On this occasion she did, for in less than three weeks she was dead, and it can surely be said, whatever the medical diagnosis of her fatal illness was, that Caroline died of a broken heart.

This last indignity and insult which she had suffered must have been the more galling by reason of the fact that in her heart of hearts she knew that she had only herself to blame. Perhaps she realized this when she was first refused admission at the west door of the Abbey; but it was then too late, the damage had been done. She must secretly have cursed herself for her folly which had resulted in her being publicly insulted, as it were, in the face of the whole nation, and abroad as well, at a time when her credit and reputation had never stood so high.

As she drove back to her home she tried to conceal her chagrin from the crowds but she could not hide it from her friends. Nevertheless, they persuaded her to carry on as usual so as to prevent her ruminating too much on what had happened.

On Monday 30th July, therefore, although she was not feeling at all well Caroline kept a long standing engagement at Drury

Lane Theatre to see Edmund Kean in *Richard III*. Although she was taken ill during the performance she refused to leave until the end. On Tuesday she was slightly better, but the following day her doctor diagnosed a dangerous obstruction of the bowel. On Thursday and Friday she was still very ill though not considered to be in any danger.

Brougham was leaving that night for York and visited Caroline during the afternoon. "I was with her half an hour," he wrote. "She spoke calmly of her case and when I told her of the satisfactory opinion which I had just heard from her medical men she said, 'Oh no, my dear Mr. Brougham, I shall not recover and I am much better dead for I be tired of this life.'"

Stopping for the night at Grantham, on his journey to York, Brougham wrote and told Lord Grey, who, he was sure, "would be desirous of knowing really how the Queen was," for there were so many rumours going about. He added the following postscript to his letter: "I suppose the King would at first be very glad at her death, but he would soon find how odious it made him."

The Queen either knew that she was dying or was determined not to live if she could help it. When her leading physician, Dr. Holland, tried to tell her that her condition was still by no means hopeless all she said was, "No, my dear Sir, I fear your kind hopes will be disappointed."

By this time bulletins were being issued and none of them gave out much hope. On the Saturday morning it was rumoured that she had died at 7 a.m., and before it could be officially denied many tradesmen had closed their shops and some theatre managers sent messengers to Brandenburgh House to find out if it were true. At 3 p.m. the report was denied and Caroline was said to be improving slightly at which there was general relief which increased considerably when on Monday morning a still more favourable bulletin was issued, and on the Tuesday no bulletin at all.

But the improvement was only a flash in the pan and on 7th August, at 10.25 p.m., Caroline "passed peacefully away", having been unconscious for two hours.

As soon as the news reached York Brougham returned to London in order to attend the funeral and found that Lushington and Wilde (two of her counsel at the trial) had had a long interview with her before she died. She was then in no pain but she no longer knew what was going on around her or what she was saying, although she talked incessantly on almost every conceivable subject for three hours.

During her short but painful illness Caroline behaved with her usual courage and continually thought of others rather than of herself. All she wanted was to die. When her condition became worse Dr. Holland said that he would like a second opinion but, she said to him, "Do what you please if it will be any relief to your own mind, but do not do it for my sake. I have no wish to live: I would rather die." To one of her friends, who kept telling her that she would soon get well, she said, "Why do you wish me to live? Life to me can be nothing but a series of sorrows and persecution. I shall be much happier in another world than in this."

Speaking of her enemies she said that for years they had been conspiring and plotting to destroy her, and at last they had succeeded, but, "I forgive them. I die in peace with all mankind." She also sent for Mariette Bron, who was still in her service, and was the sister of Louisa Demont. She told Mariette that she forgave Demont for all her "cruel falsehoods".

When Wilde had visited her she added a codicil to her will. Her first wish had been to be buried in the same grave as her daughter Charlotte, but she said, "I can have little hope that the Government will grant me this wish. I desire, therefore, to be buried in the same vault with my father and mother in Brunswick."

Immediately after the Queen was dead Lushington wrote to the Earl of Liverpool giving him the news, and informing him that she had made a will and that he and Wilde were her executors. This letter the Prime Minister forwarded to the King and advised him to remain at Anglesey Castle, where he was staying, "until after the funeral which should be expedited as much as decency would permit." Unless the Queen had given any special direction in her will as to where she wished to be buried the Prime Minister suggested Windsor but, if the King objected to that, he suggested that she should be buried privately in Westminster Abbey.

The Prime Minister even thought it necessary to advise His Majesty of the "indispensable necessity of a mourning, as in no private family, whatever might have been the faults or sins of the individual, is mourning dispensed with." That he should have thought it necessary to give such advice to the King needs no comment. George was to be, if such a thing were possible, even more callous about his wife now that she was dead than he had been in her lifetime.

As soon as Lord Liverpool had seen Caroline's will, which was shown to him on the following day, he was able to tell the King that she had relieved him of all difficulties regarding her funeral by directing in her will that she was to be buried in Brunswick and that the coffin with her body should be sent off, if possible, within three days of her death.

In a second codicil to her will Caroline had directed that the inscription on her coffin should be, "Here lies Caroline of Brunswick, the injured Queen of England". The Prime Minister told the King that such an inscription would not be put on the coffin by authority or consent of the Government and Castlereagh agreed with this.

Meanwhile preparations for the lying in state were continued throughout Sunday and orders for ceremonial of the procession from London to Harwich were issued from the Lord Chamberlain's office. They stated that Her late Majesty's remains would be privately removed from Brandenburgh House on Tuesday morning at 7 a.m. and escorted by a squadron of the Royal Horse Guard via Romford to Chelmsford where they would be placed in the church under a military guard for the night. From there they would be taken via Colchester to Harwich for embarkation.

No mention was made, however, of the route which the procession would take after leaving Hammersmith, and inquiries were, therefore, made by the Sheriff of the County of Middlesex, in a letter to the Prime Minister asking for details to be given.

The following is an account which was given by Brougham who attended the funeral:

I took Sir Robert Wilson to Hammersmith where the Queen lay in state and from whence the procession took place. His son Henry, who had been one of her equerries, was in the carriage with us. The King had gone to Ireland, and Ministers having no orders, except to prevent all honours being paid and if possible to prevent the procession from marching through the city, acted upon their own notions of fulfilling his intentions and turned out the troops to obstruct our passage.

An attempt was made by us at Kensington to move round the palace and so reach Oxford street, as we were told that we must not go by Piccadilly. But they prevented us and obliged us to go through Hyde Park intending to turn us at Apsley House. We told them distinctly that the funeral must pass through the city. Nothing occurred till we got near Apsley House where the crowd was very great. The hearse was allowed to pass and was turned into the Park Lane direction by the soldiery. They then tried to stop us but we went on notwithstanding. I heard firing and one or two bullets whistled past us. On the first noise I asked Wilson what it was and he said "it is a noise you are not used to, we are under fire." Then said I, "We must get out of it but perhaps we should do so by going on." He said, "Certainly we should not be one whit worse than if we turned round." So we went forward. Only Wilson got out and told the officer commanding who we were and that we belonged to the procession. After a shot or two more this was effectual and we escaped without hurt, though one of the bullets struck the carriage. We then got into Oxford street and found it crowded by troops who made us turn into one of the streets leading to the New Road, the great object being to prevent us from getting into the city. However we made the procession go at a round pace so as to be there before the soldiery and this was the more easy because New Road was nearly empty, while the parallel streets were extremely crowded. We then got down the street that slants towards St. Paul's and were soon in the churchyard. The crowd was enormous and furious at the appearance of the soldiery.

As we moved slowly through it, several officers, not much liking their situation in the crowd, came up to our carriage and entered into conversation with us, manifestly thinking that their being seen to be friends would make things easier with the mob, which it did, for those officers were not at all maltreated, which the others were.

We at length got clear of the city, and went as far as Ilford in Essex on the Harwich road. We then returned to London . . . I was to start early next morning to overtake the funeral before it arrived at Chelmsford. I found it had just arrived and it was deemed proper that the coffin should be conveyed to the church, but the authorities there objected and Lushington had to call for the interposition of the magistrates to overcome the religious scruples of the clergy. Next morning it proceeded to Harwich at a continued rapid rate, these being the strictest orders sent from Dublin that the embarkation must be over before the arrival of the King which was fixed for the next day.

On arriving at Harwich we found everything ready prepared for immediate embarkation. The scene was such as I never can forget or reflect upon without emotion. The multitudes assembled from all parts of the country were immense, and the pier crowded with them as the sea was covered with boats of every size and kind, and the colours of the vessels were half-masted high, as on days of mourning. The contrast of a bright sun with the gloom on every face was striking, and the guns firing at intervals made a solemn impression.

One of the sights, however, which most struck me was a captain in the royal navy, who sat on the pier and could not be persuaded to leave it; he was deeply affected and wept exceedingly. Having been in her service and employed then and ever since in dispensing her charities, he could not tear himself away, but being refused his earnest request to accompany her remains to Brunswick, he was resolved to witness the embarkation.

The crimson coffin slowly descended from the pier and the barge that conveyed it bore the flag of England, floating over "Caroline of Brunswick, the murdered Queen of England!" (it was, in fact, the injured Queen) the inscription directed by herself, and the justice of which was felt by the thousands who had indignantly seen the indecent haste of the funeral procession from London, and who felt their share in a kind of national remorse, as well as commiseration for all that had passed.

What Brougham wrote about the public's instinctive feeling of disgust for the indecent haste with which Caroline's remains were bundled out of the country before the King returned from his holiday in Ireland was quite true. The cool reception which she had received from the crowd when she attempted to gate-crash the coronation proved to be short lived, and all the former sympathy for her and disdain for her royal husband came to life again as soon as the news of her illness became known. The final insult which the King offered to his Queen by trying to boycott her last journey home from the country where she had encountered so much persecution roused the outraged mob to bitter anger.

The authorities were prepared for disturbances which they feared would take place along the route of the funeral procession and arrangements had been made by Sir Robert Baker, the chief magistrate at Bow street, to station police officers along the line of march to deal with such disturbances, and orders were also issued for the Household Cavalry to be on the alert in barracks in case of emergency. And they were needed, as riots broke out in many places when the troops tried to side-track the procession.

As the thousands who had gathered near the pier at Harwich saw the ship which carried the body of their injured Queen to its last resting-place disappear from sight, two thoughts were uppermost in their minds; a feeling of relief that all her suffering was now a thing of the past, and of revulsion for their Sovereign who had been the cause of it all.

In his book, *The Modern British Monarchy*, Sir Charles Petrie states that our monarchy in its modern form, that is to say, accepted and respected, dates from the reign of Queen Victoria, and that what it was before that is admirably summed-up in the well-known lines of Walter Savage Landor:

> I sing the Georges four,
> For Providence could stand no more.
> Some say that far the worst
> Of all the four was George the First.
> But yet by some 'tis reckoned,
> That worse still was George the Second.
> And what mortal ever heard,
> Any good of George the Third?
> When George the Fourth from earth descended,
> Thank God the line of Georges ended.

Index

Index

Index

SILT ROAD

Also by Charles Rangeley-Wilson

Somewhere Else
The Accidental Angler

SILT ROAD

The Story of a Lost River

CHARLES RANGELEY-WILSON

CHATTO & WINDUS
LONDON

Published by Chatto & Windus 2013

2 4 6 8 10 9 7 5 3 1

Copyright © Charles Rangeley-Wilson 2013

Charles Rangeley-Wilson has asserted his right under the Copyright, Designs
and Patents Act 1988 to be identified as the author of this work.

The extract from *The Emigrants* by W. G. Sebald, published by The Harvill
Press. Reprinted by permission of the Random House Group Limited.

First published in Great Britain in 2013 by
Chatto & Windus
Random House, 20 Vauxhall Bridge Road,
London SW1V 2SA

www.vintage-books.co.uk

Addresses for companies within The Random House Group Limited can be
found at: www.randomhouse.co.uk/offices.htm

The Random House Group Limited Reg. No. 954009

A CIP catalogue record for this book
is available from the British Library

ISBN 9780701186432

The Random House Group Limited supports the Forest Stewardship
Council® (FSC®), the leading international forest-certification organisation.
Our books carrying the FSC label are printed on FSC®-certified paper. FSC
is the only forest-certification scheme supported by the leading environmental
organisations, including Greenpeace. Our paper procurement policy can be
found at www.randomhouse.co.uk/environment

Typeset by Palimpsest Book Production Ltd, Falkirk, Stirlingshire

Printed and bound by CPI Group (UK) Ltd, Croydon CR0 4YY

For my mother and father.
For Vicky, always.

I went out to the hazel wood,
Because a fire was in my head,
And cut and peeled a hazel wand,
And hooked a berry to a thread;
And when white moths were on the wing,
And moth-like stars were flickering out,
I dropped the berry in a stream
And caught a little silver trout.

'The Song of Wandering Aengus,' W. B. Yeats

Paul, in a conjecture she felt to be most daring, had linked the bourgeois concept of Utopia and order . . . with the progressive destruction of natural life.

The Emigrants, W. G. Sebald

CONTENTS

CONTENTS

SILT ROAD

PROLOGUE

Last night I dreamt I was pulling fish from a pond in a city. The pond was draining fast, shrinking to a puddle in the middle of a concrete bowl, the edges of which were caked in drying mud. The sun rose high overhead and the mud cracked as I watched it. It got so hot the air started to shimmer and I couldn't stand still on the concrete – my feet were burning. As the water ebbed away fish began to gasp in the puddle, flapping helplessly in their death throes. I ran for a bucket, filled it from a tap and ran back to the pond, spilling half the water on the way. I tried to scoop up the dying fish. I couldn't get hold of one. They writhed and slid away. Soon all the water was gone and lying on the mud – the only fish left – was this vast, beautiful trout with golden skin. I could just get its head inside the bucket. The fish had been choking on silt. Clouds of black sinter flushed from its gills. I lifted it up and ran with the trout head-down in the bucket, its body over my shoulders, the bucket held with both hands. I ran through the city looking for a river. But I couldn't find one. The trout was suffocating, desperately opening and closing its gills. The bucket began to fill with blood. I had to do something quickly. I was outside a tall building. I found the stairs and climbed to the roof. The bucket was now overflowing with blood. I threw the fish off the roof of the building and jumped after it and we started to fly side by side out of the city into the suburbs. We flew along the terraced streets until the houses gave way to open country and there we fell into a small brook. For a brief moment we were half swimming, half flying side by side, skimming through the water. And then the trout was gone.

Where do I start? Any start seems arbitrary, the insertion of a marker between days. As if to say: it begins here, my story, the water's story. But the days bleed into each other (and carry freight) so that it becomes impossible to split them. And the river flows the same way, from one day to the next, changing by degrees. All I can find is a sense of possibility – as if I'm feeling for the ground in heavy mist – the start of something perhaps, as I look at a night sky splitting open like this one and imagine its space going on for ever. The sky cracking open and slamming shut. And me on the road beneath it, fast, faster.

I'm on a motorway late in the evening: the sky ahead of me lights up for an instant. A curtain of yellow snaps on and off. Not the wired, dangerous blue of Hammer House lightning, but a solid sheet, as if a sky-wide door has been opened and shut again on a spectacular sunrise unfolding beyond it. Against this yellow a card-flat tumescence of blue, the top edge riding up and down like the outline of a cloud cartoon. Looming, falling, enormous, awesome. And then gone, back to black. Black and the headlights of trucks in the other carriageway, of tail lights in mine. For some reason – it hasn't been raining – the road reflects the headlights as they flash through the strobe of the central reservation and it feels like I'm on some manic, urgent river. The trucks are ships, and everything is in fast forward, racing, pulsing. The sky flashes yellow again, only this time the brightness lingers a heartbeat longer, teasing out the edges of the towering clouds. Then black again and the river of light.

As I pull off the motorway I'm fumbling with a map, trying to work out which part of the stream I'm going to look for. I've folded the paper so that I have the river's whole course in front of me, from where it rises out of the ground to where it runs into the Thames. Sometimes it is difficult to find where the stream scurries along the skirtings and culverts of the suburbs, the trading estates and housing estates that have been laid down across its valley. The slip road peels off and under the motorway, running into a roundabout on the valley side. The driver behind is impatient to pass. I'm going slow, not really knowing which way I'm heading and so I slide into the left lane and let him go by, though we are soon side by side waiting for a gap. I make a quick decision. I turn in to the industrial estate that sits directly under the motorway and stop the car. Here the river comes tumbling out of a pipe into a staircase of concrete flumes before dropping out of sight again under the car park of a computer software company. The last time I walked this river I stopped exploring right here, assuming the pipe was the upstream limit, the spring so to speak. Standing under the motorway along which the cars and trucks drummed and rushed and from which the rain spilt in a streaking line, I felt a fascinated longing for this imprisoned stream. And now I feel this stream running through me. Much more than any other river I've known. So I find myself beside it again, at night, the timpanic charge of the motorway above me, the River Wye a black ribbon below.

3

I

BEGINNINGS

1 The River

It was when for one reason or another I'd lost my way that I began to spend days by a river, walking the streets it flowed beside and was lost beneath.

The river came to possess me, as rivers can, though none more so than this. It was a spring-fed stream which rose in a furrow in a chalk hill, and this perhaps was part of it. For as long as I can remember I've been captivated by the spring-fed streams which flow through the chalk landscape of southern England. I have lived beside them and worked with them and I suppose I must have read hundreds of books about them too. When I try to recall whatever image or place was the origin of this obsession I always come to the memory of a photograph printed in an encyclopaedia of angling, which I was given when I was eleven years old. I can still picture the clear stream brimful under banks of yellow flag iris, its gravel bed bright between tresses of water-crowfoot, a thatched miller's cottage in the distance, willows shimmering in a breeze under billowing white clouds. I was growing up in a grainy London suburb and this Kodacolor photograph had an Arcadian beauty I found utterly compelling. Perhaps I instinctively understood the precariousness of its perfection, that such a scene was already a relic from a vanishing world. There was something in the balance of that picture, the river's wildness gently tamed but not vanquished, which I now realise is all too easily lost. Looking back I might even say that much of my life since has been a hunting after that perfection, or an attempt to rebuild it. As it happens I don't have the book any more, but last summer I was picking idly through a second-hand stall at a village fête when I found a battered and coffee-stained copy. I picked it up, ready to hand over the £5 asking price scribbled on a label, but flicking to the page I had been obsessed by when I was younger I found only a disappointingly muted version of the scene that had grown so vivid in my memory, an unremarkable vignette – complete with telephone lines and a semi-detached modern terrace – of summer on the edge of an ordinary Home Counties village. My imagined river had outgrown the real one and I wondered if, after all, I was only chasing phantoms and always had been. And yet the root of this obsession must also have been more than idyll, because there was very little about that vision, real or make-believe, which would call to mind or resonate with the River Wye now. Although my river rises in a copse in an open field, flowing under the old London to Oxford road and on into a Palladian park where more springs break, no sooner has this small stream passed out of the park under yet another busy road than it is completely subsumed by the housing estates and industrial estates that sprawl along its valley floor, filling the hollow like a glacier of bricks and tarmac.

Many years ago the Wye was a rural stream for most of its course, even though it flowed through the market town of High Wycombe and a few small villages and hamlets on its way to the Thames. But the particular heritage of this stream, its valley and springs, the land which enfolds it, the timeless passage of its waters, all these things held a future that could never remain bucolic. And indeed over the last century a rapidly growing town and its attendant factories, roadways, car parks and shopping centres have so overtaken the valley as almost to wipe out all trace of the small stream which created it. Only in a few green spaces does the river express itself at all, and even there it is corralled and shamed. And where it once flowed through the town the stream now runs in dark culverts under the streets.

Maybe there was something in the trammelled soul of this river that took hold of me. I was caught up with a dreary project in London, and could get back to the river only once in a while. Even then my journeys there involved detours I could hardly explain to myself, or justify. If I was holding on to a question I did not know how to frame it. If I was searching for its answer I did not know where to look. And yet the river would not let me go.

So, it is December and I've come back again. I drive for the first time through High Wycombe and beyond, in search of two things: the springs and a grave. A beginning perhaps, or an ending. In the first of these quests I am unsuccessful: the river is dry where the channel runs under the old Oxford road. The springs, which lie only a hundred yards upstream, have not broken in spite of the rain that has washed over the country these last few weeks.

I walk back to the car. The light is fading quickly. These days are short. It is nearly four and I have perhaps just thirty minutes left before it gets dark. I drive into town

9

through the early rush-hour traffic and pull over beside a warehouse to take another look at the map. An ancient Mercedes saloon moves off, the guy at the wheel twisting to watch me as he passes. Two men walk away across the road. One turns the collar of his coat up and kicks at a can, the other blows smoke into the air. It wreathes around his shoulders and holds momentarily in a space behind his back. At the end of the road ahead of them is a hunched building, Riverside Surgery written over the door beside a glowing blue cross. I pull into the car park. Along the northern edge spindly sycamores reach into the fading light from a tangle of scrub beneath. I turn off the engine, get out of the car and push through the undergrowth.

Here, hidden inside a dark furrow, I find the stream. Its surface glints, reflecting the last of the day, the street lights beyond. I could almost walk across the river, the flow is so thin. Along the bank there is only bare soil and the trailing fronds of ivy that have peeled off the trees, piles of leaves and plastic that have been swept off the path above. It smells of damp ground and unburnt exhaust fumes. But what gets me, as I crouch down at the water's edge and reach my hand out so that all of my fingers touch the surface, is its silence. I close my eyes as if that might help. Behind me a new car has pulled into the car park. A door shuts and I hear voices. A clattering exhaust starts up in some other yard or car park nearby. Overhead the drone of a climbing jet. The beep beep of a reversing truck. A horn pressed in anger. Twice. And over the ridge opposite, the ceaseless white-noise rush of the A40, raised every few seconds by waves of traffic climbing the hill from the lights. But the river says nothing. I watch the water furl around my fingertips, delicate eddies spinning briefly until they flatten and the river moves on, unmoved.

The traffic softens for a moment and echoing along the cloister of trees I hear the distant whisper of a running stream. I have to walk across the surgery car park, along the street and back on myself to reach where the sound is coming from. Now a chain-link fence runs between this next car park and the stream. Halfway along it a ticket machine is wrapped in a bin bag and wound with tape repeating OUT OF ORDER. The sign hanging off its slumped shoulders reads: POLICE: CRIME IN PROGRESS. I walk towards this crime and the sound of rushing water. I step up to the fence and through it see the flow buckle over a concrete sill, plunging through a metal grid and into the ground. So, this is it. I've found where the river is siphoned from the landscape. As the water falls, the river speaks. And beyond this rush is the hollow, in-darkness echo from within the tunnel, the sound of water lost to a man-made drain. The sound of a river ceasing to be a river.

So, what is a river? A river is the breath of a valley. It is the distillation of everything that is washed by rain within the bounds of a line that rides the hilltops – of meadows and marsh, thickets and woods, springs, ditches, drains, of verges crushed by tyres, tarmac laid in a railway yard, antifreeze on a road, shit out of a pig farm, bleach from a sink: a river inhales it all, for good or bad and exhales the breath of a valley. A river is a living thing and it is inviolable. But beyond this grating, somehow everything is changed. Here beside the ticket machine, before the water corrugates over the sill and falls into the culvert, it is a river. It is thin, washed out, and flows over litter as much as sand. But it is a river. Confined between brick walls, drowned in shadows, half resuscitated by glimmers of daylight, still it is a river. But forced into that underground channel, to run through concrete pipes in the pitch black, unheard, unseen it has become the ghost of a river. A memory.

Here comes a kid, picking up leaves, throwing them at his dad.

I look upstream and watch a purple drinks bottle drift slowly on the current. It catches a branch, turns, bobs up and down, and drifts on towards a grating already clogged with litter. Car park lamps create pools of light now, and the sky fades from darkness to a watery band above the hill. Closer in are the harder edges of timber stores and warehouses; behind me the continuous thrum of the main road. And you'd never know there was a river between. A siren sounds and raindrops fall on the surface of the water. The river folds, fractures and drops away, a rushing hiss of white bubbles turning over and over. The river is blind, I think, feeling its way by gravity and touch, caressing the surface of things to understand them. Invisible, until you step into its world.

II The Road

Even now I am not certain what it was about this particular river that drew me in. But as the weeks and months went past I found myself going back again and again simply to walk its banks, or stand quietly beside it taking notes and photographs. I became familiar with the streets and alleyways, where it flowed and where it sank from sight, the traces of its mills and water meadows, the ghosts of the country houses, slums and factories that had once surrounded it: all those buried histories that had shaped this imprisoned stream. And slowly I became gripped by the idea that every footfall of landscape has its own story fractured within the surface of things, as if the past were hammering against ice from underneath.

It is January now. The year has turned, one into the next and I have travelled by train from Marylebone to High Wycombe and by taxi to West Wycombe Hill.

The train ride was slow, the carriage airless and soporific as the engine laboured uphill to Gerrard's Cross and Beaconsfield, the pummelling rhythm of its gears echoing between embankments of sycamores and brambles, till at a place called Cut-throat Wood we entered a tunnel through the chalk hill and moments later broke into the valley of the River Wye. The few passengers who shared my carriage slept the whole way, their heads nodding forward or slumped against the glass, and so no one paid attention as I snapped pictures of the scenery through a dirty window, brief glimpses of the valley emerging from a thin mist, the motorway riding across it on concrete stilts, lorries and cars dashing over the roofscape and below them the river seeping through a furrow in the dry dust.

And having paid and thanked the taxi driver I clamber now up the steep hill until I am high above the shrieking children in the school playground, the wisps of smoke rising from cottages in West Wycombe. The avenue of the A40, the old Oxford road, along which I have just been driven, splits the landscape like a zip, while the green dome of the chalk spur falls away below me. A fire engine siren rises from the distance, and halfway along the road I see its winking red lights. A trail of white and red eases aside, swallowing the fire truck uphill.

The source of my river lies in a cleft in the landscape below me. Its channel – still dry – slips under the Oxford

Road, and gathering flow from other springs which are still running, decorates the landscape of West Wycombe's stately park: I can just make out, through the darkening mass of trees, the glimmering expanse of the lake, the Mediterranean yellow of a Palladian mansion on the hillside above. But quickly this Arcadian vista gives way to the built-up outskirts of High Wycombe and from there the houses and workshops spread unbroken across the valley floor, row upon row of terraced semis swirling like the gathering regiments of an army. I take a photograph and lean back against the flint wall of the mausoleum that crowns the summit, sheltering under its overhang from a light drizzle that has overtaken the afternoon. The sun is already low in the sky to the south-west, and as it falls beneath the clouds and briefly lights the hilltops and the valley fills with shadow as the houses and factories melt into the gloom, I see the landscape from a time before any of this was here. I see the grassy marshland of the valley floor, its thickets of willow, pilasters of dog rose, the stream switching this way and that, braided and overflowing. The water surface is dotted with constellations of white flowers and beneath them tresses of starwort and water-crowfoot sway in the marbled currents. Here and there springs break, upwelling in domes of bright water while clouds of mayflies rise and fall in the air above them. I hear the wind in the rushes and dry grass, the restless chatter of reed warblers. And up here on the thin, dry soil of the hillsides I see the dense forests of beech and oak reaching to the distant horizon. To the early settlers of this land the valley of the River Wye, with its eternal stream and fertile soil, must have seemed like paradise.

I open my eyes to the rush of tyres on a wet road, the distant drone of aeroplanes, a train speeding through the valley, a hammer drill: all the noises of a busy town washing towards this hill as if the air is ocean, rolling like waves on to a reef of chalk. And suddenly in the broken turf of the hill, in the beech woods which crown it and the lake beneath them glowing silver in the sinking light, in the housing estates or the grey industrial units of the dim valley floor, I feel how the centuries have broken over this landscape like waves, each drawing away to leave fragments, the valley's history slowly accreting like the chalk it is built on.

I leave the hill and walk back along the A40 towards the town. Back to earth and this is my first thought. The road is a river. The real river is lost.

On this wet afternoon that idea is made more vivid by the reflections of headlights on the damp tarmac, the glinting street lights, the wide pool of green and yellow spilling from the garage at the roundabout below West Wycombe Hill. This downpour has brought to life the inverted narrative of the valley, the silencing of the old voice, the rise of the new. Each vehicle is like a wave washing down the channel of road, a burst dam of noise. I brace myself as they rear up behind me and pass. Light smashes into the rain. Noise rolls over it. And into the air behind is thrown a roiling vortex of water vapour.

The real river – if it is running at all – is hidden in the dark hollow of the valley.

Finally I reach a junction. The insane rush of the A40 recedes behind me. Chapel Lane rolls down a gentle incline, levels and climbs again, its vanishing point buried behind the branches of overhanging trees. I pass the vast, blind walls of a factory encircled by a security fence and signs that read WARNING: RAZOR WIRE. I pass an eighteenth-century almshouse set back from the road behind box hedges and a neat lawn. And then as the gradient flattens and I see ahead of me the flint walls of a bridge, all the noise drops away leaving behind an eerie silence. It stops me dead. I strain my hearing, feel I must be imagining it, or that the incessant tumult must have briefly blown back on the wind. But there is no wind. The branches above me are still. I look up the road ahead and it is empty, though seconds before it was a ribbon of cars. I turn round: nothing. The A40, of which I can see only a short section, is empty too. In this insulated silence I finish my journey and walk to the bridge. I look over the parapet and see a flat expanse of water framed by reeds and broken willows: the lower end of another park lake that seeps away under the bridge below. I look downwards. Tucked inside the hollow beneath the bridge the water is cloaked in a grainy light reflecting the sky. Instinctively I search for a window in the surface and find it. And there, as if waiting, is a vast and beautiful trout. My eyes strain to hold the silhouette but with one flick of its tail the trout pushes away from the shallow and under the sky. I can't hold on to it. I scan the lake, for a shimmer on the surface, a bow wave. Nothing. After a minute it is as if the fish was never there. And then I hear a car turn off the main road. The lights have changed. The noise rushes downhill and traffic is sweeping past again. A moorhen pulls itself across the water. A second clatters out of the reeds, leaving a trail of skimming-circles behind it. A covey of pigeons drops inside the spinney, breaking into a flutter of grey as the birds settle.

II

A GOLDEN WORLD

It is Tuesday, 15 January 2008 and I am in room 42 of the Abbey Lodge Hotel on Priory Road, High Wycombe. I slept badly last night. My throat was like a desert gully every time I woke and my heart pounded in my ears with a noise like a large industrial fan turning slowly: whump, whump, whump. Outside, High Wycombe glowed and whispered, its lights and rush talking to the sky as the river would once have done. I imagined the river flowing between snow-draped banks and wondered whether it could be heard now the town was asleep. With no moon and stars, only a deep mist forming a reflective cover, the innumerable lights of the town were trapped between the snow and the sky. All the buildings and trees, garden walls and parked cars, the church, the hill on the far side of the valley, the railway line – everything was as visible as if it were a gloomy winter's day. The sky glowed a jaundiced yellow. The snow was blue. And between, purple and orange signs stood out, etched in neon – Sainsbury's, Morrisons, BP, all visible from up here.

I woke some time in the small hours – too much beer – stood and padded to the bathroom. Glancing out the window as I went I saw, or imagined I saw, a light on in the dormer window of the house next door, and someone

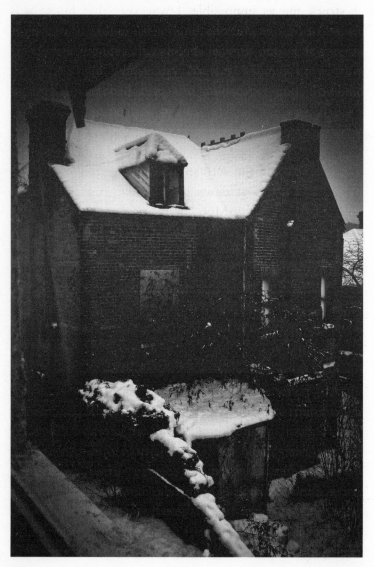

at the window gazing out over their back garden. Perhaps I was still half asleep. I don't think I had processed the thought until I was by the toilet and the fierce bathroom light and the noisy ventilator had jolted me awake. Then it struck me as impossible. I was sure that house was empty and derelict. I'd noticed boarded windows and panels of security fencing the evening before. I looked again as I walked back to bed. The window was dark and empty and the pane in it was broken. I sat on the edge of the bed for a minute, looking at that empty house, and the image in my mind then, for some reason I can't explain, was of the precise geometry of the wainscot back home as it runs along the turn in the stairs. I recalled how I had paused there at dawn the morning before, carrying the tea as I do every Monday at half-past six. With only the reflected light from the kitchen below and the bedroom above, a grey, palpable stillness between and the only sound my feet pushing across the carpet at each step of the stair . . . I remembered that we had argued the night before. That Monday morning stairwell, its mucus of newsprint grey, and suddenly the relentless plod of mornings, the days bleeding without meaning, all this stuff behind a door we contrive in a thousand different ways to keep shut: I glimpsed it for a second, felt the weight and remembered our fight, as if it was that which had opened the door. We're all running, I thought, like that coyote who has long since left the canyon road, legs pedalling wildly over thin air. And if the coyote stops and looks down, then he falls. We're miles above the earth running like fuck to stay in the screen. But stop and look, at dawn on the stairwell, your heart going like a tractor pump, then you'll see just how far is down. That's when you drop out of the picture leaving a circular cloud behind you. Peeeeow.

Vicky had been in a spin about her work, a deadline and a choice with hardly enough time to make either, let alone both. I offered the simple idea of flipping a coin. Most of the time we can see only the bow-saw in our hand and then the forest. She said it was a good idea, for want of any better. There was a pause as I washed a few more plates and Vicky wiped the side and called the dog, to let her out.

Then she came back through and said, 'So, enough of me. What are you going to do?'

'I don't know . . . Just don't fucking ask. Okay?'

'Sorry.'

And now I'd been tetchy and short. And guilt doubles the speed of the fall. It's a chasm down there and I don't know what I'll do, whether I'll pedal the air, or stop because of the dawn light and the shape of the wainscot, and glancing down see the horizon – in newsprint grey like the stairwell – come reeling forwards, getting faster all the time.

'I'll sort something out,' I said.

'Cool,' she said.

There was no one at the window. I had imagined it, or dreamt it. I shivered and went back to bed. I have, perhaps, been dreaming more than normal.

The sounds of dawn: at first the hum of the town. Then birds. One or two singular, stark noises filling out slowly until there is an all-pervasive electric chatter. Spilling inside this the coughing reluctance of a diesel van in the hotel car park, the engine turning for five or six seconds before it catches. And then its wood-slapping clatter. An alarm clock next door set for seven-thirty and ignored by the person in the bath, beeps on and on and on. Finally a drill starts up – a street or two away – and its seismic hammering propels me out of bed.

Outside, High Wycombe is cloaked in a blanket of thin, frigid air. Figures walk hunched against the cold and drizzle. I'm intrigued by this house next door. No one can have lived here or tended it for twenty years. In the garden the snow lies in heaps, over stones and piles of plastic bags and in a thick, rolling cover underneath a riot of branches: laurel, ash, beech and sycamore – all grown wild so that the full length of the garden, which reaches back a hundred yards, has become a young forest. Branches bar the white landscape with stripes of green and red. The dormer window in the roof – the one at which I imagined I saw someone last night – is broken and rotten, its white boards worn thin and fractured by the weather. Snow has blown in at the open window. Grass is growing out of the gutter.

Yesterday evening, after a frustrating day in the library, I came back from the café where I had eaten supper and spent some time looking through a book of old photographs of the town. Leafing through the pages I found images of the river flowing in sepia beside mills, bridges and water meadows, the Old King of Prussia public house where the stream swept in a broad curve alongside the walls of the building and under a wooden footbridge. I recognised the flint bridge on Chapel Lane described as 'The Pepperboxes, West Wycombe', although it took me a while to work out that the photographer must have set up his tripod on ground now buried beneath a furniture factory. In another image a boy in breeches, stout shoes and a jacket had stopped on the main Oxford road to pose, hands on hips, though his head, which was broad and smudged, must have turned at just the wrong moment. Behind him other figures had also stopped to watch the photographer as they leant against a bridge. The stream,

which ran hidden from view in a brick-lined channel, was separated from the road and pavement by black bollards and a single railing. As I studied the image I realised that absolutely nothing in that old photograph remains today. The bay-fronted Victorian villas, the terraces beyond, the rows of glass-fronted shops under awnings in the distance, the bridge that ends Brook Street, the river itself, the trees that have grown between the stream and houses – every last brick and board and leaf is gone. And so these waves of light frozen in a second are already only echoes of what they once described so forensically; the image no more than a shadow, or a scent left hanging in the air. Somehow the misty haze and the overexposure of the photograph – which only made the whole scene more vaporous – had combined to render these buildings and the river as unfixed in space and time as the boy whose head had blurred and become two, captured in the same moment.

I flicked through other parts of the book – so many of the images had faded, or were overexposed or were overwhelmed by the same misty light which seems to have permanently enveloped the valley a century ago – until eventually I was too tired and I pulled open the curtains and fell asleep.

But now as I step out on to the snowy pavement and turn to study this derelict house the view triggers a memory of yet another picture I must have glimpsed and passed over the night before. I pull the book out of my bag and turn the pages until I find a photograph of a row of private villas taken in 1907 from more or less where I am standing. There is Abbey Lodge, the same Gothic lettering drawn over the glass. And next door the same barrel-vaulted dormer window, the same colonial veranda under a sloping lead roof, the same wrought-iron pillars and railings outside. Its name is obscured by a climbing plant, as it is now by plywood, but the date – 1902 – is just visible. And so the house was only five years old when the picture was taken, but already it was half shrouded in shrubs and trees: a silver birch, a cherry, and laurel hedging. Now it is falling apart, while the villa next door has been extended to provide forty-five guest rooms, and its garden has been paved in tarmac so that the occupants of those rooms have somewhere to park their cars. And the houses uphill, semi-detached and not as grand as the hotel or its derelict mirror image, are a veterinary surgery, an accountant's office, a Conservative club, or are broken into flats.

I suppose this house must have held on to its home-liness for that much longer until it too succumbed to the weight of history. Perhaps its owners moved away and forgot about it. Or a widow grew old here with the walls crumbling around her, weeds pressing in through cracks in the windows until finally she died alone, leaving the place to her cats. However it happened, the land around the house has become a feral reminder of what was here even before there was a house. The overblown box hedging, the laurel cloaking the southern walls – these are echoes, like the building, of smart Edwardian domesticity. But through the garden where the brambles are taking hold, along with the self-sown beech trees and common ivy, the buried wildness of the hill is breaking into the open air, an isolated fragment of a forgotten landscape. I imagine this life thrusting back uninvited, before one thought gives way to another: that soon the place will be a car park too like the land next door, like the ground beside the stream; and the open hill and the Edwardian garden will be lost again under the strata of time.

It is market day in the town centre. A stallholder blows into his hands as I pass. He looks up and shouts over to someone behind me, 'Didn't think you were coming.' A tight, gaunt man in a black suit, his trousers too short, is arranging bibles on a stand marked BIBLES. He's selling nothing else. Next to him an Asian kid taps a text into his mobile. His stall sign reads ANY MOBILE UNLOCKED HERE. The traffic seems less violent this morning. I walk along icy pavements back through the town past Bridge Street and Brook Street to the district called Newland,

and then past the Wye River Studios, and on to the Oxford Road which runs in a straight line to the foot of the West Wycombe spur. I can see the dome of the church sticking up like a golden nipple from the swell of the hill. My plan is to trek back up to the Pepperboxes on Chapel Lane and from there follow the river back into town as closely as the streets and paths will allow. I've noticed on the map an expanse of green close to Chapel Lane which I guess must be a playing field or park. I've noticed also that the river runs around this open ground in two channels, having split just upstream of the Pepperboxes, only to reunite at the lower limit of the park, near Fryer's Lane, where the river seems to be swallowed back into the industrial hinterland of Wycombe. It looks as if that open ground may be the only place between the springs and the river's early grave where it runs freely, in touch with a floodplain, open to the skies: and for that reason alone I'd like to see it. But to suggest – to hope – it might be free-flowing is not the same as to say its course will be untouched. The split channel is surely man-made. But then almost every inch of a chalk stream is, they being the most malleable of rivers, the most used. I know before I see it that the straighter of these two channels will be the remnants of a leat: a conduit impounded behind raised banks to create a head of water to drive a mill. The other channel will be the original course of the river, retaining its gradient and meanderings. If my hunch is right then between the two I'll find a wide expanse of flat ground that would once have been a water meadow. Not simply a meadow by water – so many places vaguely near a river are given this generically romantic and appropriated meaning – but a meadow once traversed by a network of

27

ridges and furrows, encompassed by a maze of channels and sluices: a utilitarian water garden of the type that, four hundred years ago, drove an agricultural revolution. Water meadows were once common in our chalk landscape, though most have subsided, disused and unloved, into the land they once tamed. Seen from above, from a hillside or bridge in the low light of morning, these remnants have the appearance of a woven landscape, a patchwork, or herringbone pattern stitched into the earth. They have a geometry that to me seems to harness more than vanquish. And in their slow decay this relic of ancient farming becomes the most bewitching landscape art.

It seems, however, that there were few water meadows anywhere in Buckinghamshire – though chalk streams lend themselves perfectly to this sculpture of earth and water – an anomaly remarked on in a general agricultural review of the county published in 1794. But there were some, 'just a few in the neighbourhood of the paper mills'. In those days Buckinghamshire's paper mills stood on the Wye and Fryer's Mill, at the foot of Fryer's Lane, was one of the first on the river to make the change from milling corn to milling paper.

Though I have long been fascinated by water meadows and their history, I have never been able to discover where the very first water meadow was constructed or by whom. There are records of field names that may be descriptions of early water meadows, *Fludgatmedow* or *le Floudyeat,* and John Fitzherbert's 1523 *Boke of Surveying and Improvements* describes how a natural flood might be harnessed to the same end as was later more formally realised in constructed water meadows. Drawn patterns of water meadows appear centuires later in one or two volumes from the late eighteenth century: George Boswell's *Treatise on Watering Meadows* 1779 contains line drawings of abstract beauty, and by the time William 'strata' Smith wrote his *Observations on the Utility, Form and Management of Water Meadows* in 1806, having completed intricate projects for the gentleman farmers the Duke of Bedford and Thomas Coke, this rustic carving of the land had become a fashionable science.

But it was a soldier-veteran of the Tudor wars in Ireland who first set to writing a formal discourse on water meadows and so became their unsubstantiated inventor. Rowland Vaughan manipulated the landscape of the little River Dore, a tributary of a different River Wye in Herefordshire, in the late sixteenth century. But his strange account, with its meandering and oblique narrative threads which loop and intertwine and never quite get to a conclusion, is far more telling in its form than its content, and betrays as much as anything else the workings of a mind that could conceive of doing the very same thing with land and water. This book – entitled *Most Approved and Long Experienced Water-Workes* and subtitled *The manner of Winter and Summer drowning of Medow and Pasture, by the advantage of the least, River, Brooke, Fount, or Waterprill adjacent; there-by to make those grounds (especially if they be drye) more Fertile Ten for One* – is mostly about nothing of the sort. Rowland, who dictated his work to a scrivener in Fleet Street, used its pages to air grievances about the Court of Wards, a Machiavel of a Puritan preacher Rowland thought better fit for service as a spy; salmon weirs on the Wye; his aunt and his wife and his neighbours; and to curry favour and funds from half the aristocracy of England, amongst other things.

29

Only very circuitously does Rowland get around to describing his water-meadow system and even then in the most abstract language that never seems to nail down how it actually worked.

Not much is known of Vaughan except what his book tells us. He was born in 1559 in Herefordshire into a family whose ancestors included a knight who fought and was killed at Agincourt and by whom – as Rowland takes pains to point out – he was connected to most of the Old Nobility. He started life at court under the eye of his aunt Dame Blanche Parry, but, too tender to stand the bitterness of her humour, he set off for the easier frontier of the Irish wars. There he fought, waist deep in bogs, until the poor diet and fasting sent him home to Herefordshire, sick, so he said, with the country disease.

Published in the year that Galileo discovered the four moons of Jupiter and Shakespeare wrote his last play, Rowland's *Water-Workes* of 1610 describes a grand project which had so overtaken his mind for the two decades following his return from Ireland that, as he confessed, he scarce shot a buck in all that time, even though sometimes they would wander within yards of his stream. Rowland had fallen sick with a new illness, it seemed: an addiction to rivers.

In 1585, more or less recovered and ready to rejoin the fighting Rowland had instead met and married Elizabeth Parry, his first cousin and a country gentlewoman who owned a manor and a watermill. Two years on, bored, and fearful that his life was wasting away, Rowland resolved to find some means of sating his thirst for military glory without, so he hoped, forfeiting the contentment of his loving wife. But he never found it. The loving wife put a halt to his dreams. Keen that he should make himself useful about her estate, Elizabeth, a strong-willed woman, set him to spying on the dealings of her miller. And so it happened that in March 1587, as he strolled towards the mill along the edge of its leat, Rowland noticed a molehill from which a stream of water flowed down the shelving bank on to the field below. When he stopped to contemplate the pleasing sight – this miniature spring caused by the burrowing of the mole in the raised banks of the river – he noticed how the grass along the flow of water until it sank back into the earth was a rich green, while all around was bleached and dry. There is little in Rowland's account to explain why or how he proceeded from this curious observation to a lifelong project of civil engineering, excepting perhaps the implication that he wanted for some great enterprise that might define him. We only know that it was clear to Rowland how the constant flow had improved the grass, that richer grazing would lead to greater fortune and that he set to working out how to replicate and formalise this accidental flooding on a larger scale.

Building a system of trenches, the most significant of which he called his Trench-Royal, but supplemented by counter-trenches, defending trenches, topping and braving trenches, winter and summer trenches, double and treble trenches, a traversing trench with a point, an everlasting trench and other 'troublesome' trenches, Rowland corralled the springs and streams of the valley of the Dore to his purpose. The map that would elucidate the layout of this complex water maze was never drawn. And of the construction of the irrigation system, though his book runs to several hundred pages, he wrote just these 96 words:

> In the running and casting of my *Trench-royall* though it were leveld from the beginning to the end, upon the face of the ground, yet in the bottome I did likewise levell it to avoyde error.
>
> For the *Breadth* and *Depth*, my proporcion is ten foote broad, and foure foote deep; unlesse in the beginning, to fetch the water to my drowning-grounds, I rann it some halfe mile, eight foot deepe; and in some places sixtenne-foote broad. Al the rest of the *Course*, for two miles and a halfe in length, according to my former proportion.

It is really only possible to surmise the plan by reading and rereading Rowland's circuitous prose, comparing it to the remnants of this watery labyrinth still visible in the landscape. Rowland's Trench-Royal, it seemed, was a three-mile diversion of water off the main river, a canal built along the contour line to one side of the valley floor. At its lowest end was the Stanke-Royal, a large dam used to hold the water back until the trench was full, when the flow could be diverted via a myriad of sluices out of the Royal into a series of counter-trenches which ran a few feet into the meadows and then turned parallel to it. From these, yet more trenches were cut at right angles to traverse the width of the meadows, and small gouts in these allowed the water to flow evenly over the grassland and on into drainage cuts that finally funnelled it all back to the main river. The meadows thus enclosed were levelled like a lawn, as Rowland described them, so that no drop of water went idle, no quarter of ground received more or less water than the rest. For this watery labyrinth Rowland had no blueprint. His works took him two decades of trial and error and it is easy to imagine that sculpting the land like this – the mile upon mile of trenches and embankments raised by hand with spadework, the dozens of dams and hatches built to tame the floods of this mercurial river – would have taken thousands of hours and cost him his fortune.

'Of what effect it shall worke,' he said, 'you shall have all I know to the uttermost.'

Each winter when the river changed colour in flood Rowland would divert its flow to his meadows, playing the water across the ground so that, as he described it, the substance of fallow and dunghill settled there. As the River Nile drowns Egypt from the Abissine mountains, enriching that place to the wonder of the world, so doth the muddy floods, said Rowland, from the Golden valley improve my estate beyond belief. When the water cleared he would lift his sluices and wait for the next flood. In March he would drain the ground and keep his meadows as dry as a child under the hands of a dainty nurse. But if April followed dry, on the heels of a dry March, in May he would drop the boards and drown the land again, thereafter ministering to it constantly, ensuring that it was never too wet or too dry. Three days before mowing he would flood the ground once more and gain a fortnight of growth thereafter and grounds that were as soft as velvet or Turkish carpet. He had little time for worms and even less for moles: the blind creature that gave him his idea could just as easily undermine its physical incarnation. When once he hunted bucks Rowland now wanted no better sport than hunting moles in his meadows, their offence being 'burglary'.

The work so overtook his mind that he lost all care for the glorious military career that once beckoned, seeing himself as general instead to his grand waterworks, Lord of the natural Utopia he had wrought, but ever alert to any insurgency of the conquered land, attendant to every rise in the river or drop of rain, for it pained Rowland more than he could bear to see a summer flood run idle and carrying, as he saw it, the bounty of the land to the bowels of the sea. So much had he harnessed and enhanced this bounty that it pained him too that his neighbours, in wilful ignorance, did not follow him. Indeed, no one else in the Kingdom could claim comparable ground, said Rowland, unless he also drowned as Rowland did: because it is confessed by everyone in the Golden Vale that if the like were done throughout England it would profit the Kingdom two million pounds in a year, enough to maintain a Royal Army to the honour of Great Britain and the comfort of soldiers crestfallen for want of war.

So much had he changed his meadows through his great waterworks, Rowland also changed their names to commemorate his life's work: his meadow 'nine-days math' could hardly be called that now that it yielded over thirty. And so his grounds, divided into twelve portions, became the Pinck, the Gille-Flower, the Carnation, the Rosemary, the Mary-gold, the Gilt Cup, the Honeysuckle, the Daysy, the Garland, the Eglentine, the Cowslip and the Primrose: new names laid over the old as much as new earth. Because Rowland hoped to reshape the world in more than just earthworks and canals: his waterworks were only the start of his dreaming. Rowland wished to raise a new world, a golden world in this Golden Vale. The little river would give its bastardised name to an English El Dorado.

His Golden Vale was, said Rowland, the richest, yet for want of employment, also the plentifullest place of poor in the Kingdom. Within a mile and a half of his house at

Newcourt five hundred beggars lived intolerable lives. They survived by pillaging cornfields, orchards, gardens, hop-yards and crab trees, and being poor they could barely get a foothold in an honest trade. Thus their lives were misspent in a most miserable manner. And yet through his dream of a golden world, through his vision of this commonwealth, he could remedy their miseries if only His Lordship the Earl of Pembroke, to whom the book is dedicated, would recognise (and sponsor) Rowland's great discovery: the waterworks that would give rise to this Utopia.

Alongside the mill he would build a dining room to entertain knights and gentlemen, a buttery, a pantry, a kitchen and a larder; and, beside that, rooms for his tradesmen – the employed beggars in Rowland's wandering imagination had now become his 'mechanicals' – a surveying room, a brewhouse, a slaughterhouse, a backhouse. The mechanicals would include a clerk, a miller, a loder, a malt-maker, a butcher, a chandler, cooks, bakers, brewers, a tanner, a shoemaker, a cobbler, a glover, a currier, a sickle-maker, a nailer, a smith, a joiner, a cooper, a carpenter, a mercer, a cutler, a barber, stocking knitters, a hosier, a lanthorne-maker, a fletcher, a bowyer – here Rowland paused, red in the face and short of air while the scrivener faithfully recorded his words 'hold breath'. Breath recovered, the list goes on – a tailor, a sempster, launderers, wheelers, a card-maker for spinners, a hatter, a point-maker, as well as shepherds, hinds, dairy-people, swine-herds, two vittlers and 'a noyse of musitions with the Greene-Dragon and Talbot'. If I make a mistake, said Rowland, in marshalling my mechanicals, His Lordship must understand that I am no herald: after all, it is no great offence to place one knave before another. However they are gathered in whatever order, he continued, all these mechanicals will serve those who work the ten narrow looms, the ten fustian looms and such silk looms as might be necessary; the number of spinners, carders, wool pickers and quill winders rising to two thousand in due course, which vast number in turn will not want for anything their backs or bellies might require. And in this Lombardy of Herefordshire, said Rowland, no tradesman will rate his own commodity, but instead prices will be set by the clerk and so every tradesman will trade with every other at rates reasonable and accordant with the good of the commonwealth.

If only he had the funds Rowland would raise this Arcadian collective from the silt newly washed to these meadows by his great waterworks. Many honourable gentlemen, Rowland said, perceiving how his ability and vision exceeded his means, had wished him entreat a number of 'Contributers', persons of great worth, who would have sympathy with such an undertaking and help make it happen. And so, separating these persons from the sullied layers of society, so respectfully did he undertake the invention of this idea, Rowland invited the good Earl to become a benevolent Contributer, along with the Lord of Mountgomery and the Bishops of Worcester, Hereford and Gloucester. He also invited the Lord Chief Justice of England, the Lord Chief Justice of the Common Pleas, the Lord Chief Baron, all the good Lords and judges in general, the Knights of Bath, the Knights of the Field, the Knights of Great Britain. And in case he had left anyone out he invited all the gentlemen and esquires of all the counties as well.

Nor would these Contributers go unrewarded, for in homage to their generosity he would build a dining room, wainscoted and hung with arras, the table forever furnished to entertain forty at a sitting, a hundred Artificers to attend, twenty-five at dinner, twenty-five at supper, fifty more the next day and so on, daily and perpetually. The Artificers would serve forty varieties of meats, with a pasty of venison for dinner and another for supper. So that the commonwealth of mechanicals should know when a Contributer, or a party of them might visit – and Rowland's expectation was that they would throng to his door daily – a sentinel would be set in a turret from ten until eleven: if a footman approached the sentinel would sound a bell to signify a footman, and at the bell a drum would beat; if a horseman, the bell would be rung and a trumpet would sound. And so awoken, the commonwealth would prepare to entertain with joy and merriment and music from Bartholomew Day to mid-May.

I think I have bestirred myself pretty well, wrote Rowland Vaughan, to make the world wonder at me.

And so his strange treatise ends.

I doubt that his golden world in all its imagined glory ever came to pass, though some like to believe it did. Ellen Wood, whose 1897 edition of Rowland's book I have with me in my bag, describes his two thousand mechanicals at their looms as if his vision were a reality, though it seems to me more likely that beyond the water meadows the rest was only ever a flight of fancy. At the very least the ground is blurred between what existed and what might have existed if only Rowland could have gained the patronage of the Earl of Pembroke and others. He must have employed a carpenter to build his sluices, a miller to grind his corn, mechanicals to dig and maintain the trenches, labourers to cut the hay, to shepherd the sheep. Whether he ever kept a table furnished day and night for forty of his patrons waited on by a hundred Artificers, whether his looms were spun and tended by two thousand mechanicals, all of this is less certain. A person in command of that scale of empire might not have needed to add as the coda to his narrative the public acknowledgement of a debt of 40 shillings still owed to a person unspecified, to be paid at the end of five years from the date thereof, being 1609. Such a person might not have mortgaged his manors with 500 acres of land, or sold up his home for good in 1614, or have spent thirty years in constant litigation with neighbours and relatives over transactions to do with the sale and purchase of the lands on which he worked his watery empire.

In fact so little is recorded of Rowland's real life – that which exists coming mostly from the law courts he frequented – that imagination, as Ellen Wood writes, must fill in the gaps. And so, she continues, we must fancy the old squire in his scarlet cape, riding-rod in hand, walking down the Golden Valley from the White House to New Court to overlook the raising of the sluices and the marshalling of his mechanicals to dinner, or, as one can well conceive, reading the Riot Act to the unruly, and intermeddling with kindly officiousness in the private matters of his people. Or in later days, too old now for the walk down and up the valley, dictating his 'Long experienced Water-workes' to his admiring amanuensis; and so slips the time away, she says, till first the book and then the life draws to an end, and Rowland Vaughan sleeps with his fathers.

Rowland died in 1628 and is buried at St Dunstan-in-the-West, the church in Fleet Street next door to the scrivener who took down his book. Though his bones are in London, what is really left of him lies in the landscape of the valley where his *water-workes* were still in use a hundred years ago. Most have now vanished under the plough leaving only a few remains, trenches in whose dry courses willows grow: those fragments etched into the landscape, and Rowland's rambling, serpentine prose.

I have walked through the streets that led me here to the playing field, a labyrinthine route to match my story, along the West Wycombe road, down Victoria Street, right into Nuffield Lane, left along the Oakridge Road as far as the bridge, turning back again to the West Wycombe road, to Desborough Park Road, Grafton Street and finally right into Fryer's Lane, which soon ended as a lane and continued as a footpath until I reached a footbridge over the old course of the river.

There is a playground for children here and on the far side of the stream, in place of the cottage that old man Fryer lived in long after his family had stopped milling, is an electrical substation that buzzes and fills the air with a menacing friction. But no trace of the watermill remains. Only a car park and a tennis court. I stand for a moment on the footbridge under which the stream runs unimpeded between concrete kerbstones past a red bin for dog litter. And slowly the topography I came looking for is revealed: the steep gradient of the stream under my feet, a relief channel which once bypassed the mill; a meandering line of trees on the far-side playing fields, tracing the old course of the river; the steep bank at the foot of the hill, a long mound of soil under grass built up centuries ago to form the leat; the flat of the tennis court where this mound ends, where Fryer's Mill must once have stood. And between it all the flat land of a municipal playing field, Rowland's legacy to the landscape. Encouraged by this thought I crouch down low to the meadow and scan the surface of the football pitch – the snow has melted now – and fancy I can distinguish, picked out by the low sun, the faintest imprint of the ridges and furrows that once traversed this space. And turning back to that steep bank that was once the mill leat I see a man in a long coat, walking his dog and carrying a stick.

III

THE RIVER FLOWS
THROUGH NAMES

It wasn't any warmer when a few weeks later I walked
into Downham Market railway station and bought a ticket
south, hoping as I did so that I might steal a day or two
from this task in London and go back again to my river.
Even now it is difficult to know exactly what guided me
on my meandering walks through the valley. I reflect on
the time I spent there, the routes I walked, the books I
read in the local library, and only slowly does any form
emerge, as if a mist were clearing on an intermittent breeze.
I had found where the river vanishes into a hole in the
ground in the corner of a car park. I had walked its course
as best I could up to the springs and back downstream.
And for hour after hour back home I followed this same
passage in satellite images on my computer along a line
of trees which from high above looked like mould tracing
the line of a damp crack in an old wall: the river hemmed
in by the masonry of factories, engine sheds and workshops. That green line stopped suddenly at Westbourne
Passage where the river also disappeared, subsumed so it

43

seemed into the line of the A40 which passed through the town across Brook Street and Bridge Street, skirting the northern edge of yet more car parks, flat acres of grey ploughed with the hatching stripes of parking bays. Yet even this space-age incarnation of the landscape was out of date now those tarmac acres were buried under the vast monolith I had stumbled into that first evening when I tried to follow the underground stream beyond the sinkhole and turned the corner at Bridge Street to face a towering white wall, as if an alien craft had fallen from another world to squat menacingly over this one, and those rainbow letters glowing from the sodium darkness high above me spelling out the word EDEN. The solid finality of this construction made it difficult to imagine what lay hidden beneath: the marsh and stream, the meadows, the tenements, the slums – the buried histories that must carry the narrative of my river's untimely grave. Perhaps then it was a compulsion to dig deeper into this history, to search for what had happened, which drove me now, as I bought a cup of tea and a bacon sandwich in the station café, to think of little other than my imprisoned river and certainly not the day ahead.

I walked through to the waiting room, where I heard on the radio that snowdrifts of up to six feet had forced the closure of the Humber Bridge, and that in North Yorkshire gritters had been forced off the road while a man and woman had been arrested for the suspected murder of a six-month-old baby girl. A fire was burning fiercely in the grate and all the tables were taken. I stood by the second-hand-book case and resting my cup on the shelf, opened my small historical picture book and looked again at a grainy photograph in it of Lawrence Chadwick, a sanitary inspector of High Wycombe in the early years of the twentieth century. He had waged a campaign against poor housing, the book said, arguing with the town council that this area called Newland through which the river flowed should be cleared of its houses and dedicated to industrial use alone. The local paper once ran a feature on the man, from which I had hoped to learn more. But on my last visit I spent several fruitless hours in the library scrolling backwards and forwards through spools of microfiche without ever finding what I was looking for.

Two old ladies sat beside the fireplace. The one with her back to me wore a white coat. Facing me was red frizzy hair cropped tight around tortoiseshell specs, pearl earrings, and a white woolly scarf, all framing a wrinkled orange face that had smoked too many cigarettes. They whispered and shuffled as the northbound train pulled in signalling the imminent arrival of the southbound. I closed my book and picked up my tea. Outside in the cold I walked gingerly along the icy platform past a man who was saying to the woman beside him, 'the trouble is, it is impossible to find anywhere to get out of the cold'. A blackbird's song split the air beautifully. I stopped. The platform was lined with overhead lamps, orbs that hung like giant bulbs of mistletoe. Their lights glowed weakly against the dull grey morning, and at the end of the platform the last lantern but one flickered on and off. It was hypnotic and for a second as I stood waiting for the train, trying to keep heat in my teacup by holding it tight against my coat, it seemed to me that the light must be in touch with another time and place, coming and going between here and there. As the train drew in and brought me back to the moment I realised that of course it was just a broken light, a loose connection or a bulb on the way out. But on board the train I became transfixed by this same sensation of being outside time, or rather of time peeling away and taking me with it. I sat on the far side of the carriage and could see the light again, still flickering. A kid a few seats away began bouncing a ball, muttering to himself as his mother looked through a magazine. The train pulled away and gathered speed. I placed my tea on the half-table between the seats and leant my head against the cold glass of the window. Stale, hot air wafted upwards from the heating duct, while the landscape slid past, the earth in flayed patchwork, black flesh, green skin, exhaling birds and vapour. The bouncing ball skimmed over the fields, over the canal I had walked along with my dog only the day before. That same weathered caravan in the trees. The Fens frosted white. The frost in furrows cross-hatching the fields. Frozen rivers and dykes cloaked in ice like mottled, frigid cellulite. The Fens misty again. Always misty. I closed my eyes and the river had become a bird. The feeling of something lost, the flickering white of its wings as the bird hammered away across rain-soaked fields. Under a sky that was heavy and grey I cried out, 'You are my lifeline,' over and over until I collapsed on to my knees and fell face down in the earth, my shout echoing on and on, though the bird was now gone. Startled, I opened my eyes. My tea had gone cold. Outside the train window the mist was now so heavy it seemed to have consumed the day. The mist glowed from within. Two dozen swans scattered across a bronze field like so many white fertiliser bags that had fallen off the back of a tractor and were blowing away on the wind. Brindled ponies, heavyset, grazed their way towards a yard of mud and forgotten washing machines, an old bath, a steering wheel buried in the soil. On the far side of a field a blue tanker sailed the sea of mist, the hull of its wheels beneath the waves.

As I watched the wintry day slide by I remembered with absolute clarity a conversation I'd had beside the river on my last journey there as I walked back from Fryer's Mill playing fields.

From the site of the old mill I had followed the stream along a muddy path that snaked between brambles until I reached the point where the two streams met and there I sat with my back against a willow. Beyond a broken fence was the derelict ground of Bartlett's furniture store. A flock of pigeons rose, scattered and settled again on the ridge of the factory rooftop. The constant chatter of engines, the beep of trucks and vans reversing, the emergency sirens: all these sounds receded. And though I couldn't actually hear the river it was as if buried deep within the white noise there was the dull trace of a voice. I put my ear close to the surface to hear the whisper. It was the most peaceful corner I had found in this frenetic landscape and so I stayed until the monstrous shadows of the chestnut trees reached across the playing fields to the foot of the hill beyond. The hillside caught the last of the sun and rising in contour lines up its side, row upon row of white windows reflected the light. Close to the ridge one window stood out from the others, shining so hard, like a starburst, that I was unable to look straight at it. I closed my eyes and must have dozed for a minute or two, until a sound startled me awake. Not far away a lady was feeding the ducks. She tore off pieces of bread and tossed them on the water and the ducks scrambled after them.

'I think they are hungry today,' she said after a moment.

More ducks flew in, clattering on to the water to open long, white stripes in the dark mirror of the stream. Others floated down from under the bridge.

'They know who you are anyway,' I said, standing, conscious that I might have looked like some wino asleep under a tree. 'Do you feed them every day?' The bag which held her slices of bread had been used many times. The pattern on it was cracked and faded.

'No, not every day. Just when I have some scraps of bread spare. They look like they need it today, though. It's cold.'

Plastic bottles and a lost football bobbed at the edge of the stream.

'There are more of them this year. Last year there were very few. This year they seem to have done well.'

She paused and followed my gaze.

'It's terrible, isn't it?' she said. 'I hate it when people throw rubbish into a river. It's always full of rubbish.'

'Seems to be.'

'That's why they didn't open up the river downstream.'

It was strange that she brought up this subject though we were a long way from the culvert. Burials mean something to everyone, I thought. I told her I had found where the river disappeared under the town, at the end of the car park off Mill Street, and that I had wondered how and why that had happened.

'Well, yes it used to flow through the town,' she continued. 'All the way through. Then it was covered over. What's your name, by the way?'

'Charlie.'

'Hi, Charlie. I'm Anne.'

Anne was small, and had short brown hair, a padded jacket wrapped tight, black trousers, black shoes. The kind with comfortable soles. She wore glasses, I seem to remember. And her cheeks glowed pink in the cold.

'And I don't know why it was covered over. Not originally. Perhaps it was just filthy. The council got rid of it in the end.'

'But you mean there was a plan to uncover the river?' I asked, returning to something she'd said a few seconds earlier.

'Well, it got suggested.'

She stopped for a moment. She had thrown most of the bread away by now and some of the ducks looked expectantly up at her, while others paddled here and there across the stream snatching at scraps. She tipped the bag upside down and shook it so that the last few crumbs fell on the water to set off another flurry of paddling.

'But they didn't do it because of all the rubbish that gets thrown in. That's how I heard it, anyway. Bicycles, pushchairs, televisions, tyres. It all ends up in there, you know. All sorts of stuff.'

'I know.'

'I suppose they were right, though it's a shame. But it would have got smelly and vile. People would have thrown rubbish in again. They always do. It would have been nice in a way. But then everyone would have just thrown in beer cans, bottles and it would soon have looked a state. I saw a suitcase in there one day. Someone must have been clearing out their house and thrown that in. Why? I mean, there were clothes in it.'

'Yeah, I've been looking at the rubbish too. Loads of footballs. There's always footballs in rivers.'

'Yes. Well I can kind of understand that: they'd roll and blow in. A football could get itself into a river. But I can't understand throwing suitcases in there. Or tyres like you see sometimes.'

'People think the river will wash it all away,' I said, remembering that once I had seen a lady, the mother of a small child, stop on a bridge to unhook a bin liner from the handle of the pram and tip it upside down over the river that flowed beneath her. I remembered the child with a soother in its mouth watching, as I watched too, the paper and plastic bags and food wrappers as they fell and floated away downstream, sinking slowly.

'It's funny because the ducks seem to know it's there,' said Anne. 'You see them from time to time wandering along the pavement following the course of the river.'

'Do they? I've been trying to work out where it flows,' I said.

'The vets have to come and round them up, rescue them when they start to cause a problem with traffic. But I'm sure of it: the ducks seem to know there's a river there, underground.'

As she said this an ice-cream van chimed from just beyond the corner of the road. But it seemed so ridiculous for an ice-cream van to be out in the melting snow in a bleak commercial suburb that I stopped to listen to the noise even though I had been captivated by what she had said about the ducks and their inherited memory or instinctive knowledge of the course of the river, an image that stayed with me for days afterwards.

'Well I must be going,' she said into the silence that was left behind when the chime had finished.

It must, I thought, have been a time-keeping bell at one of the industrial units.

'Oh. Okay. Well, it was nice to chat. That's a great story about the ducks.'

'I must be going.'

'Yes. Sorry. Didn't mean to keep you.'

She walked away over the playing field to Fryer's Lane. A few minutes later I walked the same way and turned left into Grafton Street past the disused factory buildings of Bartlett's furniture store above which pigeons still fluttered and on towards the town centre through the landscape of my river, this strange hinterland where light industrial estates abut isolated rows of terraced villas, where workshops leak Radio 2 and the smell of burnt paint, where the pubs hold strip-shows at four on a winter's afternoon. I tried to stay close to the river though it slid away from me again and again behind barricades or buildings that, greedy for every last inch of land, pressed tight against the edge of the bank, so that I caught only fractured sightings of the surface. And as I threaded my way past boards and signs I made notes of the names that fill this valley, names which strung together seemed to describe the story of the landscape. The river flows through names, I thought, as it now flows through the valley, in broken glimpses. Fryer's Lane, named after the miller who lived on it. Gillett's Lane too. The Mill End Lane that leads there. Maunday's meadow now Mendy Street. Rows of terraced villas: Brookside, Mayfield, Wyebrook, Ivy Dean, Hazelwood, Beech House, Springfield. Riverside Surgery. I paused briefly by the bridge over the river where I had begun my day, the traffic now thick and stationary on the road at my back, and then walked on down Mill Street, Westbourne Street, Brook Street, Bridge Street and through the town to the railway station where I caught the train to Marylebone and headed home.

As the fading scenery flashed by, trees, terraced houses and embankments, dark against the evening sky, I imagined these names, and many more besides, all the names of the town, imprints of the past, on a scroll flowing across the screen, the parts of them that resonate water picked out so that they might become a moving image of the stream. If there were traces of the river in the street, house and business names, I thought, then traces might also exist in other ways: in the shapes described by streets, in the patterns left by melting snow, in the density and colour of grass or the cascade of rain across the roads and pavements. These thoughts would not leave me even when I was back at home and miles away: thoughts of the buried river, the route that it took under the streets, the idea that, though hidden, it might be discernible in the way fog lies at night, or that its physical presence – even underground and locked inside a dark pipe – might be still palpable, if mostly to a duck.

HISTORY IN THE GRAIN

And here I am, heading back, chasing those thoughts.

From the train station I took a long route to the library, first of all to drop my bags at the hotel in Priory Road where I asked for room 42 again. A plump girl with red hair and granny specs took my registration, said the room wasn't ready and that the bags would be fine with her behind the desk. She picked up a mint from a bowl on the counter and, licking her blue-nailed finger and thumb, flicked through a copy of *Grazia*, pausing at a story about Megan Fox and her lingerie masterclass. I stood for a moment, wondering whether or not to emphasise that my laptop was in my bag and that I would really like her to keep an eye on it, when she looked up at me again as if puzzled by why I was still there, and smiled abstractly.

'Okay,' I said, feeling I should have left already.

'I'll move the bags in a minute, pet,' she said. 'They'll be fine.'

Almost assured, I thanked her and walked out on to the snow-packed pavement, crossing the road to get a picture of the derelict house next door – its grey security fencing, grey sky above and the unbroken snow on the cold roof, a buddleia slumped under the weight of snow and drifts of dirty snow on the road out front – before walking away quickly, conscious that *Grazia* girl was watching me through the window.

All the bins were out on Priory Avenue, though no one had collected them in a long while. Snow lay thick on their lids, on the pavement and right across the road, where a few cars had compressed twin tracks of grey ice. The street was empty and quiet. There were no footprints on the path to the front door of High Wycombe's museum which stood behind a tall garden wall overlooking the railway line. The lady inside seemed surprised to see me. She smiled and said that she was amazed anyone was out on a day like today, but that I was welcome to look around. I thought I might as well, though I was there to ask a question.

'I'll be shutting early, mind,' she called after me as I climbed the stairs. 'Because of the snow.'

I browsed for a while amongst the old paintings, prints and photographs of the town, glimpses of the river in engravings of West Wycombe Park, watercolours of the surrounding woods and men at work in them. Back downstairs I turned into a room in which were arranged dozens of simple wooden chairs of differing designs and I paused to photograph one or two. The museum was silent but for the digital click of my camera and the shuffle of my footsteps on the hard floor, until a stuttering soundtrack crackled across the quiet as if a needle had suddenly fallen on to an old record. I turned to where the noise was coming from in time to catch the text 'The Chair Bodgers of the Chilterns' over a dimly pulsating image of a radio mast on a television screen. The screen dipped to black and brightened again to plaintive bucolic music and an aged, flickering image of a wooded and rolling chalk landscape. 'In the Chiltern Hills of West Buckinghamshire,' began the narrator, 'where the scarp of the Chiltern Hills slopes steeply down to the vale of Aylesbury, one of the oldest rural crafts in England still survives. But only just.' The narrator's clipped voice and the scratchy music now filled the white room: 'The brothers Owen and Alexander Dean being, so far as is known, the only two genuine chair bodgers working in the old way.' I stopped to watch for a few minutes until the television clicked off halfway through and I was left looking at a black screen.

The curator wasn't at her desk when I went to find out what had happened. The place was empty but for me and this malfunctioning television. I walked back in and strangely the film jumped into life again, but back at the beginning. I watched it through once more until the story of the bodgers and their forest craft had followed the wood which they turned, along its onward journey to a factory in town where steam-driven saws pounded like boxers, when there was a click and the film died again. I tried punching some green buttons but these started up different films, also about these chair bodgers. Again and again one or other of the films switched off partway through until I thought I'd never get to see the end of any of them when finally I traced the audible click that had preceded each shutdown to a motion sensor hidden in the ceiling above me and realised that I could keep watching only if I fidgeted in my seat.

When the last film had finished and finally I could stop rocking from side to side, I heard the curator tapping at her keyboard again and I walked through to ask after the man I had actually come looking for: Lawrence Chadwick. She looked blankly at me. I explained that Chadwick was mentioned in a book written by someone who I thought had worked here at the museum, and that the book cited a profile of Chadwick in a local paper printed in 1936. I had already spent a day failing to find this profile in the library in town. Might she know where I'd find it? Perhaps it was here? Sorry, she said. She thought I ought to try the library again. But you know what it's like, I said, looking through microfiche till the sweeping movement of the text makes you seasick. Now that I had exhausted 1936, I continued, all 52 issues taking a day of checking and double-checking, I didn't know whether to go backwards or forwards. Her face suggested she didn't know what it was like, but I thanked her anyway and feeling it was the best way to conclude things bought a copy of an old map and a DVD of the films I had just watched. And then I left.

In the garden, meltwater dripped from yew trees on to the snow beneath, the patter of drops almost the only sound, while on Amersham Hill, a road normally busy with cars and buses, the winter afternoon seemed drained of life. I walked up the hill a short way and took another photograph, this time of a house called The Grange. Like my hotel and the house next door to it, The Grange had been built in the heyday of Wycombe's grandified country houses, up high and removed from the squalor and industry of the valley floor. Here was the very grandest of High Wycombe's grand houses, a turreted Victorian extravagance built by the furniture magnate Walter Birch and landmark enough to become the subject of picture postcards. I had one in my pocket. In this picture, taken in 1905, the valley fades inside smog and the skyline is only just visible as a tumid ridge of bare downland and stunted trees, the razed earth which had built Walter's fortune. In a window on the first floor a housemaid has paused in her work and is looking out over the garden. Today, a flickering signpost out front tells shoppers how many car-parking spots are available in town, the trees that were so small in Walter Birch's garden are 50 feet high and security cameras look out from the corners of the building. The Grange is now a pupil referral unit. Like my hotel, like so many of the Victorian buildings on the hills above High Wycombe, buildings that nowadays seem to house only doctors' surgeries, Conservative associations and New Age health consultancies, The Grange was a fine country house with servants for only a few years.

And so as I walked the river and its valley it seemed that I was always passing through concentric rings of growth, ages that could be traced in the buildings, the changing fashions of their names, what they were used for. In a hundred different ways perhaps, even in the grime that lay caked beneath layers of paint on the windowsills of the reform school I was now looking at. I had searched for these rings in old and new maps of the town and by flying over the landscape with satellite images on my computer and it was clear that even the streets bore an imprint of age in their patterns, and that the patterns themselves described the passing decades: the valley floor where tracks once followed ditches, and where roads and alleyways now follow those same ancient lines; the terraced streets and Victorian villas on the contours above them, named after pastoral idylls that their sprawling growth threatened as much as commemorated, but whose footprints still record the meadows they trampled over. And beyond, high up on the hilltops, stranger shapes not drawn by any of those passive architects of the older town – its river, the meadows, the hedges and hills. Here, it was as if the town had grown out to a given boundary, burst its skin and metamorphosed into a host of new organisms: Micklefield, Cressex, Totteridge, Bowerdean, Terriers. More imposed than evolved, their roads swept in curves entirely unrelated to the land they were on, fans and circles radiating about some arbitrary apex, folding in again and again. All of these ages were traceable in maps of the town and yet the map I had bought at the museum, from the first Ordnance Survey series, showed a very different town centre from the windswept expanse of car parks I found on Google Earth now. It was as if at the same moment when those hillside estates had sprawled forth in their labyrinthine curves, the land at the centre of it all, where the river sinks into the ground, had been hollowed out to nothing, like the rotting core of an ancient tree.

The hill which had been so quiet was now a ribbon of cars and buses, their exhaust fumes thick in the freezing dusk. The air above the road seemed to be breathing vapour, like a river on a cold evening in winter, and as I turned and walked gingerly down the frozen pavement I recalled the footage of those bodgers at work in the Chiltern woods, the chairmakers in village workshops, and in cramped, inflammable riverside factories. And in the evening – the library had closed because of the weather by the time I reached it – as I played the films through again back in room 42 of the Abbey Lodge Hotel I became transfixed by the story of the Wycombe chair and by the threads of dependence I might trace from it and those lilting country accents to these aspirant hillside villas, to the bare hillsides of 1905, the windswept car parks of 2008, to The Grange and to that culvert at the corner of Westbourne Passage where the river sank into the ground.

It was already a few degrees warmer when I returned to the hotel after supper, though the TV news headlines I watched as I lay on the bed described, over images of cars slumped in frozen ditches, the glacial stasis of an icebound nation: how in Barnsley so much sleet and snow had fallen on already frozen roads that the only way people could move about safely was by crawling, how Accident and Emergency departments throughout the country were now overwhelmed by patients with broken hips, legs, arms and shoulders; how motorways, airports and schools were closed. Insulated from all this in my hotel room I opened the two or three books I had brought with me and flitting from the books to the films and back again, occasionally drifting off only to wake at a slamming door, a conversation in the corridor and even the tremor of someone snoring in the room next to mine, I fell inside the history of this furniture town.

There is little record of High Wycombe's earliest chair-makers, only the name Turner on the parish register and a bill dated 1732 for the sale of a Windsor chair to West Wycombe vestry. Nor does anyone know quite why that other Buckinghamshire town otherwise associated with a royal castle gave its name to a simple chair built to be used outdoors, one that had more plainly been called a forest chair, except perhaps that Windsor is where those chairs were first sold. In time, however, this quintessentially English chair, distinctive for the way in which the legs, arms, spindles and bow are inserted from above or below into a flat seat, became more allied to High Wycombe than Windsor, and there it was made by the thousand. Painted, it could be used in the garden. Polished, it could be taken indoors. Only a few tools and the right wood were needed to make one, and that wood grew in such abundance in the clay and chalk topsoil of the Chilterns that it became known as the Buckinghamshire weed. 'So is the country overgrown with beech in those parts,' wrote Daniel Defoe on his rural tour of the nation in 1725, 'that it is bought very reasonable, nor is there like to be any scarcity of it for some time to come.' The scarcity came, of course. It always does. By the time the photograph of The Grange was taken one hundred and eighty years later, High Wycombe was close to running out of wood, most of that weed having been turned into chairs.

The first sixty years of that transformation of the landscape passed without record until in *Bailey's British Directory* of 1784 three chairmakers are listed: the Treacher brothers, Samuel, Daniel and William, makers of 'Windsor, dyed and fancy chairs, opposite the Woolpack, Wycombe'. By 1790 the Treachers had been joined by Daniel Hobbs and William Bavin, the Harris brothers and Abraham Meade and by the end of the century fifty-eight chairmakers made their living in small workshops and sheds built over the marshy valley floor to the west of the town. By 1810 Thomas Wigington had opened a two-storey factory in St Mary Street and was employing thirty men in it. By 1823 'chairmaster' had become a term quite distinct from chairmaker and by 1830 there were twenty-one of these masters running chair factories in the town. It was the year when other farm and mill workers in the valley, their precarious livelihood threatened by a newly mechanised world and stirred to unrest by a wave of riots that swept across southern England, joined the affray over several nights and one climactic day. It made no difference:

the machine had come to stay. Besides, the displaced workers of High Wycombe became in time so many new recruits to this booming furniture trade. Though they earned less there than they had threshing corn or milling paper it was, after all, still work and wages. Ironically, the growing demand that fuelled their labour came from the men who built and maintained the machines that had replaced them. Men who lived in the terraced houses of industrial centres like Birmingham, Manchester, Leeds, Bradford, who wanted inexpensive, sturdy chairs. By the second half of the nineteenth century High Wycombe's chair factories were turning out 4,500 chairs a day. Enough in one year for every other bottom in Victorian London. Eight thousand chairs for Crystal Palace, 2,500 for St Paul's, 19,000 for a meeting of evangelists: such orders were taken and swiftly processed, so easily could the expert workforce and apparently limitless resources swell to meet demand. And so High Wycombe's Windsor became the first mass-produced piece of furniture ordinary people could afford and High Wycombe – on the main coach road between London and Oxford, the industrial Midlands and the Welsh valleys and entirely surrounded by dense forests of beech – was always destined to be the town that built them.

'Bill's father was a bodger,' said the honeyed, rustic voice of the narrator T. C. Hanks as a faded film image trembled and jumped on my laptop screen and to a weaving pastoral ditty of oboe and flute the camera panned across a rolling wooded landscape. 'It would be about 1890 when he started. His uncle who learned him the trade started in 1846 and the chap he learned off started in 1800. And that would be the time the first bodgers

CHAIR TURNERS IN HAMPDEN WOODS, GT MISSENDEN

started.' The strange term given to those woodland chair-makers may have been a nickname for an itinerant worker, or a derivation of botcher, or even a word for a sharpened tool such as might be used at a lathe, or all three, or something else entirely. No one knows for sure. But as a local papermaker said, these fellows simply 'bodged about' in the woods and so the term stuck. The Windsor chair, I learned, was made with round and flat timber, turned or sawn by hand. And so the bodger found his niche because it made no sense to carry from the woods to the town the weight of the shavings that would soon be peeled off anyway. It was easier by far to make certain parts for the chairs – the legs, the spindles and cross-braces – right there where the timber was felled, in makeshift workshops or in the open air. A fall of forty or fifty trees yielded timber enough to keep a team of three or four bodgers busy for a year.

They began by sawing the trees into logs the exact height of a chair leg. These logs they split in half with a beetle and wedge, the halves into quarters, the quarters they split again with a hatchet into eighths or even sixteenths. Sitting astride a low trestle the bodger worked at an amazing speed, clamping and releasing and spinning the billet, drawing his knife down each raised edge, long tongues of beech licking up and falling to the ground in a snow-white pile about his feet, or standing at his lathe under oil-soaked calico driving the treadle up and down as he worked his chisel back and forth until from the round, white wood a chair leg emerged. 'I worked from the time I could see in the morning, to the time when I couldn't see any more at night,' said the voice of the ancient bodger, the last of his line, as the camera showed the younger man years before stooped over his lathe in the dim light of his makeshift hut. 'And even then in the winter I saved the lathe work till after dark and stuck candle ends on the poppets and went on turning. In summer I might stop at six on a Saturday and watch the cricket on the village green and in a week I could turn four gross, making £1 profit, which together with the waste wood I sold for firing made me better off than other labourers in my village. And moreover, I was my own master, though few masters can have worked harder.'

Working all year in the woods, occasionally driving to town with a cart full of chair legs, the bodgers must have seen how High Wycombe was changing. When once they had sold to solitary chairmakers, or groups of makers in collective workshops in a rural hinterland, gradually, inexorably, it was with a new class of men they were forced to negotiate, men who built and ran the factories which were mushrooming across the valley, stuffed together side by side around the river to the west of the town. Perhaps, as they returned to their woods after dealing with the increasingly ruthless masters, passing their loads over to workers who had to rent the glass that gave them daylight in someone else's factory, they might have reflected that there was a worse life than long hours in all weathers.

The legs and braces might have been ready for assembly, but the banisters and stands, seats and Windsor tops still had to be cut from planks and so it was the workshop sawyer's job to cut them using every variant of the bow-saw, each with its own nickname: the Up-and-Down saw, the Jesus Christ saw – because he bowed to it – the Dancing-Betty – because he danced with it. This was long-winded work: the saws had to be taken down and reassembled perhaps a dozen times to cut out the pattern in one decorative piece of fretwork. To carve the seat the bottomer straddled the wood and chopped at it with a razor-sharp adze, gouging out the shaped, receptive hollow of a seated bottom: Billy No-Toes was the name of one Wycombe bottomer and very few men like Billy, it was said, had all ten after a few years in the job. To shape the delicate arch of wood that rides across the top of the seat back the bowyer stooped over the wooden form and with arms outstretched took hold of each end of a boiled stave of ash or yew and bent the timber down and in towards the base of the bow at his feet, clamping it in place while it set. And so the bodgers bodged, the sawyers danced and prayed, the adzers stooped and the bowyers bowed, arms outstretched. What they made – the turned legs, the fretwork, the seats and bows – was brought to the framer. He put them together: he bored the seats to take the legs, sticks, bows and arms, he bored the legs to take the stretchers, he cut the mortises and tenons, he glued and wedged, he smoothed and sanded every surface. You could tell the framer by the leather apron he wore on which hung his breast-bib, a bar of wood with a socket recess at its centre. All the boring was done by eye and the bib allowed the framer to lean on his borer and use both hands to turn it. The pressure exerted would burst veins in the chests of the trainee lads when they started and in his first weeks it was said the young framer would unpeel his bib in the evening from a blood-soaked chest.

Though many chairs were sold in the white, others were stained, dipped in heated tanks of woodchips and water, combed with Indian ink to imitate rosewood, or burnt in with nitric acid to give a warm, sun-kissed yellow. Staining was boys' work. Dressed in a sack with holes cut for the neck and head the staining-boy wiped on acid with rags on a stick. The fizzing, acrid slop would flick and splash, and his hands turned yellow like the furniture. The staining-boy slept restlessly, if at all, when the acid got under his fingernails. In the polishing shop the heady, warm air swam with the odours of shellac, oils, spirits and polish: it was the best place to work if you could take the fumes, because it was the warmest. It had to be for staining with boiled linseed or the full French polish, to keep the oils fluid, the wood receptive. But the heat came from live stoves and the place was a tinderbox: benches covered in jars of spirit and soaked rags and hanging round them coiling ropes of horse tail dripping in polish. In cramped conditions like these it was easy to knock a jar of spirit on to a red-hot stovepipe and the whole building would go up like a firework. Every chair-master lost his factory at one time or another

– Gomme, Birch, Smith, Bobby – to say nothing of the innumerable sheds and workshops, like piles of dry wood on Bonfire Night. It was the age of fire, they said. The local paper called it the 'all consuming element', and on many nights the sky and the faces of appalled onlookers would light up as workshop walls burst apart in the heat and dry timber crackled like gunfire and kegs of spirit exploded one by one.

On these nights the proximity of the River Wye to the sprawling hinterland of workshops and factories might have been a hastily remembered blessing. Most of the time, though, it was a curse. The overcrowded landscape to the west of the town centre had been called Newland as early as the thirteenth century, perhaps because it had newly been brought within the borders of the borough, or more likely newly drained. It is not always easy to remember, let alone imagine, the old landscape now buried beneath pavements and yards. Newland had once been a spring-sodden marsh, an impenetrable mass of willow, hazel and alder, domed stands of sedge, flag iris, grasses and wild orchids, broken by springs and rivulets and the braided channels of the river itself plaited through the thicket. This wilderness was reclaimed by corralling the river into one channel, and its springs into ditches. As the tangled mass of trees was cleared and burned, the land turned and levelled and sown with meadow grass, and finally grazed and cut for hay, these ditches became boundary drains running along the undersides of hedgerows. The hedges in turn formed the lines of farm tracks. And gradually the wild, wet landscape was tamed. The history of one meadow is the history of them all: Agnes' Mead, Bowdery's Meadow, Soulden's Meadow, the Hop Garden, sold in parcels and built on, cottages and workshops and pubs, the meadows by now visible only as ghosts of themselves, spectral imprints of their hedgerows and ditch borders in the layout of the streets. But through the middle flowed the river: not quite as reducible.

In Newland the houses were packed closely together, row on row with only alleyways, lanes or courtyards between them. Damp and cold in the winter and stinking all through the summer, these houses were built on marshland that hardly drained. Drinking wells and hole-in-the-ground privies might flood into one another with just the smallest lift in river height, during 'February fill-dyke' for example or when the caning girls threw all their cane shavings into the river and blocked its flow. Each privy was shared by fifty people, and if not holes in the ground or boxes in sheds, they hung off the backs of houses suspended over the stream or its ditches so that when the water rose and flooded back through these alleys and courtyards it was already full of shit anyway.

* * *

A man needed very little to start up in the chairmaking trade. Some tools, credit or cash for materials, workshop space, a bench in a wood-house. A chairmaker might work for one of the chairmasters, an employee by day and self-employed at night, working all the hours of the day. With a yard for storage, extra space for a small workshop of his own, he could even set up a business. Backyards and gardens were divided and subdivided again. Houses became workshops, rows of them became factories. Chairmaking businesses, said the honeyed voice in the film recalling Bill's father who had 'gawn to work in 'igh Wycum', sprang up like weeds and died back again just as quick. But a firm of your own might be a way out of the poverty and squalor inevitable in a landscape where units multiplied like cancer cells. If a growing business was the route out of this squalor to the airy hillsides, few made it. Those who had made it, the chairmakers who became chairmasters, did not enjoy the prospect of losing their workers to the have-a-go firms that grew like mushrooms overnight. The publicans and shopkeepers had the space and the capital to get an advantage in the first place and it was too easy for these masters, in a one-trade town, to run their workshops so astutely as to keep these other mushrooms from sprouting. So, the publican would pay his chairmakers on a Saturday in the bar, only he'd take a while coming himself, a few hours say, during which time no chairmaker was going to stand around without a drink in his hand, not with his week's wages as credit on the slate. The shopkeeper likewise preferred to pay in kind, wages on elastic that came straight back through the door, tokens valid only in the shop of the master who issued them. Beer and tokens for the many to build those grand houses for the few.

As for Walter Birch, I have found just one undated photograph of the chairmaster who in 1900 built himself High Wycombe's grandest house of all. It shows a youngish but portly and bewhiskered gentleman as he strides confidently along Church Street, his right hand buried deep in the pocket of a single-breasted overcoat while his left is raised slightly as if he might at that moment be making a point to fellow chairmaster Arthur Vernon who walks beside him, perhaps about Randolph Churchill's mocking jibe in the House of Commons, a comment about cheap Wycombe furniture which stung Birch onward to greater ambition over the following years: to the construction of a three-storey factory in Denmark Street; the employment of reputed designers like Punnett and Whitehead and the creation of fine Arts and Crafts furniture for the smarter London stores such as Liberty, and in the end to the commemoration of his success and social standing in the erection of The Grange (though he called it Gennheim) in which Walter lived with his wife Annie and their six children and their servant Rose Boddington. Would the ambitious Birch, who rose from flooded Water Lane to the heights of Amersham Hill and eventually to the Mayorality of High Wycombe, have had any idea, as he walked across Church Street that unspecified day when he was caught on film, that his Gennheim would become a nursing home within thirty years of its construction, or that his factory would burn down, or that finally, almost exactly one hundred years after his father had moved to Newland to set up shop, his family firm would be absorbed by a larger, more successful company to become G-Plan, maker of a new breed of mass-produced furniture for householders of modest means?

It was to thoughts like these that I eventually fell asleep in room 42, though the snoring next door did not stop or get any softer, as the final film about the chairmaking firm Ercolani rolled through to its end. Do not be sad that trees like this are felled, ran the narration, for trees have a crowning maturity like all living things, after which they decline and decay. And if you cut across a tree you can trace the history of its growth, summer and winter, year upon year. Start at the outermost ring and you're looking at the year when the first man walked on the Moon. A little further in, Hillary and Tenzing are climbing Everest. Somewhere about here in 1919 was the first flight across the Atlantic, while further in, at the end of the last century the first motor car began to roll on the roads. In 1870 it became compulsory for children to go to school. Further in to the centre we might hear the sabre clashes of the Light Brigade making their heroic charge in the Crimea. And so when this tree was a mere sapling it was more than likely that England, in 1837, was celebrating the succession of a young girl to the throne: Queen Victoria. Do not mourn the passing of a tree, the voice said, but think rather that when you touch this wood you touch something with history written into its grain.

V

DELIVERANCE

I was woken the following morning by the hiss of tyres spinning on ice in the car park and a minute or so later the rhythmical scrape of a spade across tarmac. I sat up on the edge of the bed, still tired. Outside, two squabbling blackbirds knocked snow off the roof of the house next door. Under my window the hotelier paused, stood to straighten his back and then stooped to his shovelling again. He was at breakfast too, downstairs in the subterranean dining room, re-laying crockery at tables which had been sat at already, punching again and again through the kitchen door while the drone of an Xpelair fan and the clatter of pans and plates followed every entrance and exit. As other guests drifted in and out Terry Wogan's morning radio show played through speakers over the bar: news headlines about a BA strike, jobs going at the MOD and then Blondie's 'Sunday Girl' from a lonely street: cold as ice cream, she sang, but still as sweet.

At the library I found what I'd been looking for almost immediately. My book had referenced 1936 but I'd already spent a day going through every issue of the *Bucks Free*

Press scrolling forwards and backwards on the microfiche roll without success and I had started to doubt that 1936 was the right year at all. And yet every issue had been full of diverting headlines and stories, so that it had been more or less impossible to keep on a straight path of enquiry and I couldn't have said for sure that the *Destruction of Wood Pigeons*, the *Lane End Man who was Sick of Life*, the *Beating of the Bounds at Hughenden*, or the *Man Found Shot in a Train*, hadn't distracted me at just the wrong moment. I thought that I might start again on 1935 or 1937, but at the last minute I decided to give 1936 one last look. And there in the second issue of the second roll, dated 10 July, right alongside an advert for Ryder-Rex the King of House Coals, was a column about Chadwick entitled Thirty Years of Progress. And it was as if Chadwick

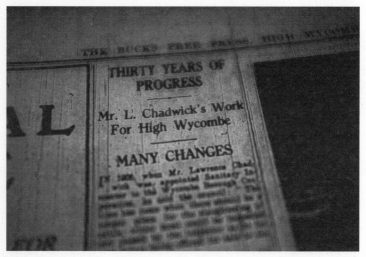

himself was looking out at me from the microfiche screen, that startled and precise man, with round spectacles over a round face and his hair neatly parted.

When Lawrence Chadwick was appointed Sanitary

Inspector for Wycombe Borough Corporation in 1906, the article read, he told the council that the time had come when there should be a proper place for the slaughtering of cattle and where meat could be inspected before being offered for sale. And yet he had now been in the job thirty years and still High Wycombe was without an abattoir. It was an important point for the council to consider, ran the article, so that it might bring its increasingly efficient public services one stage nearer to the ideal. Chadwick had long sought to achieve the public ideal in High Wycombe, a town which had evolved out of all recognition into a sprawling belt of industry reaching up and down the river's valley. This pace of change had caused his work in service to sanitation to increase rapidly over the years and most likely to keep on increasing beyond, so he predicted. In the early days Chadwick had supervised only dairies. Soon the inspection of food and drink had been added to his duties, then the inspection of common lodging houses and drainage. By 1936 Chadwick controlled every-thing eaten and drunk in the town, he dealt with outbreaks of infectious diseases, with overcrowding, the inspection of rag flock used in making paper and finally the clearance of slums. But it was this issue of housing that had occupied Chadwick most considerably of late, he told the reporter. He could still recall the first house he had closed because it was unfit for habitation: it had been in 1908, the year when for the very first time in the history of High Wycombe proceedings had been taken in respect of a nuisance in the River Wye in the centre of town, although housing had been poor in certain areas for many years and the river had long been in a bad state too. Indeed, a filthy river and unfit housing, Chadwick remarked, were two parts of the same problem and he had fought for better housing for the town's poorer residents from that day to this. 'In all truth,' he concluded, 'an inspector has to be partly lawyer, doctor, builder, farmer, architect and veterinary surgeon, to think of just a few of the things at random. I have to supervise the houses in which people live, their general living conditions, their food, their places of employment and their houses of entertainment, so that I enter very much into the daily lives of the people.'

Those lines are the only traces of Chadwick's words that I have found outside the bounds of his statistical reports, despite many hours of looking. For a man who so influenced the evolution of the town, he left few traces of himself. Nevertheless he spoke as I had expected him to, this man who approached his work so conscientiously and who found that his time had become increasingly occupied by housing in 1936. In those few recorded words, I felt his presence, as I had felt Chadwick beside me before this moment – at my shoulder as I walked the streets and the river, when I stopped to photograph some detail or scene that caught my eye. He was there, too, when I looked at the many photographs Chadwick himself had taken of the town as he documented its sanitary condition, particularly of the housing in Newland. His shadow became my shadow as I looked through his viewfinder at the same landscape – now much altered – and the shamed or defiant, sometimes smiling but often empty and hopeless faces of those who looked back at him, whom he caught unawares or who had steadied themselves just enough to hold still, or perhaps to pose. Even when, as was most often the case, his photographs taken before he gave his interview to the *Bucks Free Press* showed only buildings, empty courtyards, or unpeopled vistas along the riverside and row on row of latrines hanging over it, or broken windows, or sagging roofs, or gaps in the brickwork of cottages that appeared more organic than man-made, I sensed him all the same, his patrician gaze and statistician's intellect. Perhaps the camera was at his waist and he had perfected the technique of holding it steady and pressing the shutter as if he was still only fiddling with the dials. Or perhaps he raised it quickly to his eye, grabbed his image and moved on, waving briefly and modestly at those he had incidentally crystallised in silver iodide, as if to suggest that they shouldn't mind him, or shouldn't stop what they were doing on his account. He wasn't really photographing the people anyway and had no wish to expose them personally, though I can't help but wonder whether a little humiliation wasn't a by-product of his mission. The children were more inclined to stop and pose or stare back at this intrusion. I can see them playfully harassing this strange, smartly dressed visitor with his camera, growing in confidence as he walks through the courtyards. They stand all in a row, hand in hand or arm in arm, smiling at Chadwick or laughing with each other. Chadwick meanwhile is not quite looking at these children who have assembled in the centre of his picture: he is looking at the houses they live in. Perhaps the adults are more aware that it is their lives which are being examined, or perhaps they are just less willing to be exposed in this way, caught in the nakedness of their domesticity. In a narrow alley at Rosa Place a young woman in a floral dress and flat-soled shoes stoops to her washing. Her arms pound downwards into the tub of water. She has not stopped even to look at Chadwick.

In Janes Court on the sloping stone flags outside her cottage another woman is taking to her legs with a sponge, while a man strides past, ignoring the camera. But his face is streaked and transparent. He is hardly there. And outside Clara Cottages, where in a stiff breeze the washing flaps on the line, the only hint of a person is a blur of white across the centre of the image. It is as if the humanity captured in these pictures was only ever an ephemeral presence, of itself or to Chadwick, and soon the men and women and the children too would become nothing but a memory.

Chadwick took these pictures in 1934 and 1935 to record the terrible condition of the town's slum housing: the latrines, the airless courtyards and claustrophobic living spaces, and the River Wye which flowed under them, all crammed together in the shadows of the furniture factories. He had lamented the accumulation of rubbish by householders too idle to burn it, the old bedsteads and mattresses and other things of no use stored for ever in woodsheds and WCs, the rats and houseflies swarming over the mess. Though landlords had from time to time reconditioned some of these defective cottages, it was hardly worth the effort, he had argued: the houses were unfit for human habitation and the humans who lived in them hardly aware of the value of soap and water. The authorities needed to realise that building houses hardly touched the fringe of the problem. And here Chadwick stretched outside the bounds of his position in order better to sway the council in the direction of his vision: that it

is more efficient to spend money to relieve social ills than to ignore them and deal with the result. One can hardly blame a person for not knowing the value of cleanliness, he said, of fresh air and sunlight – and perhaps now he was thinking back to those children who had larked about in front of his camera – a person who has spent his days in a squalid court and who has never been taught the principles of hygiene or basic sanitation.

But Chadwick had finally got his way. Before moving on to discuss subjects as diverse as custard powder samples, milk supply, offensive trades, smoke abatement, and the Artificial Cream Act of 1929, Chadwick was able to write that in July a revised programme of slum clearance had been prepared. One hundred and twenty-three houses, of which ninety-nine were occupied, were to be demolished, and the displaced were to be rehoused on the Desborough Castle estate. This particular exodus had been a long while coming.

Eighty-four years earlier two men, one a doctor the other a vicar, tried to shame the town's councillors into relieving the sufferings of the chairmakers who lived in the Newland slums, which even at that time had long shrouded the River Wye and which were, year on year, spreading over the water meadows and marsh beside it. Quite by chance I stumbled on the story, written up in a little red booklet and part hidden amongst piles of leases, clippings and papers in a cupboard beside the elevator of High Wycombe library. Out of curiosity more than anything I sat down with it and learned of how an inspector, called to High Wycombe in the spring of 1849, had discovered there a maze of fever, fetid air, fogs and miasmas, weeping cesspits, rotten houses and standing heaps of excrement quite beyond imagination. And yet, although Newland was a nursery of sickness, as one doctor put it, this report, which Thomas Rammell sent to the Board of Health in 1850, described an inspection thwarted at every turn by councillors and landlords who feared neither the disease nor the shame of owning and renting out lodgings like these, but something else entirely.

No sooner had Rammell opened proceedings on 12 April 1849 before a crowd of disgruntled councillors than an objection was made that the notice of the inspection had not appeared on the correct date in the local paper. Rammell was forced to abandon proceedings before they had even begun. And that was nearly the end of the matter. But piqued by this jeering crowd of well-to-do ratepayers, who had attended the hearing only to enjoy its failure, Rammell decided, before he left the town altogether, to inspect the Register of Burials. Here he found that the average mortality, at a rate of 23⅓ souls per thousand exceeded the limit prescribed by the Public Health Act by exactly one-third. It was a sufficiency of death, he wrote, to compel another inquiry. And so he returned to High Wycombe two months later to open court again, taking care this time to show that the notice had now appeared in accordance with the law, whereupon Councillor John Nash objected that the excess of mortality did not amount to a full person, while other councillors chorused that it was absurd to split a man into parts, that this meddling was bound to be costly and that it had all been got up under false pretences. They all most strenuously objected to this interference in the town's affairs.

Assuring them that there would be no interference if indeed the landlords and councillors did have sanitary matters in hand, Thomas Rammell set forth on a tour of the town, accompanied by a representation of councillors along with the two men who had sought the inspection in the first place. Coming into the district of Newland, Rammell saw with his own eyes what his nose had already told him: that the whole place was filthy beyond belief, that the river which was used for washing and drinking and all the lanes and courtyards surrounding it were choked with excrement. Witness after witness came before Rammell to attest to the squalid conditions of these Newland slums, as if having seen them he needed any more evidence. Dr Rose, the town's mayor, described the sodden courts and pavements, the drainage in open gutters, the privy soil accumulating in hot weather stinking until it contaminated the very air, the stream overhung with privies, the endless cases of fever, rheumatism, diarrhoea and dysentery, and the fatal cases of typhoid which his work forced upon his consciousness and conscience. John Pepin spoke of there being only two privies to eleven houses, and four pigsties at the back of his court. Charles Cross confessed that he had no privy and would take the soil from his house to the gutter that ran through the street. Mary Walker told the court how the drain outside the front of her house, into which the soil of many houses was emptied, ran through the middle of Mr Thomas's house next door, through the living room and out the back into the river. And Charlotte Dowling, living in Mr Bridgwater's yard in St Mary Street, said,

My son and daughters have been ill with fever; I have been lately ill four months myself. There is a privy in the yard, within five yards of my door. There are 32 people belonging to our four houses, and from morning till night I should say there is from 18–20 men, travellers and others, because it's public, who use it. The privy is in a very bad state when it gets full. Mr Bridgwater won't have it emptied, because he won't pay for it. It's sometimes so full that we are over the soles of our shoes to get to our door. There is a well in the yard and a very bad well it is. The water is offensive, so offensive that we cannot drink it, nor yet wash with it, nor nothing. I don't know why the water is in this state except it is the privy. I believe the privy soil escapes into the well because we emptied the well so many times, and the water continued so bad.

But in spite of the deep embarrassment such confessional statements caused to the witnesses, it was the general tenor of the opposing argument, wrote Rammell, to discount such deficiencies of drainage and to attribute the unhealthiness of these witnesses of the poorer classes to their uncleanly habits. 'It is in the power of anyone to keep themselves wholesome and in this instance there is a running stream to which the inhabitants of the court have free access,' said a Mr John Turner, surgeon.

'But can you state what is discharged into that running stream?' Rammell asked him. 'Is it fit for drinking water?'

'I believe many of them use it for that purpose. It *is* a trout stream.'

'Did *you* ever drink the water?'

'I cannot say I ever have.'

'Are there not privies over that stream discharging into it, above the part where Mrs Walker would take her water?'

'I am not aware of any for a considerable distance.'

'Do you think it probable that there are some?'

'I think it possible.'

'Do you think it *probable* that there are some?' asked Rammell, wrenching the truth from his reluctant witness.

'I think it probable,' said Turner.

The opponents of the inquiry, Rammell summarised, whilst they did not actually deny the existence of some of the evils complained of, claimed that the corporation had matters in hand. Mr Wheeler, newly appointed chairman of the Sanitary Committee, cited the inspection and repair of one or two nuisance drains in Newland and the construction of a barrelled arch over what was once an open watercourse from the north end of the town to the tail of Thurlow's Mill. When Rammell suggested that these improvements had only been made as a direct result of the notice of the inquiry, Mr Wheeler objected that this wasn't the case, that they were begun as long ago as October. But I must observe, wrote Rammell, that I find no trace of any evidence documentary or other supporting this assertion: it appears that £10 was expended within a few weeks previous to the institution of this inquiry and that with the exception of £1 in the month of January no money had been expended upon these matters since the year 1846, three years ago.

'If the powers of the local Act was already sufficient,' said Rammell, 'how is it they have not been exercised before?'

'Sir,' Wheeler replied. 'When meadows are cut up and converted into private dwellings we don't know where our authority ends. I think we are much indebted to the commission for calling our power into action.'

'Are there powers in your local Act for enforcing proper house drainage?'

'I don't know that there are.'

'Are you aware that such power exists in the Public Health Act?'

'I don't know what that Act is,' he said.

'But you are opposed to the introduction of that Act?'

'Yes sir. As we understand it to be carried out, the expenses alarm us.'

In short, Rammell concluded, I could not ascertain in

the whole course of the inquiry that a single individual in the borough opposed to the introduction of the Public Health Act had read its provisions. What is abundantly clear, he continued, is that the opponents had very exaggerated apprehensions on the score of the expense which the application of the Act would involve.

After then discussing the burial of the dead, the overcrowding of the churchyard and the probable contamination of the one water pump in town by the noxious effluvia of broken coffins, Rammell ended his exchange with the councillors of High Wycombe over the issue of drainage in the swelling slum of Newland. He recommended that the provisions of the Public Health Act 1848 be applied to the Borough and Parish of Chipping Wycombe and added in conclusion that he could see no practical difficulty in carrying out, at a cost that would be spread over thirty years and would be met by a very modest weekly charge, works which would prove remedies for most of the evils he had described: water might be piped into the town, he said, and distributed through a system of pipes to every house by gravity alone, whilst for waste-water a system of tabular drains might be laid at a small cost. The expense of the whole project would be met at a rate not exceeding 3d weekly upon a house of the fourth or cottage class, he added as his final words on the subject and after, I have the honour to be, My Lords and Gentlemen, Your very obedient servant, T. Webster Rammell.

Twenty-one years later when a Mr Wagstaffe was in turn asked to write a sanitary report on the town, he was still able to observe that the whole of Newland was permeated by open sewers, the smell from which, even in cool weather, was very objectionable. And it was no surprise, he wrote, that these are the places where fever is prevalent. Recalling Rammell's report he reminded the council that water could be supplied to the people at a very moderate outlay and that the water wells were so contaminated such a supply had become a vital necessity. Rammell's report had only ever been an advisory one. The council had been free to ignore it. And they had.

Although in the intervening years successive generations of councillors had grown more conscious of the need for drains and sewers and a decent water supply, still in 1936 Lawrence Chadwick was only just realising the end of a career's worth of dreaming, if dreaming is quite the right word for the very particular vision of a man like Chadwick, as he led the dirty and sick children of Newland and their feverish parents out of the slums, away from those fetid streets up to the airy hillsides, high above the likes of Walter Birch's house, which was already a nursing home. The day of emancipation was reported in the *Bucks Free Press* that same year. An article entitled 'From Dreary Street to Bright Estate' described a week of great adventure for the lucky families. For years, it said, they had lived in damp and dilapidated houses and now they had been transported to the top of a hill overlooking the town and placed in new dwellings that were light and dry, that were palaces compared to their old, dreary hovels. These families and their belongings had been loaded one by one on to carts and into lorries and driven away for ever from the slums. Neighbours who had lived beside each other for years hoped they would not be separated on the new estate, parents worried about the distance their children would have to walk to school, whilst Lawrence Chadwick, upon whose shoulders much of the organisation of the evacuation rested, had no light task in trying to meet the hundred and one requests of the people who had come to welcome him not only as a kindly official, but as a trusted friend. Finally mothers who had found it a heartbreaking job to keep the house and family clean in buildings with damp and broken floors, crumbling window frames and little or no ventilation, who had given up in despair, could now look forward to escaping these dreary surroundings. 'I am that excited about it,' said one of them, 'that I cannot sleep and I shall be glad to have a house in which I can breathe properly.'

Yet the river which they had left behind them still could not. It might have had a little less shit in it, but it was running foul with other things, with the liquor-excrement of light industry and roads, the detritus of a town, the old bedsteads and linoleum and mattresses that Chadwick had complained of. He might have remembered, when he was interviewed in 1936, having to deal with the occasional 'nuisance' – as he euphemistically called it – in the River Wye, but it was beyond even his particular powers to emancipate the river in the same way as he had the people. The borough–parish boundary that had so vexed the ratepayers of 1849, along which a tributary stream had run, was long since covered over and had become Brook Street. The stream along Water-Up Lane which had fed that brook was now under a street too, as were most of the other ditches that had once been springs.

Only the river remained, a wraith memory of itself like the now empty townscape which surrounded it. I have a photograph of it taken some three decades later by which time the land either side, if it no longer housed people, housed little else. It is as if some holocaust had occurred in a dimension confined only to the stream and its long-lost meadows, the river held in time while beyond in the distance the town groans onwards. A bus rounds the corner along the Oxford Road, destined most likely for West Wycombe; a dark-haired man in a gaberdine coat is walking along the pavement, his hands thrust deep in his pockets. It is March. I fancy that as he walks his head is turned slightly towards the river, which has shrunk beneath its bones of brick rubble and silt like the drying husk of a body, its life departing, the only thing left behind an empty vessel. There is a lost shoe beached on a brick in the middle of the stream and beyond a duck and a drake whose young of the year – if the ducks manage to nest at all in the maelstrom that is approaching them – will be born to dry streets.

By October of the same year – 1965 – there is a dredger belonging to M. A. Dawson, Civil Engineering Contractors, Luton, in the middle of the stream along the Oxford Road beside where the man in the gaberdine coat had walked in March, its caterpillar tracks at right angles to the flow. A man in overalls sits in the cab and leans out of the side window as if to see more carefully what he is doing. Another hangs off the side of the cab, suggesting to him where next to scoop with the Bradshaw bucket that hangs by a hawser from the end of the crane. The same white bus is passing, heading into town in this picture, and on the edge of the pavement three residents of High Wycombe peer carefully over the railing to take a last look at their river. The stream below them has already been edged with steel plating driven deep into the gravel and before long Messrs Dawson will have bridged the space between the pilings and the pavement opposite and the river will have become a car park.

*   *   *

By the time I left the library the light was draining out of the day and the snow had begun to melt so that the dusk fell more heavily than it had done those past few weeks. I wanted, while I still had time, to find Chadwick's house, which I had discovered from a census had been in Queen's Road. Following what I imagined to be the subterranean route of the river I soon found his street, sandwiched between the railway line and the main A40, a row of Victorian villas and light industrial units of exactly the type which had replaced the furniture work-shops when that industry succumbed, like farming and milling before it, to the machine age. Number 29, from which Chadwick walked to work each day in his dark suit and thin black tie and tortoiseshell spectacles, his hair combed just so, was a modest semi-detached house with bay-fronted windows. From these his wife Alice or his mother-in-law Elizabeth, who lived with them, would have been able to look out during the day over the lower slopes of Saffron Platt to the Rye, the open water meadows below the town along the edge of which the River Wye still flows and there they would have seen children playing or cattle grazing. There was no plaque to record that Chadwick had once lived in this house. In fact there is little to record the life of Lawrence Chadwick at all, beyond the short profile in the *Bucks Free Press*, his annual sanitary reports and a road named after him on the Terriers estate at the top of Amersham Hill. There was no obituary either when he died on 14 July in the same year that Messrs Dawson of Luton buried the river, and three days – I realised when I found the note – before I was born. The notice in the paper read simply:

Peace, Perfect Peace: beloved husband of Alice, passed away at Amersham Hospital, aged 83 years. No flowers by request.

I turned and headed back towards the railway station. The river emerged from under a four-lane gyratory and flowed by yew trees beside the pavement, though it was too dark now to see much at all. According to the 1897 map I'd bought at the museum this new road had been built along the course of the stream between the eastern end of the old High Street and a boating lake in the grounds of what had once been Loakes Manor and was now Wycombe Abbey girls' school. In fact it seemed as if Abbey Way, along which the traffic was now pulsing as if the road were some kind of particle accelerator, had taken the top off The Dyke too, slicing an angle over the elegant curve if the lake. And there, where lovers in boats must once have taken easy turns across the water to drift back downstream again, was a busy round-about. I walked along the pavement towards the centre of town through an underpass that crossed beneath the four-lane road at exactly the same angle as the old river's course and as I walked down its long incline from the fading day above towards the eerie glow of the tunnel ahead I realised that the underpass would take me right beside the subterranean river, that I would be on the bank of the buried stream. I turned the corner into a stark space lit by a dozen yellow lamps, an oblong of blue daylight beyond. Bicycle tyre tracks streaked from the wet, melting snow on to the dry, grey floor inside. I paused. The sound of running water. But so soft as to be audible only from within the shelter of the passageway. I had stepped over it. I looked down. At the threshold of the underpass was a drain cover and from beneath it came a whisper. I bent down to listen to the hollow trickle of a sound. I held my phone there to record it too, and now, when I play the file back and listen to the rustle as I stoop close to the ground, to those few seconds of running water, the sound of my voice as I stand and say out loud to myself that I must get a picture of the underpass and its strange, yellow flickering lights, I hear another voice as I stop speaking and the shutter of my camera clicks twice: a watery echo that saturates everything, as if I'm underwater and the river is there too, trapped within the dense air of the underpass, thrumming through the concrete wall of the tunnel.

VI

A PARADISE INDEED!

The 5th of February. I woke to reports of terrible weather rolling across the country from the south, of more snow and sleet, and wondered briefly whether I should go at all. As it turned out the journey was easy and this half-frozen rain only began to fall as I dropped into the valley from the M40. Two months had passed since I first went looking for the source of my river and found only a dry channel below the mausoleum at West Wycombe, but it was likely now after weeks of wet weather that the stream's springs would have broken at last.

I had written to Sir Edward Dashwood to ask whether, even though his gardens were now closed for the winter, he would mind if I came to look for the springs that formed the upper river. 'Of course that's fine,' he replied. 'Just book in with Mary in my office. Hope I am around when you visit. Ed.' I wrote again to say thanks and to bother him with one last question. 'There is no definite answer,' he wrote back. 'The main source is a spring in the lake. There is another under the cricket pitch some-where and the upper river, which does not flow all the time, comes down the Chorley valley from a spring in the copse near the garden centre. Very occasionally the river runs from further up. Hope this helps. Ed.'

So as the sky darkened and the rain turned to sleet I drove through the gateway of West Wycombe Park and under a vaulted arch of yew trees. A Palladian mansion with walls of Naples yellow stood at the end of the drive on a rise of open ground and backed by a ridge of woody hills, the house almost luminous in the wintry landscape around it. In front was an open channel of water framed by black trees whose heavy branches met their reflections below. Beyond was the lake, flat and grey in this light, like a slab of wet steel.

Mary had been expecting me for over an hour and though I should have called to say where I was, my phone had died somewhere on the M11. I was ready to explain as much when I knocked on the door of the estate office and waited in the cold. But then I hesitated as she shook my hand and said welcome to West Wycombe and I swallowed the apology awkwardly. She showed me through to an inner office and there unfolded a large cloth-and-board-backed estate map.

'That's the statue on a plinth you will have passed as you came in,' she said. 'Immediately below it is one of the springs.' Her hand moved over the map. 'Now, the other spring is up there, in a spinney over the meadow. It's a pleasant stroll.'

I crossed to the window and looking out over the valley as far as I could trace it, at the trees, the sloping land and the lake, I asked if I could explore the rest of the park too. Mary said that would be fine and waited for me by the door, her hand pausing over the light switch. On the wall an ancient map of the park depicted the lake, the galleon, a man in a rowing boat. I told her that I had read about the galleon and the real captain whose employment was to live aboard it and fire the cannon every now and then.

'Yes,' said Mary. 'And you can see there were perhaps more streams and channels then.'

The water meadows above the lake were indeed a patchwork of streams. The artist had drawn the flowing water with wavy lines and where each channel entered the lake, a small cascade. A third spring came into the main channel from below the village . . . and another further along the Wycombe road. I lost myself for a moment exploring this beautiful map, trying to picture the park as it was then, when I realised Mary was waiting. She handed me her card so I could call her later, but said she might not be in when I returned because she was feeling unwell.

And now I am sitting in my car in the National Trust car park waiting for a break in the weather. Raindrops patter on the windscreen. Heavier drops fall off the bare branches of a walnut tree above me, drumming across the roof as a breeze whips up. I'm flicking through the guidebook to Wycombe Park that Mary gave me and I have stopped short at the description of the Temple of Venus and the Parlour which stands beside the river: 'an Ionic rotunda on a mound beneath which is a cave flanked by curving screen walls. Built by Donowell in 1748 this is West Wycombe's most notorious monument, for it is said to represent the vulva and spread legs of a naked woman, the temple above playing on the theme of the mound of Venus.' It is more surprising than it should be to discover that what a landscape suggests to me, it also once suggested to others. After all, these chalk downs are the most human of all: slumped breasts and sprawled limbs. And in their hollows, chalk streams springing from the womb of the earth. I imagine a woman. She's naked. Kneeling. Sitting back on her ankles she leans her body back too, supporting herself with her arms braced until the angle up her thigh from her knee continues over her hips, her stomach and ribs. Her breasts soften into the slope. Her knees apart, she sinks back inside the landscape. Her cunt is the spring. Her bush the spinney of trees it rises within. The river is her child. And she is chalk.

Even the word cunt, which has been so debased, derives from words that mean valley or hollow place – the Germanic *ku*, the Welsh *cwm*, and for valleys in the English chalk, *coombe* – and so, far from obscenity, cunt has in its proper meaning the idea of the earth as mother, the infant stream.

I watch rooks breaking from the wooded slopes of West Wycombe Hill across the grey sky and try to recall a few lines from Coleridge's opiate poem: *But oh! that deep romantic chasm which slanted, Down the green hill athwart a cedarn cover!, A savage place! as holy and enchanted, As e'er beneath a waning moon was haunted, By woman wailing for her demon-lover!* This unfinished fragment of verse, which has always evoked for me this same idea of the Earth as a woman's body, the source of life, came to Samuel Taylor Coleridge in the autumn of 1797. For months he had been reaching for a subject through which he might reflect on man and nature and that would quite naturally entwine the two. He found it in a stream which, as he wrote, he intended to trace from its source in the hills among the moss and bent to the first break or fall where its drops become audible and it begins to form a channel; thence to the peat and turf barn; to the sheepfold; to the first cultivated plot of ground; to the lonely cottage and its bleak garden won from the heath; to the hamlet, the villages, the market town and the manufactories. His daily walks that autumn took him over the Quantocks and among its sloping valleys, where he made studies, moulding his thoughts into verse. But although his poem, 'The Brook,' never was completed, it was on one of those walks, his imagination imbued, I like to think, with the idea of the river as the narrative cord binding man and nature, that he stopped to rest at a farmhouse near Culbourne Church. Taking two grains of opium and reading in the book he carried with him of fertile meddows, pleasant Springs and delightful Streames, he fell into a dream.

As he slept the imagery of what would become his most famous poem rose before him, two or three hundred lines perfectly formed. He woke and straight away picked up his pen and began to write. But he had transcribed only the first forty or so when a person on business from Porlock called at the house and kept him talking for over an hour. When he returned to his desk Coleridge could recall only eight or ten more scattered lines, and the rest was gone as if, so he described it, someone had cast a stone into a still stream and shattered the images thereon. The poem as it remained, a fragment of 54 lines, he published almost reluctantly nineteen years later. Perhaps in the intervening years he picked over it from time to time, but was never satisfied, felt that he could never close the gulf between what he had seen and heard in his dreaming mind and what he had managed to shape in the dull forge of the days and years that followed. My mind, he wrote, feels as if it ached to behold and know something great – something one and indivisible – and it is only in the faith of this that rocks or waterfalls, mountains or caverns give me the sense of sublimity or majesty! The landscape that Coleridge truly pined for belonged to Mary Evans, elder sister of a school-friend, a girl whom he had loved but who hadn't loved him back. Such a beauty was Mary that Coleridge could hardly look at a swan bobbing on the water without recalling the heaving white downs of her bosom. If only I could recall her song, he wrote in the closing lines of 'Kubla Khan', struggling to catch hold of the vanished singularity of his vision, 'I would build that dome in air, That sunny dome! those caves of ice!' Here Mary and the river are one, the source and flow of his word rising from the womb of the Earth, only briefly glimpsed: *And 'mid these dancing rocks at once and ever, It flung up momently the sacred river. Five miles meandering with a mazy motion, Through wood and dale the sacred river ran, Then reached the caverns measureless to man, And sank in tumult to a lifeless ocean.* And unrequited his love fades, like his memory of the poem.

*   *   *

It is almost three o'clock. The rain has stopped and it is time I got out into the park before I lose the day. Time enough to put my coat and boots on before the sleet arrives. I jump back in the car and wait to see if the flurry will pass. Snow swirls momentarily against a muddy sky, the grey hill, a black wall of trees, and quickly turns to a rain which fizzes against the window. Finally the cloud lifts, leaving behind clammy, frigid air and a settling mist. I step into it, zip up my coat and walk down into the park under dripping trees.

I find the stream not far away, trilling over stones, twisting under limbs of yew and rhododendron, slipping soundlessly through shallow pools over a bed of sand and silt. I follow as best I can along the overgrown banks. The small river feels more or less lost here at the edge of the park, though traces of its place in a pleasure garden remain: the measured meander, sculpted banks and stone cascades. It takes a leap of imagination, a stepping out of time, to see how this tamed stream is the final and lasting exhalation of the forces that carved the place it now so meekly waters. Or how in spite of its role in the newer creation – a mere something to shape the landscape in order to express an idea of landscape – the river continued to guide the hands of its architects. Perhaps then what we blindly fumble towards is also what drives us forward? *There all the barrel-hoops are knit, There all the serpent-tails are bit, There all the gyres converge in one, There all the planets drop in the Sun.* The Ouroboros, like the river, eats its own tail in an eternal circle of renewal, while that which we long for has always been with us, and as much as we chase it, so we leave it behind. Beneath Dashwood's stately pleasure dome, in gardens bright with sinuous rills the river waters an envisioned Arcady, the shadow on the cave, when the river is the source of light.

It is to thoughts like these that I wander the paths and follow the waterways and springs, which burst, one by one, through the dead leaves.

I'm inside the Temple of Venus now, or rather her parlour. My hands are too cold to write easily. My back pressed to the cold, mouldy bricks, it is as if I am enclosed in an insulated sound box. Each noise enters this space clean and separate from the others: the dull echo of the A40, the rise and fall of birdsong. My view to the world outside is through a low doorway built in the shape of a vulva. The wet turf at its entrance has been puddled bare by footprints. Beyond, dripping spruce and larch encircle an empty lawn. It might not be the time of year for it, I reflect as I blow through my hands to warm them, and keep writing, but I'm sure this parlour has been used, over the centuries, for that which it was designed to inspire. Or at least its earliest incarnation was, because this Temple and Parlour are only recreations, built by the 11th Baronet long after the original was removed by its creator's prudish and more immediate successors. The empty lawn once held twenty-five lead statues, most of them erotic, including a particularly libidinous incarnation of a satyr, bought by Sir Francis Dashwood, 2nd Baronet, in 1746 as part of a more general consignment of garden statuary, pedestals, ladders, lead urns and stone pots, blocks and rollers that amounted to a purchase price of £120. For this Mons Veneris and its attendant army of indecent satyrs and nymphs, its Mercury for a clitoris and Leda for a nipple, was just one small, infamous part of a pleasure garden that Dashwood, twenty-five years before the poet was born did, like Kubla Khan, decree: a theatrical excess of loggias and cascades, caves, aqueducts, Greek temples, fortified islands, impounded lakes and toy navies to sail on them.

This Sir Francis came to his estate at the age of sixteen by that serpentine path of fortune, misfortune and chance which entwines, one way or another, around every gain or loss over the centuries. After the Norman Conquest the Manor of West Wycombe was bestowed on the Bishops of Winchester: 23 carucates of land, seven servants, three mills worth 20 shillings and a fishery which produced a thousand eels. For five centuries it remained the property of the bishops until in 1550 their star fell like that of the Anglo-Saxon lords before them. The property was seized by child-King Edward VI and gifted to a favoured duke. Twice more in the succeeding years the Manor was taken and given: first by Mary, who restored it to the Catholic bishops, and then by her Protestant sister Elizabeth who conferred it on a loyal knight, Sir Robert Dorner. A century later the allegiance that was his family's making undid its fortunes at the Battle of Newbury when a younger Sir Robert – of whom it was said that he delighted in the looser exercises of hawking, hunting and the like, but who had taken up soldiery in defence of the King more diligently and dextrously than any man – was run through with a sword by a straggler trooper after routing a party of Parliamentarians. Robert died within an hour, the family was ruined and his impoverished son sold West Wycombe, closing the chapter of another dynasty.

The new owners Samuel and Francis Dashwood had pleased neither Church nor Crown to make their way in the world. Instead their fortunes had been made trading porcelain from China and silk from Smyrna. When the brothers fell out a few years later they were rich beyond all measure, had tired of trading and were keen to establish themselves as country gentlemen. And so Sir Francis, who eventually bought Samuel's interest, passed to his teenage son in 1724 a modest Jacobean manor set amidst formal terraces, parterres and orchards, overlooking a spring-fed canal bordered by trees. How the place would change under the visionary, theatrical eye of the young baronet. In the stewardship of his guardian John Fane who had built Mereworth Castle in imitation of Palladio's Villa Rotonda, Dashwood was given an early taste for the pastoral classicism he would so heartily embrace. But at eighteen Dashwood set off on his own Grand Tour, the first of six. He was to prove no ordinary Grand Tourist. He travelled to France, Germany and Italy, to Italy twice more, to Russia, to Greece and Asia Minor and finally back to Italy again. In between tours Dashwood founded the Dilettanti Society, a dining club for cultured rakes, the nominal qualification for which was having been in Italy; the real one, as Walpole acidly expressed it, was having been drunk in Italy. In fact the Dilettanti combined bacchanalian excess with genuine cultural enquiry. His luggage loaded with architectural tomes such as *Pitture antiche delle grotte di Roma*, or *De l'ancienne Rome* by Overbeke, Dashwood fornicated and drank his way across the Continent. In St Petersburg he masqueraded as the long-dead Charles XII of Sweden and in that disguise seduced the considerably amused Tsarina Anne. In Turkey, smoking a hookah and sitting on a heap of silk cushions he chose his concubines from among the beautiful, gossamer-clad 'houris' hired in for the occasion. In Italy, to the terrified cries of *Il Diavolo!*, he horse-whipped the penitent faithful in the Sistine Chapel and later, flushed with the rakish bravado of his jape, got so drunk that he mistook two caterwauling pussycats on his windowsill for the Devil come to claim his soul. This vision plunged him headlong into religion with all the zeal he had previously had for art, wine and sex, while his long-suffering Catholic tutor thanked his God for the mercy – though it was he who had shooed the cats away without confiding the truth to Dashwood. Back in London, Dashwood's plans for a cathedral, his rosary and his preaching wore heavy on the friends who had known him for the most hellish of rakehells. They plied the tutor with wine, extracted the truth and Sir Francis was, briefly, a laughing stock. It is said he never recovered, that this humiliation turned him back to a yet more zealous mockery of bourgeois morals and of religion.

And thus was born Sir Francis's most infamous creation, the Society of St Francis of Wycombe, or the Monks of

Medmenham, or the Hell-Fire Club as it became known, whose motto was *Fay ce que voudras,* do as you will. For several months this society of apostles with Dashwood as a mock Christ and various political cronies filling out the order, met in the cellar of the George and Vulture in London while Sir Francis cast around for a more private location to better indulge the antics he had in mind, away from prying eyes. Finally in 1752 he found it at Medmenham Abbey, a ruined Cistercian priory and Elizabethan house on the banks of the Thames not far from his home in West Wycombe. He extensively renovated this small estate to enhance the picturesque ruination and quasi-religious imagery: stained-glass windows decorated with images of the apostles, pornographic frescoes, private cells and couches upholstered in the finest silk, a library of erotic literature, a wine cellar. At one end of the dining room a statue of Harpocrates the Egyptian god of silence, at the other Angerona, Roman goddess of catharsis and secrecy. The garden, the groves, the woods he filled with statuary, temples and inscriptions and all, so it was said, bespoke the loves and frailties of the younger monks: here *a lover dies on the bosom of his lady,* there *a thousand kisses of fire are given and thousands of others returned.* In the centre of the orchard a grotesque figure clasped in his hand a flaming reed tipped with fire and underneath the words *peni tento non penitenti* – a stiff cock unrepentant. At the entrance to the grotto Venus bent to pick a thorn from her foot, and the inscription over the mossy couch within exhorted *go into action you youngsters, put everything you've got into it together, both of you; let not the doves outdo your cooings, nor ivy your embraces, nor oysters your kisses.*

Who the Monks of Medmenham were and what they got up to in the old Abbey and its grounds has been subject to much speculation. Some say Dashwood conducted only mildly salacious mock-religious ceremonies, peppered with titillating imagery. Others that the monks enjoyed feasts of Roman excess, celebrated the Black Mass on the prostrate naked bodies of local virgins, and conducted orgies of eye-popping depravity. The monks arrived at night by boat, so it was written, guided to the Abbey by the toll of a bell and ghostly organ music: men such as Sir Henry Vansittart, Governor of Bengal, the satirist George Selwyn, John 'Liberty' Wilkes, MP. Even Benjamin Franklin – who liked to parade out of doors in the nude anyway – and the Prince of Wales are said to have donned the white robes lined with scarlet and processed to the Abbey holding lighted tapers. Dashwood, their host, waited at the door and asked each the password. 'Do what thou wilt!' they replied. Inside, belladonna, hemlock, henbane and mandrake burned in braziers around the walls, while the monks chanted Latin incantations in obscene parody of the scriptures, drank sacrificial wine from the navel of the Virgin, and poured libations to the Bona Dea, a naked Venus.

Service over, the monks retired to the Roman Room where prostitutes and society ladies waited for them, masked and in brown Franciscan habits. Whatever else they took off, it was said, these nuns kept on their masks so that no misunderstanding could arise from an unexpected meeting with a husband or admirer. The Abbot of the day enjoyed first choice, and thereafter it was a free-for-all. Couples – or whatever numerical permutation their appetites might desire – would retire to one of the cells or outside to the groves or grotto, though most remained in the Roman Room and built up their appetites watching each other go to it. For the ladies, the Idolum Tentiginis, a rooster hobbyhorse with a phallus for a beak, would serve to inflame their passions. For the monks, an apothecary dispensed aphrodisiacs. One member chalked a score on the door of each cell, a record for the evening. Whatever their doctrines were, wrote Horace Walpole, who may also have been a keen attendee, they were decidedly pagan.

So the rumours flowed. But Venus and Bacchus were also more publicly venerated just over the hill, in the wholly receptive landscape of West Wycombe where Sir Francis continued with his visionary intermingling of the classical and erotic. In this parlour and on the *mons* above it; in paintings and frescoes scattered about Dashwood's new Palladian mansion; in its portico modelled on the Temple of Bacchus at Teos and the statue of Bacchus within it; and most priapic of all, in the milestone pillar at the end of the West Wycombe road, said to induce trembling anticipation in young maidens. But these were only bodies in the landscape. Dashwood envisioned the land itself as body. It was said that he transformed the whole garden at West Wycombe – by a curious arrangement of streams, plantations, hills and bushes – to represent a naked woman, that the wooded island was her cunt and two hillocks topped with red flowers her breasts and that this female form was entwined with a swan. It's obvious even now from a map, or from satellite images of the park, how the swan was cast, the lake as its body, canals to the west as legs and the long river curving as it flows downstream, the neck and head. Leda is not so obvious. Not any more.

It is too cold to sit here any longer.

From the Temple of Venus I walk across an empty lawn once filled with satyrs, under the dripping branches of spruce and larch at its edge, towards an open glade and the canal that I saw as I drove in. A few ducks paddle away from the shallow margins, their part-melancholic, part-ribald quacking echoing in the damp air. They seem to float on nothing as if, but for the shimmer and reflection, the water is air and the clouds of star-leaved weed under its surface tremble in a breeze. The head of the canal tapers towards an arched flint culvert and from this a small stream leaks water that seems brighter than the grey day around it. Flowing on towards the lake the canal sweeps away from the glade through a stand of stately trees. Ahead is the Music Temple on the wooded island. Across the water beyond two nymphs frame the edge of the cascade where the impounded waters of the diminutive Wye resume their flow. A rush of falling water floats over the still surface. All around me is this gentle susurrus of water: waves at the lake's edge, raindrops falling from the trees on to wet ground, streams over stone cascades. Much of the spirit of landskip, wrote Roger de Piles in his *Cours de peinture par principes*, published in 1708, is owing to the waters which are introduced into it. Though he spoke of painting to painters, he was as much listened to by gentlemen landscapers like Dashwood who reshaped the land itself according to their own passing conceptions of paradise. With water, land and trees they imitated paintings of a rural Utopia and then commissioned real paintings to commemorate their vision. Dashwood set William Hannan to it in 1751, and a few years later his renditions of the lake and the fleet of replica galleons on it, of the stone-arched grotto and its recumbent water god, of the naked hill above the village and the stands of half-grown trees on the island, of groundsmen with scythes and of ladies and gentlemen walking the paths, were each copied as engravings which spread the fame of West Wycombe far and wide. Through them all the tiny chalk stream played a grander role than its nature intended, though I suppose it was an Eden of sorts. An imitation of one, carved from the real thing. Dashwood's sculpting was at least tacit, human and self-conscious and different therefore from the projection of an unpeopled ideal that would one day topple his gaudy extravagance.

Above a weir I find a basin of the most crystalline spring water, though its surface is shrouded in a tangle of dense and untended yew trees growing along each bank. I press my way through, looking for signs of a spring. But for the ripples of rain dripping from the trees it is difficult to say where the air ends and the water begins. At the far end of the basin there is a shimmy on the surface, an uneven marbling and boiling coming from under the bank. Closer to, I find the broken-in brickwork of an old archway and within it another source of the river. I lean out as far as I can to look inside the culvert but see only darkness beyond the tongue of sand and flints at its entrance. And so sheltering under the yews from a new fall of snow I sit on the edge of the pool, the road at my back. In the lulls between the traffic and the shrieks of children, or when the breezes that have arrived with this new flurry push those background noises in the other direction, I hear the snow falling in crisp, melting bursts of sound on to the water of the pool. I pull my coat tight around me, close my eyes for a moment and listen to the snow. And in that warm cocoon under the yew trees, as the light falls out of the day I doze off for a moment and the music of birdsong and lapping water fills the trees and the air. Rising high above the ground I see the undulating hills, the woods, meadows stained with the colours of wild flowers, grasses swaying in a summer breeze. And through it all the river, meandering this way and that, as if by turning and turning again its waters might caress every plant, every tree, every living thing with the breath of life, until having run to and fro and with nowhere left to go, the river at last throws itself into a cavernous hollow under the Earth, vanishing beneath a grey and empty wasteland beyond. And the air above it turns cold . . .

The snow fell hypnotically and I had been staring at it, entranced by the blurring whiteness and the whispering sound, for I don't know how long when I noticed a vast trout almost motionless on the leaf-strewn bed of the channel. With a start I recalled the fish I had seen from the bridge at the foot of this very park and wondered if it could be the same one. The gentle undulations of its tail, its gills opening and closing almost imperceptibly as it held station in the flow of the spring, slowly revealed the form of this great fish. And in time with the gills a blinking sliver of white along the jaw. As I watched the fish, its presence in this isolated trough of water something I could not easily explain other than to think it had been placed here many years before and had since grown to this great size, or that I was being haunted by visions, that in fact this fish was a sacred trout such as are said to inhabit springs and fonts like this one, I realised that I had been here before, that I had dreamt this place at the very beginning when we had flown side by side along the terraced street of ancient houses, under the railings into a river in a wooded park.

I stood. The fish did not move or startle.

At the head of the pool was a carved stone font, sea monsters furled around its base, empty, dry, the copper pipe through which a fountain once poured now pinched in. I stepped back to take a photograph framing the font and trees, a slice of the pool barely visible through branches beyond, pointing my camera up at the yews to get the correct exposure and twice having to wipe away beads of rain from the lens. Finally when I got the shot, for one brief moment in the space that had somehow fallen into the composition to the right of the font, a space that needed to be filled and would have been filled had this photo been a painting, I saw a naked woman. I saw Leda leaning back against the font, her long hair, her soft breasts hanging. She was there and just as quickly was gone. I wondered briefly, madly, whether to check the image on my camera as I stood in the cold, my feet sticking in the mud, a mist of rain soaking through my coat, mist rising off the water.

And now – I am not sure if after all I was awake and standing by that font or still dreaming at the foot of yew trees, asleep in the falling snow – I heard a voice. Chalk is not a Romantic rock, Sir Francis said. He had replaced Leda and was standing in front of me in a long, black cloak. An old man with an Ottoman scarf wrapped about his head. Water is as much to this landscape as blood is to the body. It is within it. He looked right at me and with tears in his eyes he continued: Yet they think it a prodigious pity that this faithful looking-glass of mine, gentle in her attentions, should not by some magic be metamorphosed into a new River Eden, rolling over a bed of rocks! Such a quicker circulation they say would give an infinite spirit to the view, thinking if not to make nature, then at least to mend her. No, do not look for my Leda here, he said, weeping bitterly. She is raped and taken down and the spirit of the age now looks for paradise in a more . . . igneous landscape. These well cultivated plains cannot compare to their wild nature, nor Leda's soft bosom to those far-off mountains, those rocks, precipices and cataracts down which thunder the whole weight of vast rivers, dashed into foam. A paradise indeed!

In later life Sir Francis, whose appetite for Bacchic orgies had waned with the years, devoted his remaining energies to an abridged version of the Book of Common Prayer, a work that was less than half as long as the original and free from all remnants of Catholicism. He grew fond of walking alone with his memories through the pleasure gardens he had created around the headwaters of the River Wye, though it is said that he was troubled by visions there and that once he saw the ghost of Paul Whitehead, the poet and fellow monk who had bequeathed to Dashwood his heart, beckoning to him from under the trees, after which Dashwood took to his bed and died a few days later, on 11 December 1781.

In fact the world had left Dashwood even before he left it. West Wycombe, theatrical and overblown even at its creation, was by now a gilded trollop, showy, excessive, unduly erotic. The gardens, according to one contemporary description, were finished to a similar profusion of ornament as that which had pervaded the house. Temples, statues and vases by turns attracted and wearied the attention. And though, the writer conceded, the character of the place was one of beauty there was nothing grand or sublime. Only the water enlivened the place. Whether divided into several streams, expanded into a pellucid lake, or meandering between the lawns, it was more than a counterbalance to His Lordship's more trifling decorations. But even the river could have been made more lively by the judicious placement of rocks, they speculated.

Sir Francis's heir and half-brother took little interest in the place and before the end of the century the neglected park had passed on again into the hands of the 4th Baronet Sir John Dashwood-King who – mindful of changing tastes and his gaudy heritage – called on the improving services of the foremost landscape gardener of the day, Sir Humphrey Repton, who tamed Leda if ever she was there, with a fig leaf: I hope to justify, he wrote, the sacrifice of those larger trees that have been cut down upon the island, and whose dark shadows, being reflected on the water, excluded all cheerfulness.

VII

THE LOUDEST GONG

It's three-thirteen in the afternoon and I'm waiting in my car outside a cemetery in south-west London thinking about why, this year of all years, I don't want to go in. I was always going to be here, though I have missed years in between. And yet now that I am, something is . . . I don't know . . . weighing me down. As if by sitting here I might hold the seconds back and cheat time. This disconnect has been with me all day, growing, nagging.

I might ordinarily feel, if I stopped to think about it, only a resigned regret at the passing of the years. But today stands out: there is a moment I must pass through that seems both enormous and inconsequential. I have known this before, this inevitability of arrival, this reluctance to look up the line. And I know that whatever is coming comes.

It is a fine day and way too warm for February. Where this weather turned up from I don't know. The sky was heavy when I woke. From where I'm sitting I can see only the thinnest line of clouds rising above the black delta of treetops that overlook the place I went to school when I wasn't even ten years old, an age less than this significant meter: the loudest gong, marking out a life – or an absence of it. And now, decades on, another decade has almost passed. I'll walk in eventually. I'll set down my flowers and stay for half an hour or so, thinking. Or trying not to.

I simply don't want it to be over. Something will have changed when it is. A closeness. I will have drifted. I wonder if this is common, this sense that although each day, each week, month and year takes you further away, there is always a stretched and fragile scar of regret, as much as the catharsis we ought to be looking out for.

Above the clouds a vapour trail razor-cuts the sheer limitless blue all around it, while the endless rise-and-fall drone of aeroplanes – half-animal, half-machine – washes over the unseen space between. To the south-west a lowering sun is eclipsed by a brick wall along the pavement and the blue is bleached out of a sky which is still too bright to look at directly. A kid comes past with his mother. She has collected him from my old school. He is talking about pancakes. He shouts 'gobble, gobble, gobble,' as he passes my car and his mother says, 'Yeah, right!' A minute later another mum walks by with her kid. She says, 'I hope it is.' The next family pass in silence. Just the delicate rumble of the wheels of a pushchair. Then farther off another boy shouts 'Mummy! Mummy!' He's showing off by the sound of it and wants her to watch or hurry up.

I really don't want it to get to five-thirty.

Though I found springs yesterday I didn't find the true source of my river. I dallied too long in the park and it was dark by the time I got back to my car. So I returned this morning, parked again under the same walnut tree

– no longer dripping – and crossed the A40 by the yellow gatehouse. The road was unusually quiet. There were no children playing, no mothers walking with pushchairs across the sloping ground below the hill. Grey clouds rushed urgently across the sky, though I could feel no wind. The dark silhouette of a red kite turned circles above the line where trees met grass on the steep hillsides.

I found the gap in the hedge where the stream reached the road and pushed through. I had stood in the same

spot when the channel was dry back in December and the hubcap which had rolled off a passing car into the dry channel was in the same place below me, half draped in silt and lying in a tangle of branches and dead leaves. The river was flowing now. And yet no trace of it existed on the other side of the road and there was no bridge either. I stood on the edge of the wall, grabbed a branch to stop myself from falling and leant out to see what happened in between. The small stream had been diverted along a retaining wall and into a pipe, where it would have to flow for many yards under the road and the car park behind the gatehouse to reach the channel that skirts the back of the village. It was a sign of things to come, I thought, the first culvert the water must travel through after only a few yards of daylight.

I clambered down. The water rushed into a dark hole fringed with green moss. It was too low and small to look into, so holding my camera close to the surface I snapped a photograph of the inside of the tunnel and stood again to study the image: a circular concrete pipe striated in green mould, the mould fading into darkness. Stalactites of dust hung from the seams between the pipes. Where the river lapped the edges a thin reef of moss had grown and the moss pulsed in the flow like the weeds and algae on the stones under the water. But these remnants of the living stream also faded quickly. Within a few feet the water had changed. The green stones were bare and rusty. And beyond all was black.

There is a river in Slovenia with seven names. I went there years ago to write a magazine feature not long after the old regime had collapsed. I was served eggs and chocolate milk for breakfast by a hotelier who held on to my passport, and I spent the day by one incarnation of the stream, the Unica. But the river rises from the ground seven times and sinks into it six times and for many years no one could be sure that these independent, landlocked streams were all part of the same watercourse. Now the water has been dyed and traced in various ways so that the Trbuhovica, the Obrh, the Stržen, Rak, Pivka, Unica and the Ljubljanica are known to be one stream. This apparently mysterious cycle through the birth, death and resurrection of one river is caused by rain dissolving limestone over many thousands of years, creating cavernous watercourses underground, and many routes to and from the surface. The Ljubljanica, the final incarnation of this stream, though it flows through towns and cities now, and though there are sewage plants on its banks, is and was, for as long as there have been people living beside it, revered by them. Tens of thousands of ancient artefacts have been found in the shallow waters of the Ljubljanica: spears, swords, axes, keys, brooches, pistols. It is impossible to say why so many treasures like these were thrown into the river over the centuries other than to guess that each generation in turn saw the stream as sacred, a deity to whom votive offerings should be given in thanks or in sacrifice. It is not unusual for rivers to be worshipped or sanctified. But a river which rises from the grave, again and again, must hold a particular mystery.

The Wye has three names, though not for the same reason. It is also sometimes called the Wick or the Wycombe Stream, and all three names describe the one continuous river. Only now, like the Ljubljanica, it too dies and is born, again and again in its short, seven-mile course. The sinkholes are man-made, the underground caverns concrete pipes. The votive offerings old tyres and VHS cassettes.

But it is almost certain that the Wye also has a natural underground course, though chalk is softer than limestone and can't create of itself the same cavernous subterranean architecture. When Sir Francis excavated West Wycombe Hill to mine his own network of caves – perhaps as a playful folly, perhaps to quarry chalk for the old Oxford Road, replacing the marshy, winding track that once ran beside the river, or perhaps, after Medmenham had lost its secrecy, as a more private setting for his mock-monastic orgies – the miners uncovered at the farthest depths a small watercourse that came to be called the River Styx by Dashwood and his monks, though it was in fact the underground Wye. Having negotiated a labyrinth of caves rumoured to represent the passage from the womb through the vagina, the monks had to cross this river on standing stones or in a boat to get to the inner chamber where today there are wax figures of Dashwood in Ottoman dress, and his partying cronies and masked women. Of course they invested the waters with all sorts of supernatural powers. Ghostly apparitions were said to rise from them, and even now there is a fever of speculation about spectral presences in the cave and some have captured images of a ghostly white mist rising off the subterranean stream.

The original Styx watered a far darker place, encircling Hades in nine loops of swirling silver. This river of hate and damnation in whose dark waters it was said the wrathful and sullen were drowned for eternity was one of five rivers in the mythical underworld. Circling Styx, the Acheron flowed through deserts and under the Earth, while fiery Pyriphlegethon wreathed itself between these and a fourth, the Cocytus, whose black ooze passed in a great circle and fell at last into Tartarus, the mist-shrouded lake that is the inverse of the sky. The fifth river in this rat-king of entwined water was Lethe, the stream of oblivion of whose waters the shades of the dead would drink to forget their earthly life. Unlike the Styx of hate, or the bloody cauldron of Pyriphlegethon, or Acheron the river of pain, or Cocytus the wailing river of eternal regret, Lethe's purpose seems more ambiguous. Flowing through night's blackness, her liminal waters irrigate this life as much as the next: the cathartic river whispering over stones to soothe the mind and sprinkle sleep over the world.

The day is so heart-achingly beautiful, like a spotlight of spring in the dead of winter. I can hear a chainsaw. Birds. The ping, ping, ping of a pedestrian crossing – going all the time now. School must be out. The chainsaw is suddenly closer. In fact, it is a strimmer and someone is cutting the rough grass in the cemetery. The air smells of warming leaf mould and mud, of cut grass and tree stumps, pavements and shoes, back gardens, rubbish bins out for collection or stacked behind sheds. The air smells like it did when I was a kid. It smells of suburbia. A referee's whistle blasts from the playing fields beyond the graves – I scored a goal there once, a hero for ten seconds. And these planes are just ceaseless, as I remember: waking me and sending me to sleep. The birds are louder now too. I was straining to hear them earlier, but now they are everywhere, arguing in the hedgerows, in the ivy. Insects dance in the streaking sunlight where it builds blocks between garages and sheds or over warm paving. It's three forty-five. I should go in. They may close at four. I'd like to be there in the sun. But I'd like also to be there at five-thirty, when the sun will have almost set. That will be a lonely hour, I think.

I found a gate into the meadow. The stream was wide and flat there, hardly stirring the delicate, green weeds growing from the river bed. It seeped from within a spinney of beech, oak and willow, sprouting tall and thin from a cleft in the valley floor. The fields beyond rose in soft curves and either side of the channel rounded terraces slumped into the watery hollow. I climbed the wire fence that encircled the trees and walked over a floor of broken sticks and dead leaves to the edge of a bluff. And there in the silent space of that small wood I heard the first voice of the river, the uncorrupted

river as it had always been. Water wept from every quarter of the hollow, from under the roots of trees, over shelves of flint and chalk. Or it welled up within the channel as dancing lenses of water swelling over bright holes in the bed of the stream, so that the damp scoop of land became, within only a few yards, a stream. And where the stream spilled over tangles of twigs or shelves of stones, it spoke. I climbed down the bank and took out my iPhone to record it. As I write these words I hear the soft noise of the river – the only sound I was aware of at the time – and the long-drawn-out wail of a police siren. It doesn't come closer or recede, but is there, welded as it were into the softer sound of the stream. It has often occurred to me these times when

I have explored the river, when I have stood on bridges over it unable to hear the water for the traffic at my back, or when I have sat beside it in quiet corners and even there found the river silent and the rush of the roads and motorways ever present, that this ancient voice of the valley has been drowned by cars, trucks and asphalt, drowned as surely as if a dam of concrete had been built between the hills and the old river now lay ten fathoms down, mute in the pit of Tartarus. These encircling rivers of Hades, rivers of the sullen, rivers of blood and pain, wailing and regret: these rivers of myth are now real. We have built them.

These thoughts were reinforced while I was in the library scrolling through microfiche looking for information on Lawrence Chadwick. It had been impossible to keep a straight course at times, so distracting were many of the stories in the paper, of murderous wives, of feckless husbands, of invasions of robin redbreasts. But among these headlines a certain type caught my attention and having done so once or twice, thereafter I couldn't help but notice more like them and their frequency, week in, week out, headlines that told of death after death: Amersham Boy Killed; Woman Dies after Mishap; Tragedy Marks Home-Coming; Chalfont Child Killed by Car; High Wycombe Man Crushed; Wycombe Woman's Fatal Hurry; Ley Hill Youth's Fatal Crash; Lorry Driver's Death Cry; Wycombe Woman Killed; Downley Woman's Fatal Dash Across Road. I wrote them in my notebook until the writing felt ugly. Even so, as I rolled the film up and down, looking for Chadwick, the death toll went on and on until I got the idea that the roads consuming and engulfing the town really were some new incarnation of a river of damnation and suffering.

In one edition, on the same page on which the council boasted of a road-widening scheme to deal with a bottle-neck in town, a story was headed Child Killed by Lorry. The little girl was Ruth Gertrude. At twenty past eight in the evening her mother had sent her to the post office which was only about a hundred yards from their front door. Walter Craft, land agent to Lord Burnham, saw her post her letter. She glanced at him afterwards, he told the court, and then she ran back down the footpath towards High Wycombe. As Walter posted his own letters he heard the lorry go past and then moments later a shriek of tyres. He turned at this sound to see a heap in the road, a heap over which the two offside wheels of the lorry rolled. Two men ran there and one picked the little girl up and cried out 'She is dead!' She could have seen the lorry, said Walter, had she turned to look. The driver, employee of the Goodearl furniture company, described how he had pulled on to the crown of the road to pass a stationary car, how he had been dazzled by the headlights of another car coming towards him, but could not recall whether he himself had his headlights turned on. It was his habit, he admitted, to turn them off on a lighted street, though where the girl had crossed the road there was no light. He was exonerated anyway, which might imply that the fault was that of the little girl for not taking care of herself, or the mother for sending her on an errand, or that there was no fault at all really, that Ruth's death was just one more casualty to join those that had passed and the many that would come, now that these streets which had evolved to take boots, hooves and cartwheels had been over-whelmed by motor vehicles.

And then, as if it might have contradicted my growing

conviction that this saturnine river of tarmac and metal had subsumed the River Wye, I found one more story: Wycombe Mother's Plunge To Save Child. I thought for a moment that a child had drowned. But underneath, yet more headings fleshed out the details – and I knew, before

WYCOMBE MOTHER'S PLUNGE TO SAVE CHILD

Girl In Stream After Car Blow

FROST SKID TRAGEDY

Victim Crushed Against Wall

"Your efforts to save your child were very praiseworthy." said Mr. J. G. Glover, Deputy Coroner for South Bucks, to Mrs. Elizabeth Smith at the inquest

SHOCK AFTER VISIT TO CINEMA

Wycombe Couple Find Man Hanging

When Mr. Percy Nicholls, of 22, Victoria Street, High Wycombe, returned home from a cinema late on Wednesday evening and mounted the stairs he saw his wife's uncle, Mr. Fred Barlow, hanging from the doorpost of his bedroom.

At the inquest yesterday at the "Swan," Paul's Row, High Wycombe, on Barlow—who lived at 22, Victoria Street, and was 59—the South Bucks Deputy Coroner (Mr. J. G. Glover) returned a verdict of "Suicide by hang-

I had even started to read, what had happened. Your efforts to save your child were very praiseworthy, the deputy coroner had told Mrs Smith at the inquest into the death of six-year-old Doris after she had been knocked into the river by an out-of-control car. Mrs Smith, who lived in Wycombe Marsh, had taken Doris to school one morning in the winter of 1936 only to find the school closed on account of the weather. She had turned back and was walking side by side with her daughter along a pavement beside the river when a commercial traveller from Willesden Green lost control of his car, which spun around in a half-circle and pinned Doris against a wall until the wall gave way and fell back into the river taking Doris with it in a jumble of bricks, seven feet down into the icy waters of the Wye. Mrs Smith had jumped in to rescue her daughter, but could see from her mangled legs and crushed head that she was very badly injured. Doris died later in hospital. Even the mother conceded that the driver could have done nothing to avoid the accident. It wasn't his fault, she had said, because the road was icy. Addressing the jury, the coroner noted that there had been previous representations about this dangerous corner and the jury, in acquitting the driver, recommended that the council should take immediate steps to straighten the road. Later I walked to see the place where Doris had been knocked into the river. They would have been halfway home when the car veered towards them. I followed their route, but there was no river. In fact the river didn't visibly flow between these two points at all, but instead fell into the ground through a grating beside a branch of Pizza Hut above the now broad and straightened A40 and did not show again for the entire length of Doris's final journey. Perhaps this was Doris's memorial, I thought, this rearranged urban roadway and the buried stream she had fallen into along with all those bricks, and perhaps, so my thinking continued, every change like this one has been paid for by those who are briefly remembered in the local paper. Perhaps this is how we tip the ferryman.

I finished recording the sounds of the river on my phone and walked on into the heart of the copse taking pictures of the gathering currents and then sat for a while on a fallen trunk of willow. Patches of blue sky had opened up and once in a while the sun broke through them and the day lit with a hint of spring warmth. It was pleasant to sit there with my eyes closed listening to the water, the inexorable seep from this one hollow corner of the copse, that seep echoed all around in dozens of rivulets from under twigs, leaves, stones, the roots of trees. In the silence my ear began to ring out its tinnitus Morse code as it does in a dark room in the middle of the night. It was as if this spring had softened the air about it and I had stepped into a church from a busy city street. In this still corner of the valley, insulated from the noise beyond it was not so difficult to appreciate that springs have for thousands of years been places of calm, of reverence and catharsis, possessed by sacred spirits.

The Egyptians, Persians and Greeks all worshipped the deities of fountains and streams. In India among the Dravidian tribes of Assam all the deities are the rivers of the country. The Persians sacrificed horses to the rivers crossed by Xerxes. The ancient German addressed his prayers to the Rhine. The Swede appeased river sprites with a black sheep or cat. The Scot sacrificed bulls at the well of Mourie. And among the accounts recorded by Gerald of Wales when he toured Ireland and wrote *Topographia Hiberniae* were many on the miraculous nature of springs there, springs that turned beards grey or wood into stone, that ran hot and cold, that were poisonous or whose stones slaked a thirst. There is a freshwater spring in Connaught, he wrote, high up a mountainside that overflows and recedes twice a day as if it were driven by the tides of the sea, and another many miles from the ocean whose waters spring from a high rock welling up each month at the full tides which accompany the Moon's increase. There is a fountain in Poitou at St-Jean-d'Angély which is dry all winter but pours forth copious streams all through the summer. And in the

Chilterns, he wrote, there are springs which entirely dry up when crops are abundant, while in times of dearth and famine their waters bubble up freely from the veins of the Earth and, bursting their channels, are seen to overflow. He might well have been describing this spring in the Cockshoot spinney, which like many that rise from chalk, seems to flow not so much in tune with the seasons as according to its own internal and mysterious rhythms. The springs of the Wye, I have been told, flow with increasing vigour as the year unfolds, swelling even into the midst of a drought and long after the streams in neighbouring valleys have run dry.

'Tis blest to learn the principles on nature, And scan the source of good,' wrote Gerald quoting Virgil, but since bounds are set, he said, to the powers of the human mind and everything mortal is far from perfection, the causes of such things 'ye muses tell; we cannot master all'. Indeed we can't. But although the bishop describes many miraculous things and writes elsewhere about the unique types of trout found in Ireland, the Salares, which is round and fat, the Glassans which is like a herring and the Cates which is spotless, and though he describes how a salmon leaps by curling itself around into a bow, sometimes even grasping hold of its tail in its mouth so that it can spring from the water, Gerald makes no mention of the sacred trout which inhabit so many Irish springs. Though I have searched and searched I can't say whether this particular manifestation of the spirit of the landscape was much catalogued before Sir Laurence Gomme dedicated a few lines to the subject in his book *Ethnology in Folklore*. Gomme, a statistical officer with the Metropolitan Board of Works who died of pernicious anaemia in

February 1916 not far from where I'm standing, described the recession of the pagan cult of river worship across the four Kingdoms to their Celtic margins. From the coasts of Sussex, Kent, Essex, Suffolk and Norfolk, westwards through the land occupied by the South Saxons and the Middle English, as far as Wales and north to the edges of Scotland, well worship is in the last stages of decay, he wrote in 1892, though it predated and had outlasted the Aryan, Roman and Norman cultures which had overlain it. All that remained of the tradition was its widespread commemoration in the name Holy Well, or some other dim memories of the reverence in which these wells and springs were once held. Only in the west and north, in Wales, Cornwall and Scotland, was the cult still alive, he wrote: here wells are walked or danced around, pins and coins are thrown into them, they are cursed, prayed to, incanted over, until in Ireland the worship of springs is more or less universal and here the presence of animals as guardians, animals that take on the spirit of the well, becomes a marked feature. Gomme did not observe, though I couldn't help but think of it as I read his thesis, the dim congruence between what he described and the rocks over which these mythical narratives were written, the tilting, so to speak, of the psychic and the actual landscape, from the igneous to the sedimentary, from what has risen up to what has been laid down, from what has been eroded to what has been overlain: how the recession of spring worship mirrored the relative alienation of the people from the land and how this in turn had been determined by the rocks beneath their feet.

The font of Tober Kieran, wrote Gomme, rises in a basin of limestone and in that pool are a brace of miraculous trout which have lived there since the beginning of time, never changing in size or appearance. The well at Tullaghan holds miraculous trout not always visible to ordinary eyes, and likewise at Tober Monachan there is a well inhabited by a salmon which appears only to the favoured faithful. Close to Cong there is a deep pit in the limestone called the Pigeon Hole and the sacred stream running at the base of the cavern is also said to hold an enchanted trout. Gomme relates the bare bones of the story that inspired Yeats and which was recorded more elaborately sixty years beforehand by the Irish songwriter Samuel Lover, who had visited the cave to see this curiosity of a subterranean river. Setting out one day from Cong across fields of broken limestone, a landscape that put him more in mind of an ancient burial ground than a work of nature, Lover discovered the cave. Rough steps in the rock led down to the base of a deep chasm where he met a woman who had just filled her pitcher with water from the river that flowed there, deep underground. It took no stretch of the imagination to suppose her, he wrote, with her ample cloak of dark drapery and straggling tresses of grey hair, some sibyl about to commence an awful rite, to call a water demon from the river, which rushed unseen along, telling its wild course by the turbulent dash of its waters. She cast her blazing torch on to the surface of the stream and as it floated away lighting the cavernous walls of the river's underground course, she told Samuel the story of the white trout. It is a fairy trout, she told him, and he must see it before he leaves, because it is unlucky to come to the cave and not get a peep at it. And then pointing at the river she exclaimed 'There she is!' The fish, according to Lover, was a creamy white trout. 'There she is,' said the lady again. 'In that very spot evermore and never anywhere else.' Lover asked how the fish came to be there, so far from any surface river.

'There was once,' said the old lady, 'a very long time ago, a beautiful young girl who lived in the castle by the lough. She was betrothed to a king's son, but the story goes that the prince was murdered and thrown into the lough and that she went out of her mind, the poor, tender-hearted girl, and pined for him until at last, so it was thought, the fairies took her away. But then, this white trout appeared in the stream, though it had never been seen before, and there it has remained for years and years, longer than I can express,' said the lady, 'and beyond the memory of even the oldest hereabouts, until at last the people came to believe that the white trout was a fairy, and so it was treasured and no harm was ever done to it. None, that is,' she said, 'until a band of wicked soldiers came to these parts and laughed and gibed [at] the people for thinking like this and one of the soldiers said he would catch the trout and eat it for his supper. Well he caught it and took it home and the trout cried out when he pitched it into the frying pan, though it would not cook no matter which way he turned the fish or how hot he made the fire, until in exasperation the soldier lunged at the trout with a fork and there came a murdering screech such as you never heard before and the trout jumped out of the pan and on to the floor and out of the spot where it fell rose up the most beautiful lady you've ever seen, all dressed in white with a band of gold in her hair and a stream of blood running down her arm. "Look where you cut me you villain," said the girl. "Why did you not leave me watching out for my true love? For he is coming for me by the river, and if he comes while I am away and I miss him I'll hunt you down for evermore, so long as grass grows and water runs." And no sooner had she spoken than the girl vanished and there on the kitchen floor was the white trout and the soldier picked up the bleeding fish and rushed with it to the river. He ran and ran for fear her lover would come while she was away, and descending into this cavern he threw her back into the river and there she has stayed evermore and to this day the trout is marked with red spots where the fork pierced its side.'

And now, like the soldier and the poet, I too was haunted by visions of spectral trout, and I was chasing the glimmering girl of the river. It seemed impossible to me that this particular stream, though there was little sacred about its car parks and culverts, did not have its own legend of holiness. And in fact High Wycombe's sacred spring is recorded, at least obliquely, in the Victoria County History, where it is written that although Christianity had long been the creed of the Chilterns, pagan customs lingered there with some persistence, until in the late twelfth century St Hugh of Avalon, Bishop of Lincoln, put an end to well worship at High Wycombe. If there was well worship in High Wycombe prominent enough to solicit a ban from St Hugh, where did it take place? Probably not where I sat this morning, though the wind-shredded fertiliser bags wrapped about some of the trees and branches evoked the ancient practice of well-dressing with rags. I have spent endless hours trying to find anything more than one short speculative entry on the town's holy well in a book called *Strange Wycombe*, by Clive Harper. Local interest, writes Harper, was stimulated in 1984 by a letter to the *Wycombe and South Bucks Star*: 'There is a record of a holy well existing in High Wycombe in the eleventh century, but where it was, how it was worshipped and if it was connected with St Wulfstan is uncertain. Perhaps a reader can tell.' But though the request was answered by a handful of letters describing old wells, no one could say for sure where that holy well was. Yet a century before the ban St Wulfstan had healed a blind Wycombe girl with hallowed water. And it is also true that when the Church was not trying to prohibit well worship it was as often subsuming it. So it may well be that St Wulfstan used water from a spring already thought sacred. Perhaps the miracle happened – in fact or in the minds of the people – *because* the well was sacred and perhaps, either way, this worshipped spring became Christian when the blind girl recovered her sight. There are springs all around Wycombe, but only one place has been called Holywell since before the Middle Ages, even though there is apparently no spring there.

I had maybe an hour to spare and so I left Cockshoot spinney, drove through the town and parked on Keep Hill Road at the far end of the Rye, downstream of the town centre. I knew where I was headed. On this now clear, now unseasonably warm February day the park was busy: mums pushing prams, babies crying, the toc-toc of a tennis ball, shoes sliding on a hard court. I stopped to watch a sparrowhawk tumble across the football pitch and a flock of gulls lifting off the grass in waves as dog-walkers paced through them. The Holywell Mead swimming pool was built in the 1950s, a civic improvement the town was once excited by. But it is closed and eyeless now. There are plans for its demolition. I walked around the perimeter.

Emaciated weeds had sprouted between the gaps in the paving slabs. Sky-blue paint was peeling off the edges of the pool. Dead pine needles were scattered everywhere. Yet the satellite image of this place that remains on the Web is a pointillist jumble of colours; the pool is crammed with swimmers; and on the grass around the edges is a multicoloured mosaic of towels and umbrellas. Who knows when the satellite will pass over again and wipe out this remote memory with new pixels? After all, the Holywell Mead swimming pool had, in its few decades as a place where the people of Wycombe enjoyed the catharsis of water, inscribed its own history over the mosaics that were here before it. The open air pool was built on the site of a Roman villa, a building which had enjoyed the sanctity of the same spring that lies somewhere underneath all of this. Clive Harper finished his investigation with a letter, though he doesn't say who wrote it, sent to a local paper in 1955: 'many of your readers will regret', it said, 'the passing of another of Wycombe's antiquities known as the round basin. They may remember the spring in the middle of the Rye at Halliwell Mead which fed the watercress beds and flowed past Bassetsbury Manor into Marsh Green and onwards. According to tradition, in early ages this was a holy well, the site of pilgrimages connected with St Wulfstan until they were forbidden by Hugh of Lincoln. This was all centuries ago, the nameless writer continued, but the mead, the spring, these remained, known as Holywell, Hollwell, or Halliwell, to this day. Years ago I urged that the well might have been laid out in remembrance of one of those ancient spots of interest but it has now been filled in by the corporation to add to the playing fields.'

It is sometimes possible to detect the remains of structures or the ancient passage of lost rivers in photographs taken from the air, especially in dry weather and I have looked for clues in the same satellite image in which the swimmers were enjoying one final summer in the Holywell pool. But the grass in that image is a uniform green and there is not a sign of the spring anywhere. And so, the last time I was in the library I went to the map cupboard and found a series of large-sheet prints from the earliest Ordnance Survey map printed in 1875. On sheet XLVII.6 I found it.

The holy spring was much larger than I had ever expected, so much that I was amazed the council had so successfully buried it without trace. The map showed an almost circular pool in the centre of the fields south of what was then Rye Mill but is now a Volkswagen dealership. The stream then drained away from the pool in a gently meandering channel skirting the north side of the swimming pool, the site of the Roman villa, turning sharply south and east again under what is now the car park and the tennis court and finally in a slow curve it joined the stream which drains the dyke and flows on past the remnants of Marsh Green Mill. Armed with the knowledge of where it ran I looked again at the satellite photo and wondered if I couldn't after all see the faintest trace of the channel, a patchy darkening of the green. And today before I crossed the playing field I had wondered if I might find a wet furrow in the turf, a trace of my hope that of all things a spring, which should be an irrepressible source of life, cannot ever be buried. It was soggy, I suppose. But only soggy.

I'm waiting inside now, sitting on a bench some way off from my mother's grave. I've walked around the perimeter path twice, dawdling in the sun. Waiting for what, I wonder? A perfect moment, perhaps? I don't know. A short, round lady is polishing her car, a green Nissan Micra. Endlessly polishing. It's a bloody funny place to clean a car and she won't stop. The thing is gleaming. It looks new, though the plate says it is five years old. I want her to finish and leave but she doesn't. A few graves along from my mother's another lady sits on a folding camping chair, her coat pulled up around her neck, her scarf over her head. The evening sun is catching her face. She gazes out across the tops of the graves and from time to time closes her eyes. I want her to leave, too, though she is in her own world and not minding mine. But I want to be alone. And as I realise as much, I see that it is pointless. My mother's grave is my mother's grave only to me. Otherwise it is one of hundreds. The polished slate of a headstone reflects the flickering cellophane wrap of flowers on the grave opposite and reminds me of sunlight flickering off water.

The car-polishing lady has now wrapped her feet in plastic bags and is walking off, locking her car, eyeing me suspiciously. She walks up between the graves, turning back every so often. She fills a red watering can from a tap. I watch her tidying around a grave between two trees and suddenly it feels as if the weight of all this absence – of empty beds, unused wardrobes or slippers, of unset places at table – the weight of what isn't there any more, it could sink a fucking ship.

The planes that I could hear but not see earlier are completely obvious now, climbing slowly over the cemetery and up and across the south-west corner of London. The lady in the sun near my mother's grave is still there, though her eyes are now shut. Finally I catch sight of two clock faces on the noticeboard – an opening time and a closing time – and see that the place closes at four-thirty. It's four twenty-five and I haven't yet laid out the flowers I bought at Kew station. I run over but I can't find the grave. There was a young fir tree near to it last time I was there and now it is gone. I move back and forth in growing panic until at last I see my grandmother's grave and know my mum's is one row beyond, downhill. I lay out the flowers. The last rays of the sun – it is now only just above the church on the hill to the west – catch the petals and they look pretty in the soft light. I chose them because my daughter said I should choose a bunch with lots of colours. What can I say now? I have nothing to say – the weight of the moment is enough. I can feel only how much I miss her.

I look up. A young man is standing by the gates. Everyone else has gone. He's waiting to close them, but too polite to disturb me. I stand, say goodbye and walk away.

VIII

THE HILLS ABOVE

The London project had become all-consuming and I was unable to get back to the river for months. When finally I returned I was desperate to reconnect with my stream and to anchor in something physical the weeks of reading I had squeezed into so many empty-hearted train journeys. I knew perfectly well – because I have spent so much of my life walking chalk rivers and when not walking, dreaming them – the real origin of the springs which I had spent those seemingly distant winter days exploring in the Cockshoot spinney and by the old swimming pool; how rain falling on the chalk hills seeps through countless fissures and cracks, percolating through porous ground down to a sunless sea; how this underground migration is beyond complexity, for the water might travel one mile, or ten, or fifty, it might fall in one valley and rise in the next, or it might fall far inland and rise in the open sea, running blindly as it does through an almost endless subterranean labyrinth; and how at the end of this secret gestation, somewhere – in a copse, under an oak tree at the side of the hill, in a channel by an estate boundary wall, under an old swimming pool – the unknowable topography of the underworld will gather those blind trickles and streams and force them into daylight, and there a stream will, more or less eternally, be born.

As the train engine unspooled like a mad clock, and day after day the digital screen scrolled through Littleport, Ely, Cambridge and King's Cross and at random the toilet door hissed open though no one ever dared go through it, I thought about how this real story of chalk and water is no less beautiful than the myth and mysticism. Nor did there seem to be, at heart, much ground between the geology and the romance. A fork in the road, that's all. And in the journey since then, many paths crossing back and forth between. The train from my home in Norfolk to my work in London passed over a chalk landscape, albeit a ripple to the rising wave of the Chilterns. Nevertheless that patchwork earth, its fields white after ploughing, the wild grass and beech trees on the hill above Royston golf course and the luminous scar of the bypass, gave a brightness to what were otherwise dark hours, and as the landscape peeled by and the train wheels rattled, so the chalk hammered through its bridled condition a beauty as sublime and mysterious as any Alpine cataract or long-lost rite. It was the misfortune of sedimentary landscapes, I thought, to be tamed because they are so tameable, and then, having been spoiled in this way, to become forgotten, unloved and unsung.

All these thoughts owned as much time as I could give them, and indeed the books that kept me company on those train journeys concerned the origins of the ground I travelled over, but it was late April before I booked a room at the George and Dragon, the old coaching inn on the A40 in West Wycombe, with an idea to walk from the stream's source into the womb of chalk downs that feed it, making a circular trek and passing on the far side of the hills close to a village called Watlington, which I had discovered was the last place William 'Strata' Smith had visited, still looking for rocks and fossils, just a few weeks before he died.

The girl on the phone was cheerful and friendly, said they had a room and asked nothing more than when I would arrive, then added, after I asked her if they served food at the bar, that I needn't worry, they would keep me fed and watered. Four hours and ten minutes later – I had fallen asleep listening to 'Exit Music (For a Film)' in a layby on the A14 – I drove through the narrow archway in the Georgian coaching inn and parked. The only door, which was under the arch, led directly into a spartan and more or less empty bar, though a group of five drinkers was gathered at the far end chatting intently, old friends and regulars. I stood there uneasily, wondering if I'd come to the wrong door or if there was a proper reception hall in some other part of the building, when a girl broke off from the group and called out 'Sam!' Sam appeared, but started pulling pints for the drinkers and only when she had placed five neatly on the bar did she wipe her hands on her apron and walk towards me grabbing a pad and pencil as she came.

'Room, is it?' she asked. 'Just sign here.'

As we climbed the rickety staircase with its carpet that lay wrinkled, grey and thin like the knees on an old shiny suit, she said, 'You spoke to me on the phone.'

'Yes, that was me.'

'It's funny how different people sound on the phone.'

We reached the top floor. She unlocked the door and showed me in. The room was vast, diminishing the double bed at its centre which was uninvitingly stark under an inky, paisley bedspread. In a distant corner beside the chimney breast a desk came and went as the light above it wheezed and flickered on the edge of death. Sam went back downstairs. I tried to open a window to let out the sweltering, top-floor air that smelt of burnt toast and air freshener, but it was stiff and I heaved without effect until suddenly the window fell like an axe. Moments later a truck went past below as if it had driven through the middle of the room, and I suspected sleep would not be forthcoming. But perhaps the drive had tired me out, or the hotel beer and sausages were a good sedative, because somehow I did sleep through the cacophony, waking only a couple of times to drink glasses of warm tap water from the basin in the far corner.

In town the following morning, as if he hadn't moved since the last time I was there in the snow and clammy mist, the bible seller was once again beside his stall. Though it was hot today and had been freezing last time, he was dressed the same: black jacket, black trousers, black socks and sandals. A black shirt done up to its top button. He sat on a low camping stool reading one of his bibles, his back to a corner pier of the Guildhall, his stall neatly arranged beside him, bible after bible on a low bookcase and arrayed on a baize table cover. Not far away the Asian kid who unlocked mobile phones was beside his own stall, still texting.

I bought the map I needed, a notebook and pencil and with these few things in my rucksack, along with a camera and an almost certainly redundant raincoat, I set out from the George and Dragon along Toweridge Lane, climbing the steep hill beyond the village as the squeals and shouts of children in the school playground died away behind me. Following the track through the green darkness of High Wood I came eventually to the crest of a rise and a view over the vast, oceanic swell of downs and coombes which seemed to stretch away without end into a shimmering distance. In the valley below the infant river was barely visible, a frayed ribbon of blue sky in a green meadow. Cockshoot spinney, from which it seeped, was no longer the stark pubic tangle of winter, but had softened into a cloud of chlorophyll. All about were the sounds of wind in dry leaves, the background effervescence of electric cables, the crackle of a warming day, the drone of jets climbing from Heathrow and – when they fell silent – the distant wash of the motorway.

Across the ridge, through Hellbottom Wood, Denham Wood and Wheeler End, I walked for hours along footpaths worn deep into the land, under towering beech trees and through thickets burning in billows of white blossom where the air was thick with a heady, almost oriental aroma. In the hollows under domes of moss and mottled green at the surface, except where some new rockfall had exposed its white heart, was the chalk this landscape is built from. Roots of the trees fingered through the fractured mass of it and all about were piles of chalk which had tumbled down the slopes, so thick on the surface that the ground beneath my feet appeared less a plot of earth than the bed of a tropical sea. I imagined myself wading its depths, my feet stirring the unhardened marl into white clouds, while the trees high above me became vast, prehistoric plants swaying in a restless ocean current. I followed the path over the crests and hollows of the deep ocean floor until my legs began to stiffen and after one last shattering climb I lay down in the sun in a meadow below the village of Ibstone and listened to the deep croak of mother sheep, the high bleat of their lambs, a pigeon's wings. I had long since drained my small supply of water, was thirsty and exhausted. It was two o'clock and I was barely halfway.

Somehow I got to my feet and pushed on up the hill emerging through a gate into a shaded lane. The sound of a radio came from a long way off, a tinny noise over the hedges and Steve Wright's familiar voice saying that a listener had called in from Hampshire to say she'd heard a cuckoo and that spring was officially here. 'Oh, it's here all right,' said Steve. But a nagging doubt that I might not make it to Watlington had become a suspicion that I almost certainly would not and that either way if I didn't get something more to drink I would probably die in one of these beech woods. A car whispered by on the hot tarmac and I set off after it, passing only a poster about a missing cat and a man cutting a hedge, over the long mile I trekked through Ibstone to its distant pub. Dust on my shoes, beads of sweat running down my face I hesitated at the doorway until the man at the bar said, 'You look like you could use a pint.' I drained the first and sipped the second while studying my map. Although the ascent of one more ridge would take me over the final rise of the Chilterns to my goal, that last rise and fall was three or four miles long. I might get there by five, but how would I get back? Outside again I crossed the road thinking idly about the buses that passed through here and whether I might be able to catch one on the way home. But the path snaked away through bracken and broom and within only a few yards I was alone again, not quite caring if I stayed out here for ever. I startled a herd of deer and following them along a narrow rut gouged down the face of the hill I emerged into a broad, undulating coombe where the face of the down had been flayed open by the busy labour of badgers: great mounds of splintered chalk and flint, the craters of burrows between. Here and there the dried-out husk of a long-dead rabbit. Skulls. Scattered bones. And bits of flint like cannonballs.

I looked around, vaguely hoping for a fossil, aware that William Smith had done the same just over the hill. Some of the chalk shards showed the scratch marks of animals. I cracked a few of the bigger pieces open to reveal the white brilliance inside. I peered closely at the powdery surface and for a moment, as I focused on those infini- tesimal fluctuations, I fancied that I could actually make out the individual shapes of which it was composed, the billions of long-dead shellfish which in truth I could only ever have seen with a microscope and which had ossified in a hitherto unbroken mass to form this fragile, white lump. I tried breaking flints too, smashing one against another, looking for the rotted heart of a mollusc or sea sponge. Some were hollow. Others had been bored through as if eaten by worms, a strange array of shapes: spherical, bifurcated and knobbly. They shattered unevenly. But the sun was intense in that white amphitheatre on the hill and feeling dozy on two pints of beer I sat for a while, closed my eyes and soaked up the heat: it could have been midsummer. When I opened them again the world blazed. I was conscious that I needed to keep walking. I stood, half squinting. My head went light. I held still for a moment waiting to get my bearings. At my feet lay a fist of chalk the size of a Yorkshire pudding. I was sure I'd looked at it before and that my eyes having been exposed to so much glare and ale could no longer be trusted, but there on its upturned face was the inverse image of the shellfish I had been vaguely and inexpertly looking for: the remains of a kind of bivalve mollusc known as an *Inoceramus*, dead and buried for inestimable ages, while the outline of its fan-shaped shell had lasted, impervious to time, imprinted like a death mask on the chalk.

I had found what I was hunting for in the very place I came to find it, yet it still felt uncanny to come across this relic here. Why should I be amazed, I wondered, to find the fossil remains of a sea creature high on a hill so far from the sea? Maybe it is never more than partly possible to grasp and hold a conceit like this as fact, that the high dome of chalk I had been walking all day was once at the bottom of an ancient ocean, but such things as seashells on dry land, I thought, must once have been truly strange. The ancient mystics had the world born out of dreaming, or the Word of God, or the unformed void. But Xenophanes saw a shell on a hill, just like this one, and in shaping what he thought to what he saw, puzzled through the enigma that was, perhaps, the birth of geology. The sea, said Xenophanes, must once have covered the surface of the Earth. Fifteen hundred years later Abu Rayhan al-Biruni meditated on the soil and couldn't help but think that India was once all ocean and had been formed by the accretion of stones carried from the mountains by streams. And Ge Hong described how the East China Sea had slowly transformed into a land where mulberry trees grew and would one day become mountains and dry dust. But it was Shen Kuo, a Chinese polymath of the Song dynasty who foreshadowed the knowledge that came only slowly and clumsily to Western thinkers when in the Taihang mountains only eight years after William the Bastard landed at Hastings he observed different strata of specific fossil shells and described how the cliffs there had once stood beside the sea and had slowly moved hundreds of miles inland and that this layered landscape had been formed over an enormous span of time.

In the Dark Ages such insights were totally lost to European minds. And though Leonardo da Vinci recognised fossil shells as the remains of real animals and deduced that changes had taken place to the landscape and the sea, it wasn't until the profusion of empirical science in the seventeenth century that ideas concerning the evolution of the Earth began to proliferate in the Western mind: in October 1666 two fishermen caught a shark near the coastal town of Livorno in Italy, whereupon the Duke of Tuscany ordered its head to be sent to Nicolas Steno, the Danish natural scientist whom he had befriended and housed in the Palazzo Vecchio, in return for which Steno had been charged with assembling for the Duke a cabinet of curiosities. Steno noticed that the teeth of the shark were almost identical to objects found embedded in rock formations and named *glossopetrae* by the academics of the day, objects which Pliny had suggested were stones fallen from the Moon, and others had said were the spontaneous, ossified secretions of the cosmos. Steno saw them for what they were and questioned how any solid body could become embedded in another. He published his theories in 1669 in *De solido intra solidum naturaliter contento dissertationis prodromus* where he formulated the tenets of stratigraphy, the building blocks of the Earth and the way we study it. At the time in which any given layer of rock was being formed, he wrote, none of the strata above it existed. However the strata might lie now they were formed parallel to the horizon. And these strata continue uniformly over the surface of the Earth. Most significantly Steno suggested that the stratification of fossils was a chronological record of once-living creatures.

Since long before Steno British meditations on the origins of the Earth had been coloured by the unquestioned need to reconcile that which was observed with unassailable truths which had derived from myth. Myth that may contain as much truth as truth itself, but which only derailed empiricism. Although George Owen of Henllys recorded seams of coal, limestone and glacial till in Pembrokeshire in 1603 and in so doing became the father of British geology, his notes imply that ideas concerning the origins of the Earth had gone unrecorded long before him and that always men had used what they knew to explain what they saw: it was the opinion of country people, he wrote, that the marls thereabouts had been gathered in the rolling and tossing of the waters of Noah's flood. How the common people came to the opinion, he did not know, but it was very likely to be true. And while Owen made observations that have proved in time to be more or less perfect descriptions of certain geological progressions, they did not amount to a system or thesis. A further ninety years would pass before John Woodward attempted the first.

Woodward was born into a well-to-do, but not wealthy, Derbyshire family in 1665, when the last great plague was still ravaging the country. At the local school he showed some promise in Latin and Greek, but scholarship being a luxury, he was apprenticed to a linen draper at the age of sixteen. It was out of this draper's future that King Charles's physician plucked him and by coaching Woodward in the arts of philosophy, anatomy and physic awoke in the young student an intellectual zeal and a curiosity about the workings of the natural world that would lead eventually to a great new thesis on the origins of the globe. The countryside around Sherborne, wrote Woodward of the studies he made there, abounded with stone quarries where the Earth was laid open and where he was able to see, intermingled with the rocks, seashells and other marine creatures which had turned into stone. So taken was he with this discovery that he resolved to pursue the phenomenon as far as his energies, reasoning and powers of deduction would take him. The result was *An Essay towards the Natural History of the Earth,* which though it runs to 300 pages in six parts was only ever intended as a short schema for a much larger project, one which was, perhaps, too ambitious and was never completed. In this essay he observed that throughout the world the land is divided into strata, just as in England, that those strata are divided into parallel fissures and that enclosed in the stone are the remains of seashells and other creatures of the sea and that these are the real spoils of long-dead animals.

Woodward's collection of fossils and the elaborate catalogue he drew up, including careful descriptions and the precise localities where the fossils had been found, placed him far ahead of his time. Had his mind not been inclined to theorise, or had he not felt compelled, like his forebears, to reconcile the evidence he had gathered with the unassailable truths of the Bible, truths that had perhaps been made more real to him by the religious fervour of his sponsor, he might have anticipated by over a century the discoveries of William Smith. But instead, Woodward devised a system to explain the stratification of the ground and the fossils within it, one which amounted to something of a geological romance in which empiricism and spiritualism blur inseparably, as much, in fact, as did the elements of the terraqueous globe in Woodward's cosmic washing machine. He imagined the centre of the Earth, the great

deep of Genesis, as a spherical cavity filled with water
like the pit of Tartarus, and that at the Deluge this water
had burst forth, fracturing and dissolving the Earth until

Coupe de la Terre dans son Diamètre.
1. Le grand Abyme.   3. Superficie de la Mer.
2. Les diverses couches selon l'ordre 4. Communications intérieures de
ou les Terres se sont affaissées après   la Mer avec le grand Abyme.
le Deluge, dans les quelles sont com- 5. Superficie de la Terre.
pris les Metaux et les
Mineraux.

Idée du Sistême de M. Wodward
Sur la Structure presente de l'interieur de la
Terre.

the rocks and stones, flints and chalk had lost all solidity.
The whole confused mass of creation, all the rocks and
shells and animal bodies and plants, became a rotating
orb of fluid, until, as the floodwaters settled, so did all

the suspended matter which fell through the depths in order of specific gravity: 'so that those Shells, and other Bodies, that were of the same specifick Gravity with Sand, sunk down together with it,' he wrote, 'and so became inclosed in the Strata of stone which that Sand formed or constituted: those which were lighter, and of but the same specifick Gravity with Chalk (in such places of the Mass where any Chalk was), fell to the bottom at the same time that the chalky particles did, and so were entombed in the Strata of Chalk; and in like manner all the rest.'

Chalk features frequently in his account, probably because it is the material that dominates southern England. But Woodward offered no insights as to its formation. He got closest to the truth only when haughtily dismissing the theories of those who had gone before him: the Ancients, he wrote, had built their theories on groundless speculation, for in their enquiries scarcely a man of them thought, or so much as dream'd, of the Universal deluge. They concluded unanimously that the sea had been there, wherever they met with any of these shells, and that it had left them behind. Having little to trust other than their own imagination it was no wonder that they fell into gross and palpable mistakes. The sure guide forever at Woodward's shoulder, by contrast, was the truth as brought to light by the Bible, and that which he sought was a comprehension of the perfect order of things, an insight into the constitution of paradise.

At first, he said, his reason was at a standstill. He could hardly assent to the strange and amazing, the horrible and portentous catastrophe that so levelled, unhinged and ruined an elegant, orderly and habitable world. Only a deliberate and careful examination of all the circumstances of these marine bodies could convince him that they could not have come into those circumstances by any means other than a complete dissolution of the Earth. And though the whole series of this extraordinary turn, he wrote, may seem at first view to exhibit nothing but tumult and disorder: nothing but hurry, jarring, and distraction of things; yet if we draw nearer, and take a closer prospect of it: if we look into its retired movements, and more secret and latent springs, we may there trace out a steady hand; producing good out of evil; the most consummate and absolute order and beauty out of the highest confusion and deformity.

In this metaphysical regard, I thought to myself on that bright hillside, if not in its physical application, who is to say that he was wrong?

The *Essay* went through four editions in Woodward's lifetime. Though Woodward passed out his years conducting genuinely insightful experiments in botany, during one of which he discovered transpiration and from it made predictions about the effect of vegetation on the climate, his *Essay* was, he thought, his greatest achievement. His esteemed collection of fossils was in much demand from other learned men of the day, although Woodward compelled guests to wait for hours in his reception room, to call and leave and call again, before finally agreeing to their audience, whereupon visitors were met by a man with screwed-up eyes and an affected air, still in his dressing gown late in the morning. Even then he would shave and make hot chocolate, feed his dog and shout at his servant and only after some time would he ever consent to show his collection. This however was worth the wait. 'He showed us first all kinds of precious stones,' wrote

Uffenbach, the German bibliophile, when at last he won a viewing. 'Not only was the quantity amazing, but the specimens were select and fine. He had also many stones containing fossil plants of all kinds; very many fine ammonites.' But Woodward's collection and his vanity were on a par. 'The maddest thing of all,' Uffenbach concluded despairingly: 'he has many mirrors hanging in every room, in which he constantly contemplates himself.'

Dr. WOODWARD,
From an Original Picture in the Family of his Executor, the Late Col. R.ᵈ King.
Pub. 1 May 1774 by W. Humphrey.

Woodward died in 1728 and was buried according to his own instruction – with little pomp and expense – alongside Sir Isaac Newton in Westminster Abbey, in the London clay that would have been, according to his theories, one of the very last substances to settle after the dissolution of the Earth. In his will his executors were ordered to convert his personal estate, his library and his antiquarian collections into money, to buy with it land worth £150 a year, and to use that income to pay for a lecturer at Cambridge who would ever after deliver lectures on the work of John Woodward. Although he made no distinction between his works in botany, geology and philosophy, it is also clear he could make none between his scientific endeavours which were mostly right and those which were wholly wrong. Even if he had, Woodward's geological fancies were superseded even as he drew up his final wishes and commemorated with them one thin and somewhat flawed stratum of thought in the earth that would forever amass above it.

Woodward in his tomb of clay and in his flights of fancy became two parts of one metaphor for the ground he had spent so long studying. It was not so different for those who followed him: Woodward's successors have all been somewhat wrong as much as they have also been somewhat right, so that one is made to wonder if the truth will always be Zeno's target or indeed exactly what the truth comprises. Woodward, after all, was in his greatest folly only reconciling the world as he found it with an inclination to wonder, and when three centuries later we can say with greater certainty – even though the science that allows us to do so seems at times a tapestry which unwinds at the back as fast as its weavers can work the loom at the front – how this chalk *was* formed, wonder is no less appropriate.

It was Thomas Henry Huxley, a sallow, beetle-browed man, with leonine side whiskers and small, bright eyes, who delivered to a working men's association in Norwich in 1868 the lecture *On a Piece of Chalk*, and thus revealed the true origins of the rock which had silently determined the histories played out across the soil above it. Huxley's lectures drew such crowds that many were turned away, while inside the audiences packed themselves to suffocation. Huxley struck a match: burn chalk and the result is quick-lime, he said. Carbonic acid gas flies away and all that is left is lime. Experiment another way, said Huxley, and the result is the same: put the chalk in vinegar and there will be much bubbling and fizzing, and finally a clear liquid and no sign of the chalk. This time the carbonic acid gas is betrayed in bubbles and the lime has dissolved in the vinegar. Both these things have happened, he said, because chalk is this: a pure carbonate of lime. Which tells us little about its true origins. So is the fur on the inside of a kettle. To see further we must look at chalk in another way by placing it under a microscope, when the lime from a kettle and the chalk will appear utterly different. Limescale is laminated, whereas the chalk is made up of a multitude of the tiniest bodies, none bigger than a hundredth of an inch across and most much, much smaller, so that a cubic inch of chalk, a lump of the size you'd use to scratch out a word on a wall, contains incalculable millions of these granules. But turn the lens in closer and the granules reveal themselves as the most beautifully constructed bodies of various forms, though the most common looks like a badly grown raspberry. They are known, said Huxley, as *Globergerinae* and it so happens that chalky, white skeletons exactly similar to these are being formed right now by minute living creatures which flourish in multitudes more numerous than the sands of the seashore over that part of the Earth's surface which is covered by the ocean.

But in 1868 the deeper ocean was as remote as the Moon. The information from which Huxley was able to derive the true origins of chalk, after so many centuries of fanciful speculation, was only very recently and fortuitously available.

Samuel Morse had been the first to imagine a cable linking Britain with America, just one year after Cooke and Wheatstone introduced the world to their working telegraph in 1839. By 1850 England was linked to France, and two years later the first ocean cable was laid in America from Prince Edward Island to New Brunswick. One vital component of the plan to link the two continents was a careful survey of the ocean floor along which the cable would run. Ocean soundings were a long-established necessity of life at sea but the sounding lead with grease on its base yielded information too imprecise for the needs of the cable pioneers. It was an American naval officer who devised the machine that was able to take accurate samples at great depths and the British Admiralty who commissioned Huxley's old friend and one-time shipmate Captain Dayman, to undertake the survey. Dayman completed the work in the summer of 1857 and sent samples to Huxley. The result of all these operations, said Huxley, is that we know the contours of the North Atlantic as well as we know the dry land. It is a prodigious plain, he said, one of the widest and most even plains in the world, covered by a fine mud, which, when brought to the surface dries into a greyish white, friable substance. This deep sea mud, he concluded, is simply liquid chalk. *Globergerinae* of every size are found in the Atlantic mud, and the inner chambers of many are filled by a soft animal matter, the remains of the creature to which the *Globergerina* shell owes its existence: an unimaginably simple being, a mere particle of living jelly, without a mouth, nerves, muscles, organs. And yet this amorphous particle is capable of feeding, growing and multiplying; of separating from the ocean the small proportion of carbonate of lime which is dissolved in seawater, and of building up that substance into a skeleton for itself according to a pattern which is unique.

Huxley's *Globergerinae*, tiny though they were – you might fit a dozen in the eye of a needle – were the bigger particles in this Atlantic porridge. Looking again at his samples under a microscope Huxley was amazed to find that the finer granules which made up the considerable bulk of the chalk and which Huxley had assumed were merely the dust and powder of ground-up *Globergerinae*, had a distinct, intricate shape of their own. Huxley named these tiny bodies coccoliths, the product of the most elemental of sea creatures, discs of calcium carbonate which a single-celled alga amasses about itself like microscopic armour plating.

Huxley was asking his audience, to whom the constraints of knowledge and belief which had shackled Woodward's imagination were still very much alive, to believe that the ground on which their meeting was taking place was once at the bottom of the sea, and that the rolling white downs they called home – low enough in eastern Norfolk but which tower to almost a thousand feet over the Vale of Aylesbury – were built up by the accreted remains of sea creatures too small even to see, let alone comprehend.

I think you will agree with me, said Huxley, that it must have taken some time for the skeletons of animalcules of a hundredth of an inch in diameter to heap up such a mass as that. An inch of it must have taken more than a year and the deposit of a thousand feet must consequently have taken more than twelve thousand! Even as he made this astonishing claim to an audience many of whom had been schooled to believe the world was exactly 4,004 years old as revealed in the Bible, Huxley conceded this was in all likelihood an underestimation. One day, he said, we may know the truth.

We are at least closer to it. We now know that the chalk accreted at the rate of just one millimetre in a century, a centimetre every thousand years. A small lump of chalk such as the one I was holding on that hillside bearing the imprint of a long-dead *Inoceramus* represents a greater span of time than has elapsed since the last ice age. And this lump was to this landscape as ten thousand years is to the length of time it took chalk to accumulate. The Cretaceous epoch – named after the rock itself – spanned the almost impenetrably enormous sum of eighty million years. Less time has elapsed since, and yet the world is incomparably different. When chalk was laid down South America, Antarctica and Australia were recently broken parts of the same vast land mass, slowly drifting apart. The Atlantic and Indian oceans were newly formed. Most of Europe was under a shallow, tropical sea. Dinosaurs roamed the land, ichthyosaurs, primitive sharks and reptiles the seas. The unsettled Earth spewed enormous quantities of carbon dioxide into the air and calcium into its oceans. In this global greenhouse great blooming masses of algae soaked up and trapped that burning, tropical sun and dying fell in a ceaseless white rainstorm of calcium, the microscopic skeletons cascading in their incalculable millions until they became the vast undulating plain of whiteness that once covered Europe from the edge of Ireland to the shores of the Aral Sea.

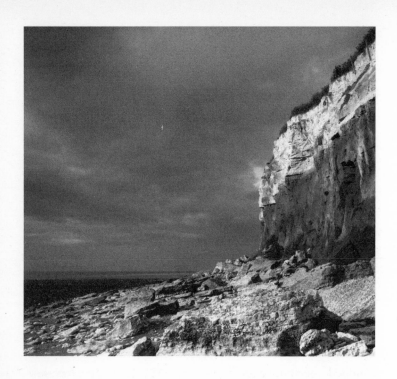

Who can say how best we approach the truth of things: through flights of fancy or the slow accumulation of empirical observations? Or even where or whether the two ever truly divide? John Woodward, in trying to square his God with his notebook conjured to mind something so far-fetched that it came – in the case of the chalk which rained into the deep from the brighter ocean above, settled and turned to rock – very close to the truth.

A small beginning has led to a great ending, said Huxley, closing the lecture to his enraptured Norwich audience, and if I were to put the bit of chalk with which we started into a hot flame of burning hydrogen, it would presently shine like the sun. It has become luminous, he said, and its clear rays, penetrating the abyss of that remote past, have brought within our ken the story of the evolution of the Earth.

Time has drifted on. The white skin of this flayed hillside has burned in the April sun with no less brilliance than Huxley's chalk in a flame of hydrogen, but now the light has softened and I get a sense of the day unspooling towards evening. I check my watch. It's four-thirty. I've reached the final rise – two or three miles through Blackmoor Wood to Watlington Hill, and the scarp face of the Chilterns, a cascade of chalk 500 feet down to the springs at Shirburn, Pyrton, Cobditch and Britwell, the little Chalgrove Brook and the flat expanse of the Thames vale beyond.

Why William Smith? Why Watlington? The reasons are not big ones. Perhaps only because he was a geologist who when he came to Watlington to look for fossils touched the landscape of my river. Perhaps also because he was the man who first saw what Woodward had been blind to, that the stratification of the Earth *is* the story of the Earth, that it needs no greater narrative. If Smith owned this bigger insight he was reluctant to set it down: it was as if ordinary expression was insufficient to capture the vividness of his ideas, as if he feared the labyrinth of connectivity he could perceive in the abstract would shrink to nothing in the telling, as if the serpentine wanderings of his mind, his inability to pass over any curious detail without weaving around it an excrescence of wonder and speculation, as if all these things forever undermined the clarity of what he might give to the world. At last he painted what he had to say, and perhaps I am here for that reason most of all, because he drew the map that turned this narrative into something tactile, something that could be walked into understanding. Smith was some walker. He would have made this easily, but I can't. I can't reach Watlington and get back before it turns dark. I've stopped too often. And I don't have the clothing to make the night in one of these woods a comfortable one. I sit down in a meadow near a farmyard, lay the map out on the ground and work out how I'm going to get back.

My notebook runs out with the following short entries in cramped handwriting: 'Crippling climb back to Ibstone. Hell Corner farm. Flint everywhere. I have no time to walk and note. The backs of my knees are tightening. My feet are hot. Through Hartmore Wood and out onto open ground. Across newly ploughed fields, white with shards of flint and chalk. Penley Wood now. Another tortuous hill. Legs so fucked that it is almost funny. At least five, maybe six more miles to walk. Red kites again. Perfect light. Immense trees. The wind has turned and the motorway is mental, a meteorite storm of noise.' After which I stop noting altogether, resorting to my camera for a series of snapshots to record my progress, to remind me of what I have seen: the towering beeches in Great Wood, an old cart track worn deep into the chalky land, hollow saw-pits in Bottom Wood, a pudding stone in a clump of bluebells, seven red kites riding the thermals high above Great Cockshoots Wood and finally the stream again shining from the deep green shadow of the valley as the falling sun lights the hillside beyond and across it the serried terraces above High Wycombe where a thousand windows catch the dying light and echo in stratified layers of luminance the brighter imprint of the land beneath.

*　　*　　*

The following day, back in London, I took a taxi from Bury Street to Millennium Bridge. The driver asked me where I was heading, what I was doing. We got on to the subject of the river and he said how fascinated he was by the history of what came before – 'all those lives played out before us,' he said. 'There's the Hatton of Hatton Gardens.' 'There's a Lamb of Lamb's Conduit Street,' I said. We turned off Puddle Dock on to Castle Baynard Street. 'It's sad,' he continued. 'All this history is there, people making places significant for reasons we have long forgotten, how we bury it all and move on.'

As I unlocked the door and stepped out on to the pavement trying to get the right change he told me about a construction engineer he had given a lift to who had been working on the Jubilee line and had found a body in a Sixties suit, someone who had perhaps been bumped off long ago. 'I asked,' said the cabby, 'whether they had reported it. And they hadn't, which is out of order. But this bloke said to me that if they did report stuff like that they'd never finish their work. They're always finding stuff, he said.'

IX

THE SONG OF THE MILL

I love this piece of road. I've been coming along it since I was a child, curled up in the back of my parents' car, late Friday nights, asleep till we reached Littleport where we'd stop for fish and chips at a café on a bend in the road. I'd have milk. My parents would drink tea. We had buttered white bread with the fish and chips. As cars passed by, the yellow orbs of their headlights would sweep across the edge of the road catching the messy grass kerb, a signpost, the base of a big chestnut tree, and then bouncing over the rolling bumps that all Fen roads seem to have collapsed into, they might briefly skip across the sides of boats moored along the banks of the Ouse. I remember only a few details from those journeys, but the punctuation of these ritual suppers stands out. I can recall, to the point that I could almost draw the scene, where we parked, the gritty glare of light from the steamed-up windows of the café on the bend. I remember the quiet as the engine finally stopped, the tick of cooling metal as we stepped out into a fresh night, the warm fug of frying. I can picture the matronly lady who brought our food to us, her upholstered two-seater chest, her striped apron. The memory looms up at me most times I pass the sign to Littleport. I tried once to detour through the village itself and find the old café, but the place seemed so much bigger, nothing like the little stage-set in the dark I had fixed in my mind. It was light and I thought that perhaps if I went back at night . . . but the experience threatened the memory in a way I didn't like. The rest of those journeys stretch out into a taut emptiness, like flights through the night, though towards their end as the roads quieted down to the very occasional rise and fall hiss of a car passing the other way – laid out across the back seat and half asleep I'd only ever hear them – my father would always remark, with mock indignation, that the back route was a bit crowded tonight. It was a standing joke that reinforced the pleasure my parents took escaping the busy city and the treadmill of the week for a couple of days rebuilding the decayed Georgian pile which had been passed on to them by a military uncle who hadn't much wanted it.

Although in the light summer evenings I sometimes asked my parents to stop at one or other of the two little bridges over the two chalk rivers we crossed towards the end of our journey, I wouldn't have had any more than an instinctive idea that as we headed north on a Friday evening every fortnight we drove more or less exclusively across a chalk landscape. The hills are not high once you pass Luton, hardly hills at all in the flatlands around Cambridge and Newmarket, though the fact that we were on a raised plateau and not at sea level would finally have shown itself as we came over what passes for a scarp edge at Stuntney, Ely Cathedral looming over the flat skyline ahead like a giant stone ship, the conning tower and cabins of a Gothic tanker sliding across a sea of rape and grass, poplars and willows. For the next ten miles or so past Waterbeach and Littleport we crossed the level Fens and the chalk was only visible as reefs of low downland on the far horizons. Then we made landfall again at Downham Market and from that point until my father switched off the engine – it was a V8 and sounded great rumbling over the undulating landscape – we were back on chalk. Great blocks of it came out of the garden whenever we tried to plant a rose, or a tree.

More or less all that remains of the wide plain of chalk that once spread unbroken from the coast of Antrim to the Aral Sea is this single rolling wave rearing above the inundated English landscape and frozen mid-moment. I have spent many hours flying over it, gliding the 400-mile sweep of downland on my computer screen, from Lulworth in Dorset to Flamborough Head in Yorkshire, tracing its valleys and the patterns which repeat again and again as if a child kneeling on a vast canvas had fanned out an image with stained hands and outspread fingers. A few years ago, when I was redecorating a house in which my mother, grandfather and great-grandmother had all lived, I peeled a sheet of old wallpaper off the wall revealing fragments of layers behind it, other wallpapers reaching back, as far as I knew, to the time when my great-grandparents first bought the house as newly-weds and – just a few years before he died on the Western Front – my great-grandfather went to work in the family brewery down the road. Showing at the surface in torn shards, one on top of the other, were the epochs of redecoration: a plain blue, a green, a white, a paisley, sheets of newsprint and an intricate illustration in sepia of the type you might expect to see on a tea service. I couldn't bring myself to remove this little vignette of my family's history and so I smoothed off the edges with sandpaper and varnished it. I don't live in that house any more and suspect that its new owner will have erased all trace of the memorial, but it occurs to me now, as I drive up the weathered scarp at Stuntney and over the level plain towards Soham that the story of this landscape during the millions of years in which that *Inoceramus* lay entombed, until it was scuffed into the open by a badger, is not so different from that wall of layered wallpapers, built up then torn away and sanded smooth. Spewed from volcanoes, dumped by rivers, rained from the ocean above, one by one each newly formed skin of the Earth ossifies on a restless magma whose spiralling boils bend and buckle the surface towards the sanding belt of time: frost, sun, wind and rain, great bulldozers of ice, rivers. Stratified layers of rock laid down over millions of years become a swirling, marbled pattern like the growth rings of a tree exposed on sanded wood, and the chalk that remains is the lighter shade swirling through the middle, pinched between the limestones that came before it, the sands and clays that came after. But only when the lens is turned in tight can we begin to see those hidden threads of dependence that link the rocks beneath to the lives above, which tie the strike of a particular hill or the ceaseless flow of a particular river to a thousand human histories.

The flicking red lights of a plane crossing the sky. Among the parked cars opposite two faces behind a windscreen turning opaque with fug. I've pulled into a car park at the corner of the King's Mead playing fields. A lady passes in a red coat, Tesco shopping bag, black dog. Birds bang out their electric chirrup though the sound is muted by the grey air. A grebe clatters away from the reeds by the river.

There was a mill here once: King's Mill, or New Mill when it was built in 1725, an arriviste among mills in the valley. Now nothing is left of it, just the Biffa service depot, though the steep gradient in the stream and the depth of what would once have been the mill leat above give some clue that a white weatherboard mill and a red-brick miller's house once stood here beneath a spreading Scots pine. Only a few hundred yards downstream at Loudwater there was another mill, though it is unclear whether it was the mill's first owner, Thomas de la Lude, or the swirling, hollow churn of water as it rushed across the breastshot wheel which gave the district its name. Like the other Domesday mills of the valley Loudwater ground corn for several centuries before falling prices at market and competition from windmills forced a change. Thomas de la Lude and his successors washed woollen cloth for several centuries more until in 1638, chasing the money once again, its new owner added the metal bed that was needed to turn a fulling mill to a paper mill. By the turn of the twentieth century the mill had sprawled over three floors and its weatherboard walls bulged as if at any moment it might fall over. Even so, the mill could not rival for height the chestnut tree which towered over it under whose canopy the children found a place to play on the earth banks above the race, while carts drew up on the dusty white road out front to collect finished reams or to deliver 'half-stuff' from other mills nearby.

I have a picture taken only a few years later: the chestnut is gone, Station Road is paved and the kids now stand with their backs pressed hard against the railings at its edge. And another where Loudwater has become a serrated white block under a looming chimney stack from which smoke billows into a clear sky, a cartoon icon of thrusting industry blurred in the shimmering heat over a cornfield. The whole place caught fire in 1945 – the history of so many mills on this river ends in conflagration of one sort or another – and in its place there is now only a car park built over the top of the stream. The river emerges from beneath it and runs secretly in a furrow of brambles and ivy under the windows of the Bucks Free Press until it dips by the Loudwater Tyre Depot under Station Road. The stream flows on between a footpath and the back gardens of terraced houses down to a small park where kids are throwing bread to squabbling ducks and a man in a grey coat stands motionless against a footbridge staring at the water rushing beneath his feet. The rush marks the race off Treadaway Mill, a corn mill turned to paper mill by William Turner in 1687. It too burnt down, a few years earlier than its neighbour, although by then the wheel had ceased to turn altogether and the building had become a furniture shop. All that remains now lies behind a broken fence and a shroud of sycamores at the foot of Treadaway Hill: a few bricks in the water and the stream itself chattering down the steep incline.

The motorway is thundering above me now, a dark behemoth under which little grows. The air smells of pigeon shit and rat piss and the road clatters and whooshes:

an echoing, structureless rhythm of tyres slapping gaps in the concrete, a background roar that feels unhinged. In its shadow a concrete weir, a deep pond of silt above, and a wall make up the remains of Snakeley Mill, paper mill from 1670, blotting paper manufactory from 1875, demolished in 1976, though the elegant miller's house still stands, most recently the offices of a security company two of whose employees watch from the window with some suspicion as I wander through their grounds snapping pictures. Beyond the motorway the river bursts into daylight again, tumbles down a concrete staircase and is gone, lost beneath Ultra Electronics and its car park, the site of Simon Hoched's eleventh-century corn mill, the mill that made tent cloth for King Edward's Scottish wars, the mill that housed the very earliest automatic box-making machine.

It is difficult to imagine, now all that remains of these buildings is car parks and the valley is one unbroken deluge of suburbia, that the town and the villages around it were more or less defined by their mills, or that the era of milling which has faded to nothing only in the last few decades had lasted for over a thousand years. The mills made the market and the market the town, wrote former town clerk John Parker in 1878. And the river made the mills.

Chalk rivers were always good milling rivers: uncorrupted, their springs flow all year long. And though these springs might be denuded now by public-water pumping stations so that many are dry and many others hardly flow at all, even so the Wye stands out. It still flows while its neighbours seep away to nothing, is swifter and steeper than any river nearby. The chalk stream to its south, the Hambledon, is nearly four miles long and yet it turned just three mills. To the north, the River Misbourne, which nowadays flows only in the wettest of years, had nine mills along a course three times the length of the Wye from source to mouth. To the north again the River Chess supported only one mill each mile. On the Wye the roll call reads: Park, Francis, Fryer's, Lord's, Ash, Flint, Temple, Bridge, Pann, Rye, Bassetsbury, Marsh Green, Bowden's, Wycombe Marsh, Beech, King's, Loudwater, Treadaway, Snakeley, Hedge, Clapton's, Glory, Lower Glory, Soho, Princes, Gunpowder, Hedsor and Bourne End: three a mile in their heyday – which might have been any time between the eleventh and twentieth centuries so adaptable were the mill buildings, metamorphosing as the centuries rolled by from corn mills, to fulling mills, to paper mills – all on a river that is only nine miles long.

Who knows what variations existed across the beds of sandstone and clay that became the foundation of the Cretaceous sea floor, or what fluctuations in the ocean currents above might have determined the chalk's accruing complexities, or the precise ways in which that white plain was later covered – as the land buckled and lifted and the shoreline closed in on what was once deep ocean – by the marbled outpourings of prehistoric rivers, only to be worn away again, all to create this particular place at this particular time? The strata of landscape, each described by what came before, each describing what comes after, seem to build a surface as specific as it is arbitrary. If this metamorphosis of the Earth was played out again would the chalk be here at all, or would the River Wye exist? Would it be a river valley that – precisely because of where it is and how it is – could only ever have held this particular future?

Three dry chalk coombes join and dampen to become

the Wye beneath West Wycombe Hill. Only the middle one contains a river of any sort, the ephemeral stream that rises in Cockshoot spinney. The Piddlington coombe is waterless, except underground, and drains instead into the spring that rises under the cricket pitch in West Wycombe Park. The Bradenham valley is the same. The water which falls there emerges in that yew-draped canal by the font, no more flow than can be accommodated in a broken pipe. And yet the Piddlington and Cockshoot coombes each rise 500 feet from where the water breaks to the surrounding watershed on the high hilltops, while the Bradenham valley doesn't really rise at all: it is no more than a slow incline through the hills to the vale beyond. Though its spring is just a tributary now, what remains above is a dry valley that once belonged to a longer, much larger river. And the ghost of that ancient river is still there flowing through the confluence of surface and time that wrote the Wye. Perhaps the venerable old trout which lay that winter day in the park fanning its fins in the flow of the Bradenham spring sensed or distantly knew this proto-river, which flowed through hills that have receded like the tide, draining a watershed that has vanished. Now only its valley remains. But its valley is everything. Without it nothing would be the same: the housing estates, the furniture factories, the paper mills, the car parks: none of these things would be here at all. It is hard to imagine now, when the motorway strides the lower valley on stilts and levels the ridge above in a cavernous incision, the critical importance of an easy path through hills. For reasons it would be almost impossible to determine, the interplay of chalk bedding planes and fissures, seams of clay and flint in the rocks around and beneath, and the infinitely slow, infinitely complex weathering of time over this geological canvas created a beheaded waterless furrow, a route through tall hills and flowing from it a river whose springs swell long into the summer while those to the north and south fade away, and which would always have been the most favourable river for miles around – and in a porous landscape there are never many – for grinding corn, for fulling woollen cloth or mashing rags to make paper.

The last working mill on the Wye, Marsh Mill, listed by William's commissioners, the property of Elias Gynant of Wycombe in 1175, once subject to a lease of 10 shillings and thirty new-caught and seasonable trout, closed its doors in the year 2000: an appropriately round number for a mill that was almost certainly grinding corn exactly one thousand years earlier. Its long history is etched into the sculpture of a roller-plate on the pavement beside the river, and a branch of Pizza Hut stands where the mill once stood. For a thousand years Marsh Mill had been more adaptable than most, but finally it too gave in to the combined pressures of cheaper, better power than a river can provide, a lack of domestic grain and a transport network that, with the invention of the internal combustion engine, was able to reach across the landscape almost completely unbound by the fetters of gradient.

Fryer's Mill is now a tennis court. Lord's Mill faded into disuse in the nineteenth century, though the mill wheel and axle remain, set in concrete opposite the Bird in Hand pub on the Oakridge Road. Ash Mill was demolished in 1939 and all that remains to commemorate it is the concrete spillway where the river now disappears into the ground. Temple Mill is lost beneath a roundabout in the centre of the town, along with the river. Rye Mill lies under a Volkswagen car dealership. Bassetsbury Mill is a block of flats. With the exception of a very few, most of these mills faded from existence, were burnt out or demolished or lost to a brand new identity just before or after the war and we would know little or nothing about

them if it hadn't been for Stanley Freese, who is looking at me now, his eyes magnified by a pair of tortoiseshell specs, his thinning white hair swept back as if he has just stepped off his bicycle, his ears, cheekbones and upper lip patchily hairy. In most of the photographs I can find of Stanley he is on his bike or just beside it. Here he is on a Chubb racer, his white shirt open at the front and yet curiously tucked inside a pair of striped football shorts. His socks are rolled down and on his feet are stout, black military shoes. His forehead is beaded with sweat. One hand is on his hip, opening a lean white chest to the camera, as if he's proud of how fit he is. No doubt the picture was taken by his brother on one of their cycling tours into the countryside near their home in Great Missenden. Stanley and his twin, Cyril, were both artists. They shared a studio in London and throughout the 1920s made trips to sketch the countryside, bringing home scenes they later worked on indoors. They drew quickly in pen and ink, filling sketchbook after sketchbook as they pedalled over the hills and along the valleys of Buckinghamshire. Stanley had particular affection for rural scenes which cast something of a backward glance, for icons of a bygone era set in an unspoilt landscape: a tumbledown, weatherboarded watermill beside a stream; a windmill on an open hill, its majestic sails still turning. Then in the early 1930s the brothers each bought cameras and Stanley embraced this new technology with enthusiasm. Sketching gave way to photography and to the forty or more drawing books he had already filled he now added hundreds upon hundreds of black and white pictures. His eye was attracted by the same subjects he had enjoyed sketching and there is in many of these new images the sense of composition Stanley had developed as a draughtsman. A black horse and a white horse pulling a hayrick across a field of stubble, the blur of a hay bale caught mid-air as it is thrown on to the rick. A bow-topped caravan parked in a muddy lane in winter, its horse grazing in the foreground and the lane broken by the long shadows of bare trees. A ploughman bent to his work on a misty morning, rolling chalk hills fading into a white distance behind him. Yet other photographs by him are curiously empty. They are arbitrarily composed to the extent that it becomes difficult to discern what it was that had attracted his attention and compelled him to press the shutter. And there is in these pictures a haunting absence, as if what Stanley was trying to capture was the thing no longer there, an emptiness trapped within the solitary objects of the picture: a bare field; a path worn through grass leading to a black copse on the horizon; a gate set in an overgrown hedge; a dead tree ossified within a cloak of ivy; a signpost; a silent crossroads. None of these images are compositions in the traditional sense and the two bodies of work – his photographs of a fading world and his photographs of nothing in particular – amount to almost the opposite of the photographic process, when the image appears before your eyes in the developing tank. In Stanley's photographs the world slowly disappears until it seems that there is nothing left to interest him at all, and he too has become as insubstantial as a stretched shadow across the foreground.

In the mid-1930s Stanley met a fellow enthusiast of the past in Herbert Simmons. Stanley had already illustrated *In Search of English Windmills* for the author Robert Thurston Hopkins. Simmons was also working on a study of windmills, concentrating on Sussex, and this encouraged Stanley to develop a more rigorous approach to his own rural tours in Buckinghamshire. With his camera and his notebook he set out to discover the history of every wind- and watermill there, some of which even then were already in ruins, some no more than empty spaces. Let us tilt our pens, he wrote, at the decaying mills and ply the worthy Old Inhabitants with questions while the titbits of wind-mill lore are yet stored amongst the treasured memories of their youth! The result of his work, more or less complete by 1939, was a manuscript far longer than a novel, illustrated by Stanley's unpopulated photographs. Each mill was described in turn, the book structured geographically and by catchment. Unfortunately for Stanley his plans for the project were overtaken by events on a bigger stage, and eventually forgotten. The war also put an end to Stanley's rural tours, his photography and his career as an artist. He took a job on a smallholding and soon after that began working for the Bucks War

Agricultural Committee. When peace returned Stanley did not go back to his bicycle, his camera or his mills, though in joining the ratings department of the Inland Revenue in High Wycombe he would have been able, on lunch breaks and after work, to walk through the town to the river's edge, and heading upstream or down find himself very shortly beside the remnants of one or other of the mills he had described in his comprehensive survey: Pann Mill, or Bridge Mill, Temple or Ash. He would have, for a few years at least, been able to relive old memories with one or other of the retired millers he had met in those years, though Stanley wasn't getting any younger either, and the millers themselves, those who were left, were mostly very old men.

Sometime in the early fifties Stanley, perhaps inspired by one of these walks to ensure the history he had spent so long compiling was remembered in some degree, took out of a drawer his manuscript of double-spaced type, extensively scored through, re-ordered and rewritten in his own pinched and careful handwriting and walked with it and a box of photographs to the Buckinghamshire County Museum, where he left it to posterity. The part dedicated to watermills is in two sections, the mills on tributaries of the Ouse and the mills on tributaries of the Thames. Of the latter, the mills of the Wye make up by far the largest section simply because there were so many. Mill by mill Stanley travelled, always downstream, gathering more or less as much history about each building as he could possibly find. He spoke to millers when he could. He drew sketches, took photographs. He noted the measurements and exact workings of mill gear. He studied old maps, topographical guides, county histories, the Domesday Book, trade directories, sales and lease particulars, estate records, parish registers. The results of all these enquiries, dates, names, conversations and anecdotes spilled out in no common order and piled one on top of the other; the links which dictated the flow of information unexpressed or unfathomable or locked away and long since turned to dust in the mind of Stanley Freese. It is as if at some point the weight of

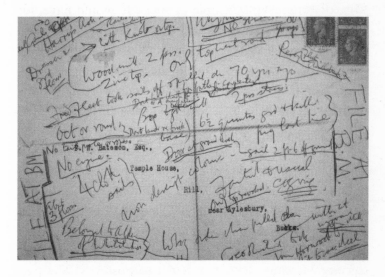

the material overwhelmed the vision, as if he could no longer determine amidst all these dates and names and crown-wheel dimensions precisely what it was that had started him out on this trail. Even in his two appendices, an introduction to corn watermills and to paper and millboard mills, where the reader now hungrily searches for some kind of overarching narrative to tie the whole thing together, there is only another eclectic and arbitrary journey through assembled milling facts and anecdotes. One can only imagine how the enormity of the task he had set himself weighed on Stanley, and reflect on how in the end it becomes almost impossible to find in the formless ocean of the past the seams of history that build one upon the next to become a story that is anything more than an abstract and dim reflection of what was.

But perhaps in the unsorted effluvium of Stanley's great manuscript something closer to truth does emerge. Certainly it is as if with each pass one is stepping further back from an image that is just too large or fragmented to recognise up close, and Stanley's own work slowly merges into one more fractal of the history he was recording. The painstaking technical descriptions of mill workings become the machines themselves, the burnt-out, rotten or demolished machinery transposed into a new life on the page. Names echo downstream and across the centuries, working families who never left the trade, but moved up and down the valley following a livelihood to wherever the mill owners would employ them. Mills roll through identities too, are bought with intent and hope, sold in despair and debt, only to be recycled again, a self-contained dream of independent trade for sale, a reality of water wars and poor corn, diseased rag flock, disgruntled workers, price-fixing and cartels. And scattered throughout are conversations Stanley recorded with the last of those millers without which their lives would now be forgotten.

Stanley's heart, if it lay anywhere at all, lay with the corn mill working in the good old-fashioned way, as he described it. His words linger over unspoilt settings, mills seemingly oblivious to the industrialisation of the surrounding valley, whitewashed and wooden-walled, their breastshot wheels still lapping, their stones still grinding corn. He was able in 1939 to describe only one mill on the Wye in this way, with the word 'working'. Some others are 'power driven factories'. The rest are classified as 'gone', 'all gone', 'dismantled', 'derelict', 'standing empty' or 'burnt out'. Remarkable that it should still be at work, wrote Stanley, of Bowden's Mill, where I now stand, for seldom has a miller had a greater struggle to make a 'do' of a mill than the late James Saunders who came from Stone Windmill in 1865, taking Bowden's Mill in the hope of finding more scope for business. 'The neighbourhood was already overrun by millers,' Stanley reported Saunders as saying. There were ten flour mills in the valley before he started; many of them paper mills converted back into flour during the bad spell for paper-making, so there were almost as many millers as bakers. Bowden's Mill had been shut up for years so that every bit of trade had gone elsewhere and the machinery was permeated with dry rot. And so most of his years at Bowden's were years of threatened ruin. They were not all alike, there were brighter gleams amongst them here and there; but the work, the struggle and the anxiety it would be hard to tell, said Saunders. The work never hurt me, but the incessant harassment for money to meet payments, the dread of collapse, and perplexities of another nature got to be more than I knew how to bear. To continue the same struggle year after year, when you are losing money and the contest looks hopeless, this is what tires a man. It is one thing to march along a difficult path when one's steps keep in time to the music of success, and the sunshine of hope surrounds you. But it is quite another thing, he concluded, to plod wearily along that same road when the song of success has changed to a dirge of failure, and the sunshine of hope has passed into night.

The clouds are thickening and it is almost too dark to write now under these trees. I have walked back up the valley along the back-stream past the sites of Treadaway, Lower Marsh and Beech Mills to the old railway cutting that crosses the river not far above where Bowden's Mill once stood. There is a spring here, quite obvious to see, upwelling a dome of swirling water into a clear pond beneath the railway embankment. The old sewage works and Bowden's Mill are downstream beyond a fence of white boards covered in black and orange graffiti. Every so often the flashing lights of a bulldozer blink through the mist, or the sharp metallic rasp of a drill or stone-cutter breaks over the soft rush of water. That noise in turn is not coming from the river, but from a grated culvert out of which spills a frothy, somewhat milky torrent of treated sewage. I am at a confluence of water-ways, some natural and some man made, this still pond and its spring at the centre and serene in spite of the noise from all around, much as Bowden's mill was serenely oblivious to the encroaching industry of the valley when Stanley came to live here in 1939. As it turned out, Stanley's favourite mill remained in the valley exactly as long as he did. In 1964, the year before the Wye was buried, Bowden's Mill was demolished and Stanley left the house he had lived in since he was six years old and moved to Suffolk. There Stanley resumed his passion, this time a book on the history of Suffolk windmills. He had hardly started when he died on his seventieth birthday. Now even the sewage works with which the corporation surrounded Bowden's Mill at the turn of the last century is no longer there, and – still trading on the serenity of this oasis on an island between two streams – the next phase in its history is under construction. A hammer drill has started at the far end of the building site and a diesel motor groans under a heavy load.

X

A RIVER'S RIOT

I stayed in that spot for a while sheltering under the yew tree against a drizzle that slowly turned to rain as I wrote the last few lines of my notes. Every so often someone would walk past along the embankment above, blue or red coats blinking on and off through the trees, a man gently whistling after his dog, a jogger breathing heavily. Then a cool breeze licked along the lane and ruffled the branches overhead, shaking loose a cascade of water. I put my notebook in my pocket.

Along Bowden's Lane raindrops smacked into puddles on the rutted track and as I reached Holywell Mead the birds which had been singing through this damp afternoon fell silent. Everything dropped to stillness leaving only the soft rattle of rain falling from a windless sky. For a moment the sun broke through the gathering clouds and lit up the trees along the stream. In the distance the dome of the church on West Wycombe Hill shone like a star against the black sky. Two boys kicked a football along as they walked back towards town and the green expanse of the Rye glowed unnaturally. And then the star went out. A shadow fell over the town and the clouds above melted into the hills. The trees turned from green to black and the rain came down as if a curtain had been drawn across the valley. The boys had picked up their ball, and were already running. I had nowhere to go. I was miles from my car. I ran after them towards a town lost in darkness.

Along the streets cars and buses slowed to a crawl as they bulldozed through streams of water and deep pools in the road. Headlights, office lights, shop lights, all blinked on one after the other and shone dimly through the rain. I ran into the underpass thinking I might find shelter but streams of water rushed with me down the sloping pavement and the tunnel was already ankle deep in water. I waded through. Its jaundiced lights flickered and lightning flashed from the gloomy space beyond. There was no point in running now. I was soaked anyway. I walked on through empty streets not really sure where to go until I reached the bridge on St Mary's Street where I took cover under a tree on the corner. The river smelt of petrol and, swollen by the storm, had become a menacing, oily brown, sliding from the culvert under the town like the waste from a factory.

Every gutter and drain was feeding the spate now with a toxic brew of dirt and diesel. The river might as well have flowed, I thought as I stood there under the tree, from the pit of Tartarus itself. The rainwater of course had nowhere to go. In earlier times it might have rained for forty days and nights and yet still the surrounding mass of white rock would have soaked up the deluge and still this river would have flowed ceaselessly unchanging: but these chalk hills have been cloaked in pavements, roads and car parks and now the rain fell on them as if it were falling on glass. The streets overflowed with water. This was a river's riot, I thought, against the oblivion it has been forced to endure. With these angry thoughts buzzing around my head I watched the water streaking over the pavement and suddenly realised that the buried river was there in front of me, that I only had to follow the rushing water and I would be walking a stream that no one has seen since 1965. Beyond the covered precinct I picked up the flow in standing puddles and cascades along the pavement outside Tesco. There it was, the lost stream, all too briefly reunited with the world above. I waded through the ephemeral flow, this reminder of a long-buried life, around the northbound turn of the round-about by the library and along the southern gutter of the A40 past Sainsbury's, over the underground confluence of the Hughenden stream and on past Bridge Street and Brook Street to the sinkhole where I had begun my journey so many months before. I pushed through flowing water the whole way, until I reached the Venus de Milo willow where a foaming torrent plunged angrily into its subter-ranean coffin. Waves of water spilled over the top of the grid and joined the streams of water spilling from the A40 and along the pavement.

I don't know how long I stood rooted to that place feeling the dispossessed soul of the river surge through me, its rage made all the more awful by my own para-lysing, hopeless despair at its fate. What it must be like to have no recourse, to break out in ways you might hardly comprehend, let alone control. It was this thought which gripped me as the rain beat down and the river boiled and foamed at the gateway to its prison, this thought and the river's history mirrored in the lives of its people.

Soaked through and no longer bothering to hunch against the rain, I stood there until the storm began to pass and a band of brighter sky appeared over the hills to the west. But I was miles from the car, transfixed by the river and in my mind the light of dawn had hardly broken over the opposite horizon on a winter morning in 1830. The mill workers of the Wye valley had gathered on the heath above the town. I was beside them. The hunting horn sounded and they advanced on this very place, to what is a sinkhole now but was a paper mill then, determined to destroy it and all that it stood for. But what could I rail at? They had machinery to break. I had only a disappearance. They had hammers, pickaxes and crowbars to smash at the Fourdriniers and rag cutters, the newfangled machines dispossessing them, replacing the work of people with the tireless pounding of metal, steam and gears, driving down wages, turning worker against worker and workers against mill owners. I had nothing.

The rioting had already spread like a fever that fateful summer and autumn, from Paris to Kent, across the Sussex and Hampshire downs and finally north here to the Chilterns in Buckinghamshire. Night after night desperate farm labourers had dragged into the open fields the threshing machines and chaff-cutting engines which had become the very symbols of their oppression, and there, illuminated by the blaze of flaming hayricks and in orgies of violence, they had smashed at them with hammers and burned the remains. Landowners foolhardy enough to resist lost their barns too. But these riots were not without cause or reason. Most often the destruction was preceded by letters of warning, letters signed in many hands but all in one name, Captain Swing, the mythical figurehead of the movement. And behind the threatening words and the destruction that was almost wholly restricted to inanimate objects was a wretched hopelessness that could find no other outlet. These impoverished workers might have been after smashing expensive machinery but would have argued that the greater crime had been done to them. And so the protest song ran: *They hang the man, and flog the woman, That steals the goose from off the common, But let the greater villain loose, That steals the common from the goose.*

The Enclosure Acts of the eighteenth century had stripped rural labourers of the common land where traditionally they would have grazed cattle or geese, gleaned or picked berries and thus been assured of at least some independent means of subsistence. Bit by bit these formerly shared lands had been cut out and entitled to the benefit of wealthy landowners on whose occasional employment the labourers became utterly dependent. But labour was not in short supply. An abundance of it allowed the landowners to pay more scantily and on harder terms year after year. When once a worker might have expected payment in kind, a seat at his master's dinner table and a contract for a year's work, by 1830 it was cash only, and monthly contracts at best, and the worker thrown back on the mercy of the parish relief system as soon as he could be dispensed with. The invention of machinery that could obviate their work altogether was the spark in a dry tinderbox.

The first Wycombe fire broke out one Tuesday in November in a barn on an unoccupied farm in the village of Nash, a godforsaken place where local farm labourers had been reduced in their search for employment to digging and sifting gravel. The next day a stack yard went up in flames, and over the weekend threatening letters were received by mill owners and farmers. The valley was soon gripped by fearful anticipation. One farmer could stand it no longer and set fire to his own threshing engine. Another took a hammer to a machine that had recently cost him £100. On Friday 26 November a meeting of folk anxious to preserve their property was called in the Guildhall, High Wycombe, but no sooner had it begun than a crowd – papermakers amongst them – came in, tipped the chairman Dr Scobell out of his seat, and began to break windows and chairs. The papermakers of the Wye valley had been caught up by the same riotous fever, for their lot was little different from that of the farm worker. Scanty wages. Too many workers for too little work. And now new contraptions to mechanise the process of paper-making and get rid of them altogether. From the Guildhall they set out for Ash Mill, a few minutes away by foot, intent on destroying its machinery. Following the river they rounded the corner of Brook Street, heralded by the sounds of marching boots, and cries of 'Down with machinery!' Men, some of whom must have been friends or colleagues but who would increasingly have become rivals for dwindling work and wages, now erupted as one. They must have enjoyed the solidarity, and the taste of what felt like justice, when they saw fear on the faces of the powerful. The mill was spared that evening only by the coincidental presence nearby of a troop of the Bucks Yeomanry and by Scobell's assurance that the millers' grievances would soon be heard. The angry crowd dispersed after a while, muttering, so it was said, dark threats of vengeance as they went.

But the weekend that followed was a long and violent one: gangs of farm labourers rampaged through the local parishes smashing and burning any machine they could lay their hands on – threshers, winnowers, chaff-cutters. To spare barns and farmsteads from the fires wiser farmers moved their machinery into the open fields. The braver stood their ground. But not for long. The mob had their way, and by dawn on Monday it was the millers' turn.

The High Constable of the town saw them coming and, grabbing a local butcher named Veary, raced ahead to Ash Mill, knowing it would be the first in line. The mob arrived to find the door locked and the Constable, the butcher and the millers the far side of it. The crowd tried to smash their way in with axes and hammers. Thirty minutes on they had done no more than break a few holes in the door through which the defenders could now see the angry faces of their attackers. One of them – witnesses said it was Veary – carried away in fear for his life at the hands of this mob, hurled vitriol through the holes in the door, repelling the attack for only so long as it took for the scalded men to rush to the river and wash off the burning acid. Doubly angered they returned and knocked the door through in no time, got hold of Veary and half drowned the terrified butcher in the stream. A shot was fired from inside. Badly burnt by the acid the ringleader retired, but Thomas Blizzard, who had stood beside him, forced a path through to the machinery – a cylinder armed with knives used for chopping rags – and utterly destroyed it.

Job done at Ash Mill, the papermakers turned downstream. Hangers-on and bystanders now joined the throng as it tramped through the town and soon the mob was a torrent, hundreds strong. Zachary Allnutt appealed to them to spare his machinery but they made short work of it even so, smashing their hammers to drown the voice of the local vicar as he read out the words of the Riot Act. Deaf as the crowd seemed, these notorious words gave them an hour to scatter, or else each would become guilty of a crime with the most serious consequences and those who took up arms against the gathering would be entitled to enforce an end by whatever means it took. A mile or so further downstream John Hay heard the oncoming crowd and in a panic had gone at his own machinery with a spanner. Too late, he stood at the doorway to Marsh Green Mill and tried to assure the crowd as they pressed through that he had begun the process of dismantling the machinery himself. He invited them to see for themselves that he wasn't lying, pleaded with them that the destruction they intended would do no more than put fifty men and boys out of work. They let him have his say and when he was done pushed him out of the way and destroyed his machinery anyway.

And so it continued, from mill to pub and pub to mill. The Riot Act was read aloud once again as the mob came out of the Red Lion to march along the turnpike road towards King's Mill. But no one was listening to it. This miller might already have given his assurances that the machinery there would not be used until he had reached an agreement with his workers, but the papermakers were drunk now as well as indignant and nothing could appease them.

By early afternoon news of the riot had spread downstream and a message for urgent assistance was despatched to Beaconsfield. There thirty newly sworn in constables quickly rallied and made their way to Glory Mills hoping to intercept the rioters. But beer had slowed the flood of discontent and all was quiet at Glory, as it was at Clapton's Mill upriver: only birdsong and the lapping of the mill wheel in the falling stream. A horseman was sent ahead. A mile upriver he caught sight of a vast crowd making their way across the water meadows. He heard voices raised, shouts of 'Down with machinery!' The small troop arrived at Snakeley Mill, over which the Dreams PLC warehouse now stands, reinforcing the exhausted band of local constables just as the angry crowd advanced across the grass towards them. Sullivan, a county magistrate, unaware that the Riot Act had been read twice already tried again from the top of his horse and was answered with a hail of bricks and stones. Rushing with hammers at the constables the mob broke through a thin line of resistance, driving most of the lawmen into an adjacent meadow, while a handful of papermakers broke away and headed to the mill. Here too the miller stood at the doorway and like others before him tried to reason with the oncoming crowd. Again it was no good. Within minutes half a dozen papermakers were flailing away at the hated machinery, smashing wheels and gears and copper pipes and cylinders, the din of hammers on iron carrying outside over the noise of what had become a pitched battle. His Majesty's Staghounds who had been hunting nearby in Wooburn piled into the melee in support of the Beaconsfield constables. Shots were fired. One rioter was wounded in the chest. Two others were carried off the field, apparently lifeless. One of the stag hunters rode through the crowd brandishing a sword and over the top of two women, breaking the ribs of one of them in the collision. Losing his mount, he was lucky, so it was reported in the paper, to escape with his life. John Sarney, an aged publican in sympathy with the customers to whom he sold so much beer, made much play of his intent to break the heads of the constables, threatening several though never landing a blow, until finally he was arrested. By now the mill machinery had been destroyed and Blizzard along with his partners in crime came out of the mill jeering and swearing victoriously, indignantly, at the constables. But the battle had turned. Losing energy, interest or pluck, many of the crowd had fled into the nearby woods and finally the constables were able to arrest a handful of the ringleaders. Sarney tried to bribe his way to an early release. 'It would have been better for me if I had been at my work,' said a contrite rioter to his captor as he was taken away to Beaconsfield prison, his apron still bulging with the rocks he had carried with him to the riot. Their fury sated, those who did escape scattered, only to be arrested one by one over the next few days, at their homes, at Sarney's pub in Flackwell Heath, when they showed their faces in town.

Sobered by a month in gaol the papermakers could hardly explain when the trials began on 10 January 1831 to themselves or to anyone else, exactly why they had rioted. These normally peaceable men had been driven to violence by impulses they hardly recognised. The people of High Wycombe could not believe that so many good citizens might well face the gallows. Even the ringleaders were given references of good character: James Miles was a peaceable and quiet lad, William Shrimpton a man who had worked tirelessly for years and only with the greatest of reluctance ever applied for parish relief, Smith a poor, harmless boy, his only flaw a slight deficiency of intellect.

And yet the contagion of the riots had alarmed the government. The Home Secretary Lord Melbourne had publicly stated that the judges in Kent, where the first trials took place, were being too lenient. Examples must be set, he said. Justice Park was part of a Special Commission set up by Melbourne to do just that and Park took trouble to point out that he could not give any opinion as to whether the machines did cause unemployment or if they were the background causes of the riots. His job was only to impose the law.

When, on the fourth day of the trials, all the prisoners placed before the bar for the indictment of rioting at Marsh Green Mill and King's Mill pleaded guilty to what they knew was a capital offence it was a sign of contrition that momentarily placed Justice Park in an awkward position. Park took a moment to confer with his colleagues before he turned to the prisoners at the bar and told them – in a grave but noticeably relieved tone – that because they had shown contrition in this way his learned brothers felt able to accede with him to the request of counsel that a sentence of death be recorded, but not passed. 'The meaning of which is that your lives will be spared,' Park explained to the prisoners. 'And I therefore beg you will consider this a most merciful boon, and that you will show, by the future conduct of your lives, your gratitude to man and to God for the mercy extended towards you.'

Nineteen other papermakers, those who had already pleaded not guilty, still awaited their sentencing. That they were present and had broken machinery in the riots at Ash Mill and Snakeley had now been established beyond doubt. But they had not had the advantage of counsel's lately considered advice to show contrition by pleading guilty. And yet still Justice Park was inclined to show mercy. It was too dreadful to contemplate, he said, such effusion of blood and sacrifice of life taking place. Once again the sentence of death was recorded and not formally passed and as before Park took pains to advise the prisoners that on what terms their lives would be spared was for His Majesty to determine. The oppressive tension in the courtroom lifted as the magistrate spoke. Not even Park's ominous hint that a fate not so far removed in severity from the gallows might yet await these unlucky papermakers could suppress the utter relief that transported itself through the courtroom and outside into the packed streets beyond its doors.

Finally, Thomas Blizzard and John Sarney were placed at the bar. They too had been found guilty of destroying machinery, Blizzard at the scene of every riot, Sarney the aged publican more by implication than action. But his boasts of skull-breaking and machine-smashing had not, it soon became apparent, served him well. Neither man appeared to be ready for what happened next, for they both shrank visibly, in sudden and wretched despair, it was reported, as Justice Park and the other judges placed on their heads square pieces of black cloth.

'Prisoners, the most painful part of my duty yet remains to be performed,' Justice Park began. 'We have considered every case with the most anxious and painful attention, we have endeavoured to show leniency as far as we could and have struggled anxiously to prevent the sacrifice of any human life. But on the deepest and fullest consideration we found it impossible, consistently with public duty and the solemn obligations which we owe to society, to spare yours.'

John Sarney clasped his hands as if in prayer, realising almost before the words reached him that he and Thomas Blizzard, who cowered beside him, were to become those examples the law demanded as the price of mercy to others. In this sense, could Sarney have foreseen it, he and the river he had railed beside would some day become one.

As he spoke Justice Park was deeply affected and while passing the awful sentence was completely overcome and wept aloud. The solemn tone in which he spoke, it was written, and the distress of mind under which he laboured, produced a deep impression on all present, and very few could restrain their tears.

'The sentence of the court on you, Thomas Blizzard and John Sarney, is that you be taken to the place from whence you came, and from thence to the place of execution, and there be hanged by the neck until you are dead and may God have mercy on your souls.'

The prisoners were struck dumb with grief and astonishment. Sarney cried bitterly though no sound broke from him. Blizzard's head drooped and he was so bowed down by an accumulation of grief that he had to cling to the bar for support. The two men looked at each other for a moment, though not a word was spoken. Sarney began to shake. Blizzard groped about the dock, doubled up and quite unconscious of where he was going or what he was doing. The trapdoor was opened, and the prisoners were led down the ladder out of daylight and into the underground passage that communicates only with the gaol.

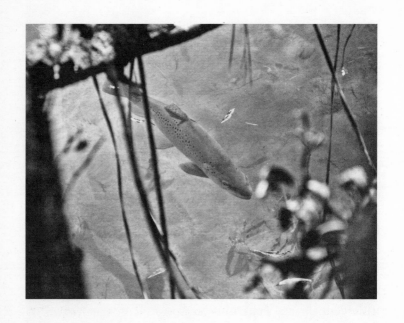

XI

THE SPIRIT OF THE PLACE

I went back to the river again last night and stood beside an ornamental stone cascade and the river was flat grey and mist rose off its surface as the water poured through faces in the stone, old faces worn almost beyond recognition. Vicky was beside me, kneeling back on the grass bank. Her head on my shoulder. It was hot now. A burning summer's day. In the pool below the cascade was a trout, iridescent in its spawning colours. It was swimming awkwardly, though, could hardly stay upright. I jumped down into the water to catch it, scooping the trout from under a raft of water lilies, only to find that it had been flayed. The spawning colours were its crimson flesh, its skinless flanks. In horror I turned, but Vicky was gone and I was alone. A rushing, hollow churning sound grew louder and louder. I was no longer by the cascade. I was standing instead on the concrete sill of the sinkhole. 'I am seeping into the next room, cell by damaged cell.' The voice came through the deafening sound of the water. I wanted it to stop and held my ears. But the voice was inside my head and the words kept repeating.

I woke. It was as if I'd shouted out loud. Vicky stirred next to me. I kept quiet and still. I must be crazy. It was okay, she was still asleep. I could hear her slow breathing. I decided to get up. I walked down to the kitchen and got a glass of milk from the fridge. Then I went upstairs, and splashed water over my face and neck. I looked up at the mirror. The light in the corridor lit my face from the side. I looked so old. I looked like a ghost.

The words just won't do it. Won't wrap around the feeling, bend to it or inhabit it. Stuck inside I can't be bothered and when it has passed I can't remember. So I start with words – one at a time – and every one seems wrong even as I draw their shapes on the page. Start again. Don't start. Don't bother. It hurts. It actually hurts to leave them there, like a fly stuck on fly paper. Buzzing and flicking.

It's as if I'm trying to shape words around space, around an imploding star, when every one is either pulled inward or apart. All I can say is this. That I lose altitude pretty quickly. That always surprises me. It's the one thing I can step back from and know: the clarity of surprise. I feel then that I have fallen far and fast.

Once a gull fell to the ground beside my car outside the Kentucky Fried Chicken in King's Lynn. I was waiting at the lights and this massive white bird spiralled to the ground like a broken helicopter, like a sycamore bud: one wing out, the other tucked in, turning round and round the apex of its body – and then it thumped into the pavement right next to my front left wheel. The one wing outstretched – its feathers were spread open like fingers. Its head hanging off the kerb. I looked up and there were other gulls wheeling in the air above the car. But what the hell had brought this one down? Had it collided with another bird? Or had its heart just stopped? I looked at the bird again. It could have been there for days.

I needed to get out of the house before I smashed my head into a wall or drove Vicky crazy. I'd sat in my study all morning tapping out one paragraph. One hundred and thirty-seven words in four hours. I read them again and felt sick. I don't know what I'm doing, I said to her. I just don't know. You think I'm working but I'm not. I'm sitting at a desk shitting out introspective banalities as if I'm passing kidney stones – hour after hour, getting nowhere. I could hear myself getting obsessive now. You just need to get out, she told me. Get out and walk the dog. So I went out, but not with the dog. I drove and kept driving and didn't stop until I was here by the edge of my stream. Then I walked for miles: from Snakeley Mill under the motorway and up the hidden path by the Biffa service centre to King's Mead and beyond to Marsh Green, round the back of the Pizza Hut where the path now runs between chain-link fences, waste ground on one side, new flats on the other. Back gardens, sheds, allotments. Clouds of midges rising and falling in the convection of warm air. Sunlight reflecting off the water, throwing patterns on the trees, the warehouse walls, an old sofa parked by the stream. The river floating above the earth. And me floating too as I walked it, insulated from everything. Finally on a bend in the stream I stopped to call home. As we talked I abstractly watched a torn shard of brown plastic waving in the current between two stands of green water-crowfoot. I took a longer walk than you might have imagined, I said. Sounds like you did, she said. And at those words the plastic moved up and sideways and became a fish. A dark and ancient trout. Leopard spots. Pectoral fins like wings. It turned, swam down to the corner with one thrust of its tail, its body stiff, arrow straight. There it turned again and in slow, languorous oscillations it forged back upriver until it lay once again between the green weeds. A fish back from the dead. Or from exile.

I must have gone completely silent because only after a while did I hear Vicky's voice asking if I was still on the end of the line. I am still here, I said to her. I have just seen my fish again.

Your totem, she said.

The sun was low now. The air had thickened, the white noise had receded. And this vast trout rose in slow motion and took a fly off the surface of the water and the viscous ripple which radiated across the river was an echo of the kissing sound that brushed over me and fragmented into the evening air.

For as long as I remember I have been in love with this fish, the trout. I can still recall the first I ever saw. I was ten or twelve years old on holiday in Normandy. My father hooked it in a small stream beside a meadow where we had stopped for a picnic and the trout jumped high out of the water as soon as it was hooked and held in mid-air, seemingly for ever. We brought the fish to the bank and laid it on its side in the grass. I can recall the shining scales, its butter yellow belly, a line of fiery red spots along the side. It was so pretty. I already knew the poem – only because I had been made to learn it at school by a headmaster whose shoes squeaked when he walked down the corridor – in which the immortal Irish god Aengus catches a trout which haunts him with its beauty for all eternity and like Aengus I have now pursued her 'through hollow lands and hilly lands' ever since, held in the spell of her perfection. Unlike any other fish the trout has a beauty which seems to far surpass function. But while its spots and colours, which vary so endlessly, appear almost gratuitously decorative, in fact the fish's markings are the result of the most acute adaptation to environment, are written by the trout's ability to absorb and project the subtlest nuances of habitat that exist along the length of one river, or even within the confines of one pool. Its spots can be black or blue, vermilion, gold, blood red: an infinitely varied kaleidoscope of colours, jagged and irregular like the stones they imitate, broken shapes against a background of sand, or marl, or peat, or silt. This patterning is so diverse that no trout is ever the same as any other. Anglers will tell you that it's quite possible to recognise individual fish by the arrangement of spots on the gill cover or along the back and sides. And so, given all this, it is hardly surprising that Dr Albert Günther, Keeper of Zoology at the Natural History Museum in the mid-nineteenth century and author of its comprehensive *Catalogue of Fishes*, wrote that there is no other group of fishes which is so difficult to classify, and that no one, however experienced they may be in studying other fishes, will easily navigate their way through the labyrinth of divergent forms.

Izaak Walton observed as early as 1653 that there are several kinds of trout, which differ in their bigness and shape and spots and colour. The great Swedish naturalist Carl Linnaeus, writing in his *Systema naturae* eighty-two years later, defined three: *Salmo trutta* the Swedish river trout, *Salmo eriox* the sea trout and *Salmo fario* the brook trout. In a subsequent starburst of scientific curiosity and discovery the next century saw a proliferation of differentiations between supposed species as naturalists began to seize on the subtlest deviation as an opportunity to name a new type of trout: *Salmo ferox, Salmo cumberland, Salmo fario loensis, Salmo faris forestensis, Salmo islayensis, Salmo saxatilis, Salmo taurinus* . . . until it seemed as if there were as many different kinds as there were rivers and lochs and scientists to name them.

Not until Francis Day published *British and Irish Salmonidae* many years later did anyone dare suggest that these myriad forms of trout encompassing all the incarnations that look so very different from one another might all in fact be just the one species of fish, Linnaeus's first-named *Salmo trutta*. As with chalk so with trout: the prosaic fact proves more wonderful than, but not so very different from, the fancy. From a mountainous outpost in north-west Africa to the shores of the Aral Sea, and from the west coast of Iceland to the northern tip of Norway this single species of trout colonised a once icebound landscape on the flowing hem of glacial meltwater, until as the ice sheets retreated and the seas and rivers grew

warmer, the trout, which can only live in cool waters, forged upstream to survive in elevated, snowy hideaways, in high mountain lakes or in rivers which flowed to impassable waterfalls. Even where they could reach the sea and where, north of a certain latitude, the sea was cool enough for them to thrive – for trout can live quite easily in fresh or salt water – the trout remembered the rivers of their birth and went back to them every year to spawn, so that over thousands of years the fish adapted to whatever river or loch or lake it and its ancestors called home, coming to reflect each place with abstract perfection.

And here again was *this* trout which had been haunting me. This fish, which was both a ghostly projection of my mind and a real creature defying the odds in a filthy, corralled and broken river was the spirit of the place, *was* this valley. I think I said something to Vicky then about the journey I'd taken the winter before, looking, I suppose, for this transported spirit. It was incredible, I said, to find this life still here, in spite of everything, to find the goal of that journey right back where I started.

I still remember that first dawn very well when finally I wangled a commission from a travel magazine and flew across the world to Tasmania. I was, of course, more captivated by my personal quest than by anything I might write about the hotels and the sights. But the turn of events that had fetched me there was a complicated one and so some complication in the final journey didn't seem too much out of place. For the river that took hold of me, I had read and written its name years before in a story called 'Trout of the Empire' published in the millennium edition of *The Field*. In that article I described how in the unusually cold winter of 1864 a great fish had been netted from a millpond belonging to a man named Thurlow – a keen trout angler and gentleman miller – and how the trout had been stripped of her ova, and how those ova were sent as a gift from Francis Francis, then editor of *The Field*, to an Australian called James Youl, who was at the time packing a steamer bound for Tasmania. It had struck me as an incredible story, not just the transportation of fish by homesick colonists to the far side of the world, but the story of that very first successful voyage which I could barely do justice to in a short piece in a magazine. Not long after the millennium issue was published I received a letter from Tasmania. It was from Michael Youl, the great-grandson of the man who had made that voyage a success. I tucked the letter away in a drawer for safe keeping, thinking that one day I might go and visit him and write a book about it all. But then we moved house and the letter was lost and somehow the project faltered and died. And I hadn't yet focused on or even really discovered the one detail that became all consuming. Not until I made a journey across the Chilterns photographing chalk streams. As I drove down into the valley of the Wye that first day, some memory stirred: was *this* the river that great fish had come from? Sometime later I went back to the British Library and rediscovered there an obscure little book by Arthur Nicols, *The Acclimatisation of the Salmonidae at the Antipodes*, which I had skimmed through half a decade before. I took it to a desk in the rare books room and began – over the next few months in stolen hours at lunch or between work and the journey home – to piece together the story of the great trout of the Wye.

It was a Captain Chalmers of Richmond, Tasmania, who first gave expression to the outlandish idea of shipping salmon and trout from the Old World to the New. The year was 1841 and he might as well have imagined taking them to the Moon. Suggesting in his letter to a fish breeder in Scotland that to get these noble fish to Tasmania their ova could be placed in a basket of gravel and stored on deck in a bucket of water he showed only the dimmest understanding of fish or quite how difficult it would be to transport them to the far side of the world. Though the fad for animal acclimatisation was in full swing, though there were pet monkeys in Hobart Town and deer, pheasants and hares feral in the Tasmanian landscape, salmon and trout could not be taken there in a cage on deck. And their ova, which remain viable only in a cold stream in the dead of winter, were not likely to survive in a ship's water tank cooking slowly off the coast of Africa. The manager of the Duke of Sutherland's salmon fisheries underlined the problem when he wrote back, several years later, to another Tasmanian who had asked about the same thing: it would be a grand undertaking, admitted Mr Young, if it could be done in the time between extracting the eggs and their hatching: if, in other words, it could be done in under a month. But since the fastest ships sailed to Australia in three, and travelled through all seasons and all weathers to get there, the idea was impossible.

Still, the fantasy would not go away. It is difficult to conceive, now the world is so much smaller and the strangeness of the exotic so dulled, the sense of absence and longing that must have stalked those early colonisers and convicts. The soundless dawn. The sun breaching a north-east horizon. So many things unfamiliar and so much that they were used to beyond reach. Adorning this alien world with those most-missed components of the land they had left far behind, though dressed with the call of utility – a salmon fishery promised many things besides romance – was as much as anything driven by homesickness. How the settler longed, as one writer confessed, to hear the nightingale singing in our moonlight as in that of Devonshire, to behold the salmon leaping in our streams as in those of Connemara!

The first ova left port on 31 January 1852: 50,000 salmon and trout eggs in a 60-gallon wooden tank, encased in lead, into which were poured six gallons of fresh water every four hours. Gottlieb Boccius, amateur inventor, fish keeper and author of the scheme, fixed on 15 and 20 April as the dates when the trout and then the salmon would begin to hatch. They beat him by a month and a half – when the ship was west of Dakar on the African coast. Fry were seen swimming in the tub, but soon the warming water became thick and putrid. By the time the *Columbus* docked in Hobart there wasn't a trace of fish or spawn. The men who drained the fetid tank observed only that perhaps ice was needed, and although the Tasmanian Governor commissioned another voyage with this one modification in mind, a cruel British winter froze out Boccius's chance of harvesting spawn and, for a while, the dream of Tasmanian salmon along with it.

The years ticked by and although the subject was raised from time to time it is difficult to say precisely how the vision became fixed in the head of James Youl, a farmer from Symmons Plains in northern Tasmania. Perhaps Youl had followed the fate of the Boccius shipment. Or perhaps he became infected by the fervour of acclimatisation when he moved to London in 1854 and met a group of fellow Australians, Edward Wilson among them, editor of the Melbourne paper *The Argus* and a vocal supporter of the craze. One way or another Youl became fascinated by the idea of transporting salmon and so began his own experiments with fish eggs in the ice house at Crystal Palace. Youl's plans were ambitious and it took some years for this association of friends to raise the £600 they needed to commit to a voyage. On board the chosen ship Youl planned to build two rooms, one within the other, both lined with lead, the space between packed with charcoal; a 200-gallon water tank linked by a pipe to the ice house below it; the pipe wrapped twice around the ice. Thus cooled, the water would fall into an inclined trough on the inside and trickle across the fish eggs. All this to replicate a cool Highland burn in the hull of a trading ship. Luminaries of fish culture maintained that the scheme was doomed: 'All I wish is that you understood salmon spawn as I do myself,' wrote Robert Ramsbottom, respected salmon breeder, to the stubborn Australian who had asked him for salmon eggs. 'You may as well try to fetch Australia to England as to carry spawn to it in moss.'

Though he doubted the sense of it all, Ramsbottom accepted the task of collecting ova – 30,000 of them from the River Dovey – and on 25 February 1860 the SS. *Curling* left Liverpool with the eggs nestled in Youl's ice house and under the care of a personal attendant.

The voyage did not go well. The passage was long, the ice melted quickly and the ova were knocked about in rough seas. Their guardian did his best to pick out the dead ova, to prevent their fungal decay from spreading like mould through the hatching trays, but it was futile labour. Within sixty-eight days the ice was gone and every single salmon egg was dead. The one consolation was that the ova had at least reached the southern hemisphere, far enough perhaps for the dream to have entered the realms of the possible. And far enough also to rekindle the interest of the Tasmanian government, which agreed to fund another voyage. All that was needed now, surely, was more ice and more care?

But ice was not a popular load with shipowners: it is heavy and awkward when frozen and destroys other cargoes as it melts. A winter slipped by and only after much searching did Youl find a willing, if small, iron steamer – the *Beautiful Star*. Within five weeks the apparatus was built. The ice house, tank and pipes were much the same, though the troughs were mounted differently this time, one on gimbals, the other on a swing, with gravel laid in the base of each. Ramsbottom's son William accompanied the cargo: 80,000 eggs from the Dovey, and a lot more ice. The ship sailed into a storm, was imprisoned off the Isle of Wight, and no sooner under way again than it was forced to retreat to the Scilly Isles for repairs. The gimbals were a disaster and the whole tray was lost on the first day at sea. The swing tray worked better, though the ship laboured so violently, so Ramsbottom reported in his log, and the apparatus swung to and fro with such force, as to render it dangerous to approach. When he could get close enough he picked out the dead ova as best he could. For those that hatched, it was a struggle to keep them alive as the temperature steadily climbed. The ship made slow progress. By 7 May the ice was almost gone and the ova were dying in droves. On the 8th Ramsbottom went into the ice house: 'The ice having got very low,' he wrote, 'I discovered a little box of ova embedded in it by Youl before we left London. The lid was broken off, but the ova in it were well covered with moss and among many dead, there were some living.' Ten days later, with no ice left, even these were gone. The whole cargo had at least lasted longer than on the *Curling*, though the *Star* was no closer to Australia when the ova died.

The Salmon Commissioners, appointed by the Tasmanian government to oversee the enterprise now that public money was involved, blamed failure on Youl's choice of ship, on the construction of the ice house, on the tanks that stored the water, on Youl. The voyage had cost a small fortune. Even the young Ramsbottom, who had shepherded the cargo, distanced himself from the failure, claiming that had the experiment been made on a faster and roomier ship – and it was Youl who had chosen the ship – many thousands of ova would surely have survived. It was Ramsbottom who returned to London charged with the next voyage.

But Youl was ahead of him. The ova inside the little pine box which he had packed in the ice had survived without gimbals, swing trays, gravel or piped water and without an attendant picking at them with a goose feather day after day. If the ice had lasted, so too would have the ova. And Youl knew the ice would last without piped water to melt it. He knew he had the answer. Stung by the criticism he vowed to pursue his idea with private money. He tried for space the next winter on the SS *Great Britain*, but it was too expensive. He bargained a better deal on the *Dunrobin Castle*, made all preparations and was ready to build his ice house when the shipowners backed out, worrying about the mass of ice involved. Finally, with no way to transport them he took his ova to the vaults of the Wenham Lake Ice Company, and there with the eggs packed in pine boxes under blocks of ice he shipped them without shipping them, to prove he was right. We exhumed one of the boxes, wrote Youl later, containing ova that had been buried – as many prognosticated in their icy graves – and as the moss was removed our little friends were found alive and perfectly healthy. The ova had lasted 144 days. Youl wrote to the Commissioners with the results of his experiment. The Commissioners could do nothing but authorise another shipment.

And so, the winter of 1863 rolled in and with it the familiar nightmare of futile negotiations with shipowners, a desperate search for salmon spawn. For a while it seemed that Youl would not find his ship, and then having found it – a clipper called the *Norfolk* due to sail to Melbourne on 20 January – he could not find his ova. Every single salmon taken from the River Ribble had already spawned. Ramsbottom set off in a hurry to the River Dovey. Others to the River Tyne. Youl wrote to *The Times* appealing to readers for help so that, wrote Youl, I may not lose the only chance I ever had of fairly trying to get this noble fish out to Australia. Excepting one brief note thanking those who had offered to help him, but with the doleful PS that as yet no ova had been obtained, Youl did not write again until the day after the ship had sailed. That there was anything aboard was nothing short of a miracle, so deep was the frost into which the country had been plunged in the fortnight between. Rivers and spawning grounds froze solid. At one time I nearly despaired of success, Youl wrote, for up to the 14th we had nothing. Yet within a day the fishermen employed in Scotland, Lancashire, Worcestershire and Wales simultaneously obtained ripe fish, full of spawn and, stranger still, they all arrived within a few hours of each other laden with ova at Southampton docks at dawn on Monday the 18th. Now in freezing conditions Youl and his helpers packed pine boxes against the clock, charcoal first, then ice, a layer of moss, the ova poured over the moss from a bottle, another layer of moss on top, another of pulverised ice, and then pure water until it streamed out from all the holes. Finally, the lid on each box was screwed down tightly. One hundred and sixty-four boxes containing 100,000 salmon ova were placed on the floor of the ice house and on top of these was piled the Wenham Lake ice to a height of 9 feet so that as long as any was left at all, meltwater would continue to trickle over the egg boxes below it.

It is mentioned almost as an afterthought – most likely because it was an afterthought in Youl's own mind – that thanks were also due for two late gifts: one of 1,200 trout ova from fish netted in the River Itchen by Frank Buckland, a noted naturalist of the day who later claimed credit for the entire enterprise, and the other of 1,500 trout ova delivered by Francis Francis, editor of *The Field*, half from Spicer's Mill at Alton on the River Wey and half from James Thurlow's mill in High Wycombe on the River Wye, or the Wick as it was then almost universally known. These last ova were the finest he ever saw, wrote Francis, taken from a magnificent 10-pound trout that had all but finished spawning. The size of fish from this river is most astonishing, he wrote, for what is little more than a good-sized brook.

I was nearly for pitching them overboard into the dirty water of the docks, Youl confessed later. Salmon proprietors persecuted trout back then, a predatory pest in their sacred salmon streams. And though these fish were from chalk streams where trout angling was revered by sophisticated London gentlemen, Youl had no desire to watch trout compromise his scheme. But Youl was also now a London gentleman and too polite to refuse the gift, unwanted though it may have been. He found space for the trout, left instructions with the young Ramsbottom that they were to be dropped off in Melbourne, and finally, with her fishy cargo aboard, the *Norfolk* sailed, one day later than planned on 21 January 1864.

Eighty-four days later she docked at Railway Pier, Melbourne, where her journey ended. The cargo now fell into the care of Edward Wilson, Youl's friend from the Australian Association. Though he was almost blind Wilson couldn't wait to see what lay inside the ice house. He and Ramsbottom opened the door and to their delight found ice and ova. More than three-quarters of the cargo had survived and Youl's plan had worked. 'The salmon is safe and your statue is secure,' wrote Wilson to Youl in London. 'It will be erected over the future fish market in Hobart Town, and you are to be in the attitude of the Medicean Venus, with a salmon instead of a dolphin. My eyes are failing me but my heart is still in the cause; and even with one foot in the grave and the other in a pan of salmon ova, I say three cheers for Youl and the *Norfolk* and Money, Wigram and Ramsbottom!'

The eggs, though, were still far from their destination, a three-day voyage across the Tasman Sea, up the River Derwent and overland, the egg boxes – trout included, Youl's instructions forgotten – slung under wooden poles and hauled over miles of rough ground to the banks of the River Plenty to the hatchery prepared in advance by the Salmon Commissioners. There Ramsbottom unpacked the ova, picked out the dead eggs and counted the rest: 30,000 salmon and about 300 trout had survived. The first of these – a trout – hatched on 4 May. It was joined by a salmon the next day. The first trout and the first salmon ever to swim in the southern hemisphere. Soon there were 200 young trout and several thousand young salmon. James Youl had triumphed against the seemingly inviolable laws of nature.

The fry were kept in their hatching trays until August when they were flushed into a large pond, the trout into their own rill. Both flourished and grew. Some salmon escaped when the pond sprang a leak, but in the autumn following – March 1865 – the grating was lifted and the remainder were liberated into the River Plenty and onwards to the Derwent and the open sea whence – it was hoped – they would eventually return. Did they? Perhaps. Perhaps not. But with so much money spent and so much hope invested the colonists soon began to look for evidence that the long-hoped-for salmon had blessed their new Eden. Reports began to circulate of silvery fish cavorting above powerful falls, jumping and showing their glittering sides. One of these leapt into a boat. Its corpse was examined and then eaten, and though it had looked rather more like a sea trout than a salmon, the flesh proved a deep pink and the flavour delicious. Since no sea trout had yet been exported this particular fish, so it was thought, must have been a salmon. Later the same year the impatient appetite of the Governor destroyed another silvery incarnation of the conclusive evidence the ichthyologists were looking for. And although the Governor announced that it was as fine in taste and appearance as any Tay salmon, no one could quite say for sure that it *was* a salmon. Time and again silvery fish were caught, examined and sometimes eaten, while their captors invariably declared that the fish was

– almost certainly – a salmon. But when Arthur Nicols published his chronicle of all this in 1882, he and the colonists were still looking for the proof they so desperately craved: none of these catches and identifications had really assured anyone. They were, to a man, hoping for salmon. What they were catching looked puzzlingly like sea trout. 'The handsome fish which is now so numerous in the estuary of the Derwent is, within certain limits, a most variable form,' wrote the noted ichthyologist R. M. Johnstone, 'some being almost identical to salmon, others to sea trout.' Even the great Albert Günther was troubled. He had identified captured specimens as salmon . . . or perhaps, if it were possible, one or other of the types of sea trout he was cataloguing for the British Museum. 'It is clear to me,' Johnstone concluded, 'that the prevailing form is a mean between these.' So unassailable was the belief in a limitless mosaic of sub-species that eminent authorities like Johnstone and Günther inclined to conjure a new hybrid rather than admit to the evidence before them. They were all trying, though without quite knowing it, to turn these fish into salmon by wishing.

But really the salmon were lost. Though the oceanic habits of Atlantic salmon remained a mystery for another hundred years, we know now what all those dreamers could never have guessed at then: that the young salmon's instincts would have taken them into the wide expanse of the Southern Ocean, and there in currents completely unlike those of the North Atlantic the fish would have swum around and around without end until they died of old age or exhaustion, quite literally lost at sea.

These visions of men with fish on the brain were doomed from the start.

But if the silver fish leaping Tasmanian waterfalls were not salmon, what were they? They were – plainly – the sea trout that they looked like. And though none had yet been exported and hatched, the sea trout were there in such abundance because the sea trout is the same fish as the trout. Gunther's pantheon of varieties were all the same thing: *Salmo trutta*. A fish that when it goes to sea, as a few always do, turns silver to blend better with the sun-soaked ocean in which it hunts and is hunted. It grows large too and, being silver and large, looks very much like a salmon. At the far end of forty years of hope and effort these leaping fish had blurred into one. It was the unsought and unwanted gift, the trout eggs from three Home Counties chalk streams – and I like to think from the Wye in partic-ular – which had come close to a dunking in the harbour, had been included reluctantly on the voyage and had somehow reached the hatching ponds at Plenty: these were the start of the cavorting silver tides of the Derwent estuary. It was the unlooked-for trout that gave rise to the elevated hopes, the hybrid theories and wishful thinking and hope against hope that the lordly salmon was finally there colonising the rocky streams of the New World. And yet even while the salmon runs failed, thousands of trout ova were distributed from the ponds at Plenty to rivers and hatcheries throughout Tasmania, New Zealand, Victoria, New South Wales and Western Australia. And from those points of introduction they spread further still: by the hand of man, or by swimming. From the Derwent they swam upstream, all the way to the lakes of the Tasmanian highlands, where they thrived and grew to such proportions as to defy the credence of anyone who knew the same species in its indigenous Old World setting. All – excepting perhaps those few who knew and fished the little Buckinghamshire Wye.

Sometimes things turn out as if you've been heading their way all along: I met Ray over a beer on a travel-writing assignment in New Caledonia, learned that he was from Tasmania and asked him if he knew any Youls. 'The Youl whose grandfather shipped salmon? Yeah, I know Michael,' said Ray. Michael and I got talking – again – by email this time, mine always the longest. Michael needed only a hundred words to invite me out there to join him in his fishing cabin on the shore of the Great Lake. 'Ray knows where it is,' he wrote.

Van Diemen's Land they called it when the Wycombe paper-mill rioters were sent there in 1831, though it was Tasmania by the time the fish arrived. It was Anthony van Diemen, the Governor-General of the Dutch East Indies who sent Abel Tasman on the voyage of discovery that fetched him here. To me there had always been something demonic in the name, while the island itself was a horned skull and its most iconic creature a devil. Van Diemen's Land had conjured in my mind a stark, windy wasteland cloaked in fog.

I remember that first dawn well. I woke early and couldn't get back to sleep. The highway below Ray's house groaned occasionally with fleeting cars. A strange croaking, that could have been either a frog or a water pump, punctuated the near-darkness. The sun was peeping over the ridge of hills to the north-east of Launceston over the Tamar estuary, casting an orange halo around the branches of the pine tree, throwing the fencing on the veranda outside the window into stark blocks of orange and black. Against this a giant spider hung off the net curtain, wreathed in this sunlight coming from the wrong direction, diaphanous and ghastly all at once. It must have felt like falling off the edge of the

Earth to those early settlers, so homesick they shipped skylarks and roses and oak trees and trout here. Of course I looked at it from my end of history and thought that it wasn't falling to hell, but the opposite. They were lucky to

leave the poverty and privation behind them, they – John Sarney and Thomas Blizzard among them, spared at the last by a judiciary besieged with pleas for their pardon, and letters signed one after another by the owners whose mills they had destroyed – were lucky to set foot on this land-scape of the possible. But then, while I'm sure this possibility was palpable, it must have been different.

That evening after we had climbed the switchback road to the Highlands we stopped beside the Great Lake just short of Michael's place. Black furrows rippled across the surface of the steely water and slapped into the stones along the shore. Across the bay two dark figures sat beside a blazing fire. In the grainy dusk and the cold – so cold I needed a piss as soon as I got out of the car, jumping from one foot to the other trying to get it out in a hurry – it was as if the four of us were the last people in the world. The Great Lake, Michael told me over supper, had once been about half this size. But it had since been impounded to run hydros and so is nothing like the lake those first trout had swum up to. And now that it hadn't rained properly for so long, he said, the lake was shrinking again, year after year, leaving this margin of bleached, broken timber around the edge.

Michael gave me sheaves of papers, letters and news-paper cuttings to read. The amazing thing to me about James Youl, Michael said, right at the outset when he first entered into the business, and I don't know why he wanted to send salmon to Australia or what got into him, is that he was quite certain the only way was to delay the hatching of the ova. The very fact that he was so convinced that he had to delay the hatching – I honestly think that was a magnificent decision, Michael said. We drank Michael's

Shiraz and with the television on and the sound of cricket commentary as backdrop, we talked into the early morning about Michael's family, how they had come to Tasmania, how his great-great-grandfather, despairing of futile attempts to convert the pagan King Pomare in Tahiti, became the first minister in the north of the island, how he had ministered to condemned men on the scaffold and died more or less of exhaustion when he was only fifty-three years old, but had in his last few years acquired the land which his son James Youl farmed so ably over the next two decades that he had made a fortune by the time he bought Waratah House in south London and began his experiments in salmon-breeding.

The following afternoon after fishing with Michael on Arthur's Lake I drove – in a hurry and somewhat late because it is never easy to leave good fishing behind – down the dirt road that connects the high country with the south, heading to those hatching ponds at Plenty. The orange track wound for miles beside countless lakes, through groves of eucalyptus, the scrub either side studded with blasted trees, fallen trunks and branches, and paraffin bushes over a fractured pavement of rocks. Lakes glowed a golden green in the sun, which burst in a nuclear flare from under a ceiling of cloud. And the ancient forest seemed to reach over every horizon. The road rolled downhill like a marble run, a fairground ride between loaf-of-bread mountains which fell in steep escarpments to the river tucked inside the folds below me. The River Derwent meandered between these interlocking spurs, steadily growing as it and I neared the sea: the river that inspired the phantom dream of a salmon fishery in a new Eden. In my own dreams I suppose I would have found at

Plenty a few tumbledown huts, water trickling over cracked brickwork, as if the place had been shut up and forgotten once the spawn of the trout and salmon brought here from England, Scotland and Wales had grown on and escaped into the wild. Michael had said I might not think much of the place. Now, standing by a bubbling pool in which blimpish albino trout swirled at kibble thrown by kids I understood what he'd been hinting at. I took a walk and found myself on a path which led under towering trees down to the banks of the River Plenty. Here at least, away from the trimmed lawns and the ice cream and the trout-shaped aprons and ties for sale in the gift shop, I was able to sit for a while alone and in silence beside the tannin flow of the Plenty. A soft breeze lifted in pulses, breathing through the sultry afternoon, rattling leaves above the river. It was ironic, this mild outrage I felt, this sense that the place had been intruded upon by these vulgar, stew-pond fish. The ponds were, after all, an intrusion in themselves, the consequences of which I had enjoyed and would, though not quite guiltlessly, enjoy again. Even then Nicols had seen the flow of things: long before the end of this century, he wrote, when manufacturing interests and a growing population will have driven the salmon in disgust from most of our rivers, the sportsman will take his rod and seek among the deep tarns and pools of Tasmania and New Zealand, the noble quarry which has found a congenial home in the Antipodes. The noble quarry proved to be a trout not a salmon: the infinitely various, infinitely beautiful trout, which did find a congenial home here . . . and in South Africa and Kenya, and Argentina and Chile, and Kashmir and Bhutan, places where it is still possible even in the twenty-first century to touch through those trout a wildness quite lost to where they came from. But I wondered – as I watched a small insect drift downstream on the current only to vanish inside the splashy whorl left by a rising trout – when we extended the range of this trout to encompass the infinite possibilities of undeveloped landscapes all over the world did we lose sight of the value of the rivers they came from? Did we export along with them our sense of the possibility of the wild on our doorstep? Is that a part of how we trample and bury what exists at our feet, even as we yearn for the wild that, it seems, we must always look for elsewhere?

It took a particular mindset to look upon the indigenous fauna and call it impostor, as Arthur Nicols did when describing the fish which swam in these Tasmanian streams before the trout. No one ignorant of anatomy, wrote Nicols, would suspect the remotest connection of these fish with the noble stock. This family of freshwater fish so derided by Nicols is known as *Galaxiidae*, small, elongated and scaleless creatures which had evolved in their various habitats for such vast tracts of time that the kaleidoscopic lens through which taxonomists were so keen to regard the single *Salmo trutta* should rather have been applied to this 'ignoble' fish. The *Galaxiidae* had adapted separately and perfectly to fit a multitude of ecological niches within the Tasmanian landscape, some in fast-flowing rivers, others in swamps, or shallow lakes with sandy beds, or in lowland lagoons fringed with lilies. And yet of the fifteen separate species found in Tasmania, eleven are now critically endangered. The Swan *Galaxia* is confined to a few miles of forested streams in the headwaters of the Swan and Macquarie rivers, which for one reason or another the brown trout has not yet colonised. The same is true of the Clarence *Galaxia*, found in a region of lagoons and interconnecting streams on the Tasmanian uplands where the limits of its distribution are now precisely mapped by the presence or absence of brown trout. Even where some species of *Galaxia* and trout do manage to coexist – the Arthurs and Saddled *Galaxias* in Arthur's Lake, the Golden *Galaxia* in Lake Crescent and Lake Sorrel – their abundance, which once would have been determined only by the relationship between the fish and its natural home, is now more directly linked to the relative numbers and sizes of trout, or sometimes to how clear or turbid the water is and therefore to how well they can hide from their new hunters. There are some who would like to turn back the clock, calling the trout underwater rabbits. But who knows what state of virgin purity you choose when entertaining such ideas? Or how you trace a line, a border perhaps, between the wild land and the people who use it? Though the story of the *Galaxiidae* might find its parallel in innumerable instances worldwide where invasive species have overwhelmed their native competitors, none will mirror it so poignantly as the eerily similar interaction between the white settlers and the few thousand Aborigines who had called Tasmania home for tens of thousands of years before them.

In the course of looking into the story of the millers and their transportation aboard prison hulks and clippers to Tasmania, I corresponded with Jill Chambers, who had researched the fate of each convict and written books about the Luddite rebellion. Unknown to me, Jill passed on my address to Professor Geoff Sharman in Youngtown, Tasmania, who very kindly and out of the blue sent me a small booklet about a part of the island in which he – and James Youl – had once lived: it was called *A History of Evandale* by K. R. Von Stieglitz. Geoff, who is descended from one of the rioting millers, thought I might find useful the short entry in that book on the Youls of Symmons Plains. In fact the book was full of fascinating narratives – on Jefferies, the Cannibal Bushranger, or The Tragedy of John Batman, and many more. But one in particular caught my attention, perhaps because it showed me the thought I had been reaching for in my story of the transportation of trout and of the *Galaxiidae*: how any paradise, be it a grand house on a hill, or a new Eden, has a foundation stone in hell.

The story was called 'The Black Line'. Almost to the day that the High Wycombe millers rioted against the machines which threatened to obviate them, the Aborigines of Tasmania, who had been driven from their land, whose wives and daughters had been stolen and enslaved by lonesome stockmen, rioted in their own way, burning homesteads and crops, attacking the white men with spears. It was one more incident of conflict in a so-called war that had begun years before as the white man settled the Aboriginal island. Governor Arthur, who had made a reputation in the British Honduras for his kindness towards slaves and his protection of the indigenous peoples there, became exasperated with the constant, needling violence, with how, in spite of all his efforts to civilise them, the Aborigines refused to wear clothes or live in houses, but persisted in ranging unrestrained over the high ground and across the plains. He decided to drive these troublesome natives once and for all off the land the white settlers had claimed from them. A cordon was formed, so Stieglitz describes, of soldiers and men from the towns, convicts too, a line which stretched from the Western Tiers to the east coast. As the troopers advanced through the country the Governor himself rode back and forth along his 'Black Line', encouraging the men who, drenched by rain and lashed by the cruel Tasmanian winds, footsore and dog-tired after a time, might otherwise have lost heart. Some Aborigines were caught. Some were shot as they ran away. Even so, they slipped through time and again, so well could they hide even in open ground, disguised as burnt logs or simply invisible against the brush. Though the Governor praised his men for their zeal and activity, when finally the line closed at Sorell it had failed in its main aim of rounding up all the blacks. But it had at least, wrote Stieglitz, shown the natives how helpless they were in opposition to the constantly increasing population of white people. Their resistance was broken. In the end, it was George Robinson, an ardent Christian who had learned the native language, who brought in the last of the stragglers so that they could be shipped over to Flinders Island and out of the way. Never again, so Stieglitz ended his tale, were the valleys and rivers, the hills and forests of their own country to echo with the sounds of their hunting and singing.

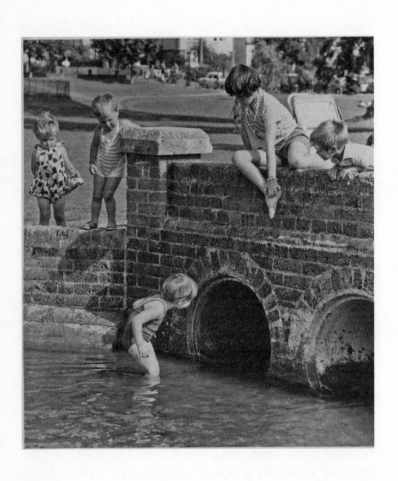

XII

CAN WE HAVE
OUR RIVER BACK?

Ruaridh: 'The last great wilderness is not out there,
it's in here.' (He points to his head, or heart.)

from *The Last Great Wilderness*

For a long time I did not know, nor did I think I would
ever find a way of knowing, exactly where on the River
Wye Thurlow's great fish had come from. Not until I read
the milling manuscript by Stanley Freese did I discover that
for half a century from the 1820s until the 1870s the
Thurlow family had owned Bridge Mill. They were gentlemen
millers, wrote Freese, and James Thurlow who was the best
fly fisher in the town was in the habit of going up to Mr
Fryer's of an evening to throw his line. Bridge Mill had been
a corn mill from the earliest of times and was one of the
six Domesday mills at High Wycombe. The mill is no longer
there, of course. Not long after I found the Freese manuscript
I scrolled my way on the microfiche machine in the library,

by chance, to a pair of photographs printed in the *Bucks Free Press* on 13 May 1932. The left-hand photograph was of a timber mill, weatherboards under half-hipped roofs, a footpath leading to a side door and at the darkened window over the river a person dressed in white, or perhaps covered in flour. The photograph on the right was of a mass of broken and charred timber, black against a pale sky underneath the caption Big Fires at High Wycombe.

Several fires broke out that weekend and children were suspected as the arsonists, but the fire at Bridge Mill was one of the fiercest seen in the borough for some time, it was reported. Late that evening a passer-by had noticed flames on the ground floor. He went to the fire-alarm corner and summoned the brigade, but it was soon clear that the mill was doomed. Flames rose to a great height and the glare could be seen for miles around. Hundreds of people from the surrounding countryside flocked into town to watch the spectacle. Residents of the neighbouring cottages threw their belongings into the street: chairs and tables, a grandfather clock, a pianoforte. Much was smashed or damaged in the panic, though the cottages never caught fire. It was a mercy there was no wind, reported the paper, but even so the flames burnt brightly until the early hours, forcing spectators back into the cool of nearby alleys and courtyards while the brigade who worked until after three in the morning returned again at dawn on Saturday to dowse the smoking timbers. Much of what remained, though spared by the fire, was thrown into the river by vandals on the Sunday when the mill had cooled down enough for hundreds more to visit the scene. Elsewhere in the same paper under the heading Mill of Memories James Thurlow's grandson, who had once lived there and was himself over seventy years old, described something of what the town had lost. The mill, he wrote, must have been grinding corn in the centre of High Wycombe since the river was first diverted and impounded to create a head of water, perhaps as long ago as the time of the Roman occupation, when a villa was also built beside the sacred spring a mile or so downstream. With the mill were buried many secrets some of which my father and grandfather might well have recalled: the vast trout caught under one of its arches and presented to the Prince of Wales, the many celebrities attracted here by the Wye's famous trout, the continuous warfare between the millers and the rats, the annual visit of the hunted stag which would run upstream to the mill tail, the heavy storms and flooding, the tragedies revealed year after year by the rake that worked the weed rack above the mill, the hundreds of incidents some humorous, some pitiful, all of which the mill might have recalled. All of these combine, wrote Thurlow, to make one feel that we have lost a valuable link with the past, one which could ill be spared. He did not mention, probably because the fact was recorded only in the pages of a small and mostly forgotten book, that the mill might also have told of the great trout stripped of its spawn and the new Eden to which they were transported.

I opened the steel cabinet of old maps kept in High Wycombe's library and compared the 1899 sheet with a satellite image of the town I had downloaded on to my laptop. I saw that Bridge Mill had stood immediately downstream of the St Mary Street bridge, straddling the river between what is now the police station and the Liberal Club and only a few yards from where the river re-emerges from under the streets. It was late winter, I seem to remember, and cold outside the library. I walked through the town to the place where the buried stream breaks into daylight again beside the Swan Theatre. Here the river trickled thinly over gravel and plastic between sheer edges of brick and reinforced concrete. Snow began to fall. I remember a snowflake dropping on to the screen of my phone as I spoke into the voice recorder. The sky was a dusky grey like the river that reflected it. As I walked on to the bridge and looked over the glassy pool I saw a disturbance in the water. A ripple, a swirl, something breaking the surface. It could have been a diving bird, but then I saw a fin cut through the water, flicker and slide under. Pulling my camera from a pocket I walked quickly round to the side of the stream behind a hedge of forsythia and ivy that draped over the railings. There below me in the water were two trout, one much larger than the other, sparring, lunging and biting. It seemed for a moment as if the smaller, more agile fish might already have driven the ancient one to exhaustion. The monster lay motionless on the bed of the stream, its jaws heavy and bulging, its eyes milky, its tail ragged and torn, as the pretender circled. Suddenly the bigger fish came from underneath, caught the other one across the belly and clamped down, driving forward across the river, the smaller fish crippled and helpless in its jaws, and then down until the victim was pinned against the bed of the stream. Still the bigger fish kept forging ahead, with long sweeps of its tail fin, grinding its rival into the mud until both fish had disappeared from view but for the enormous fin scything above a cloud of silt, and to the side the writhing head, jaws gaping open in agony. And then all became still. The bigger fish backed downstream, drifting with the silt until the cloud dispersed from around it, while the other trout gasped at the surface and – mortally wounded, it seemed – floated downstream and out of sight. I checked my camera. I had pressed the shutter five or six times during this drama. All but one of the images were blurred, indecipherable. But one had frozen the scene perfectly, the moment the bigger trout attacked. I could see even then on the screen, and later when I had downloaded the image, the way the body of the smaller fish had been crushed between those jaws.

I looked back upstream again over the rectangular tub of open water to a concrete culvert topped with a brick wall at the head of the pool. In this flat-beamed bridge, from which the water imperceptibly seeped as if it were leaking more than flowing, as if the egress had been grudgingly allowed, there was no dignity at all. There was nothing to suggest that what this amounted to was a rebirth. I had wondered, I suppose, or imagined, that if the utilitarian argument that forced this river underground had been so overwhelming, then at least the river's reappearance might be celebrated. As if the culverting might be an acknowledged but necessary wrong. But that is not how these things happen. A thin lip between the concrete and the bricks above had given enough purchase for a fringe of feral weeds. Ferns grew out of the recesses on either side too and along one bank a line of buddleia seemed to have taken root between the bedding planes of the concrete. But otherwise the entire tub was hard edged and soulless and the river seeped through it silently. I paused at the culvert and watched the snowflakes fall on the water without so much as a ripple. Lodged on a nook in the concrete below me was a lost, black shoe.

In *Camera Lucida* Roland Barthes writes that there are times when he might come upon a place and feel not only as if he had been there before, but that he was always supposed to return to precisely that place. This feeling comes from a kind of second sight, he wrote, that seems to bear me forward to a utopian time, or to carry me back to somewhere within myself. I don't believe I had ever seen before I dreamt of it that drying pond in a city with only one fish left there, and yet here it was and here was that fish, as if I had always known this place, as if I were always going to come back. Only now there would be no rescue. The ancient fish had to take care of itself in the toxic flow.

Instead of returning to the library, I walked through the town in the direction of the station planning on finishing my notes on an earlier train. I reached the bottom of the hill and crossed the road past All Saints church, remembering it from Rammell's Sanitary Report: there was a water pump here. The only pump in the town, it used to take groundwater from beneath the cemetery, and gravediggers complained about how the stinking liquor from the coffins they uncovered or broke as they dug new graves would sink into the ground and corrupt the water, making everyone sick. I had passed the place often enough by now and not been drawn to go in and yet today, almost absentmindedly, I walked up the steps. As I approached the glass doors I saw a man at a table inside, his eyes closed, a name tag hung about his neck. I took my cap off as I pushed through the door. He opened his eyes without moving his head, as if I had aroused a mystic gatekeeper.

'Good morning. Have you come to look around the church?'

'Yes, I suppose I have.'

'Here, let me give you a leaflet,' said the man whose tag revealed that he was called Peter. 'We did have a guidebook but' – he gestured to a makeshift enclosure in the corner – 'we've had some work done on the kitchen and now they're all locked away somewhere, or at least I can't find them. It doesn't tell you an awful lot, but there is a brief, sort of selected history in there,' he said.

I thanked him and walked along the aisle, looking up at the wall, the stained-glass windows, the memorial stones. In Memory of D. Barry Ercolani 1921–1992 Furniture Maker of High Wycombe – carved beneath a window depicting Luke, beloved physician, in his hand a quill and a bunch of flowers, a brown cow behind. The window itself was dedicated to the memory of William Rose, born 5th Feb 1776, died July 1st 1846 and created by his surviving children, one of whom I was sure would have been the Rose who commissioned the sanitary report of the town which referred among other things to the corporeal remains of his father corrupting the water supply. Again and again I recognised names from the histories I had read of the town and its river. Here they all were, commemorated in stone one after the other, layered like the rock their town had been built on and shaped by.

As I walked through the church reading these inscriptions an elderly couple came in behind me. They passed silently and while she slipped coins into a box, he picked up a candle and fixed it alongside others on a large, iron candelabra. I glanced across to see his face in stern concentration as he tried to get the candle in place, his features softened by the dancing orange lights. She had turned and was watching him too, motionless. When he had finished they waited a moment longer, then he turned away and nodded at a brown and bare conifer, its trunk sunk into a hub of concrete, fallen needles on the mat and on the floor all around it.

'I see the old tree is still there,' he said.

'What?' she asked, catching up and standing beside him.

'I see the old tree is still there,' he said more deliberately, adding as they walked away, 'and Dr Fenton's display over there.'

'What?' she said.

'And Dr Fenton's display over there.'

'Oh yes,' she said. 'Flowers are gone, though.'

'Yes,' he said. 'The flowers are gone.'

I crossed the nave. A paper sign at the entrance to the chapel on the far side read 'Welcome to the quiet garden'. Here the air was suffused with the soft whisper of an electric heater, and the incongruous noise of running water. A tiny stream trickled down a tower of stone, backlit with fairy lights which had been draped through the leaves of a potted plant. I sat down to take these notes. Jotting down the inscriptions from some of the epitaphs I turned in my chair to study a few more on the row of stones set in the floor and not covered by the carpet. Reading the farthest from the side and partially upside down I saw the name on it and, feeling that my mind must be playing tricks on me, that it might be my imagination on a day that had already proved somewhat out of time, I stood up and went over to look more closely. The stone was large, six feet long, three feet wide. At its head was a carved shield that I recognised from the *ex libris* stamp in books I have that once belonged to my great-uncle, some of which I had read recently – the tour by Defoe, Cobbett's *Rural Rides* – while hunting for old references to High Wycombe. A plumed helmet over a shield, three dogs on one side, a lion on the other. I had always thought the shield an affectation of William's: though his sweaters were full of holes and his appetites modest, he had a fondness for the ostentatious. But beneath the shield the stone read 'Here Lyeth the Body of Thomas Archdale Esq, who departed this life August 19th 1711, Aged 36'.

We have a slim book at home called *Memoirs of the Archdales*. It belonged to William, who was an Archdale. Like my mother and her father. I knew only that they were brewers from Norfolk, but they had come here, I later discovered when I got home and dug out the book, from High Wycombe where they had lived until the year 1700 at Loakes Manor – a few hundred yards to the south of Bridge Mill. In the *Memoirs* there is only one short description of their home, written some time after they left, and it mentions the river:

A beautiful grove, divided by a serpentine walk, conceals the house from the town; At the side of this runs a transparent river with a smooth walk on each bank. Beyond this a level lawn, then the house with sloping gardens behind it; above these is a lofty hill, near the top of which is a lovely wood, having a grassy walk along just within the skirts of it.

And now it is 18 July 2011 and I am on what feels like my final journey, travelling again by bus and train from a Georgian dower house in Norfolk that, it turned out, was part of the estate that Thomas Archdale bought when he left Loakes Manor, High Wycombe in 1700 to marry Jane Turner the daughter of a King's Lynn merchant. Who can ever say how much where we have come from dictates where we go?

I'm heading to the council offices this time, looking for an answer to the question these lines have led me to: how is it that we could ever bury a river?

I have learned enough to realise that such a thing cannot be ascribed to one soulless decision based on one bleak assessment of the needs of, say, urban planning – that the imposition of a prison sentence such as this one, which after all would seem to be a suicide of the collective spirit, or at least a fatal resignation, is built upon accumulated layers as complex and contradictory as any subterranean strata. But there *is* a tipping point. And into that moment is buckled every seam of history that has led to it. And perhaps an answer. Which might be as much as saying this burial was inevitable. The weight of evidence would make it seem so: rivers are lost under towns everywhere. But it might only uncomfortably illuminate quite how far we have fallen: once buried how is it that we could, years later, bypass the chance to exhume this river, building instead beside its underground passage a shopping centre we chose to call Eden?

The irony of the name given to this waterless canyon struck me that first night when I came down here having found the sinkhole upstream at the site of Ash Mill where the riots began. As the evening came on I tried to follow what I imagined would be the underground course of the stream along the Oxford Road past Sainsbury's, past the Alamo Car Hire and Lloyds Bank arriving at the corner of Bridge Street by the bus station only to find in front of me, straddling the valley, a vast face of glass and stone and the name EDEN glowing brightly against the winter dark high above those rows of buses waiting to ferry Christmas shoppers to the hillside suburbs of Sands, Terriers and Cressex, or further down the valley to Bourne End and Loudwater. Inside was a vast shopping precinct: Waterstones, H&M, Next, La Senza, HMV, Starbucks, Costa, one after the other at the base of the canyon. Lights and Christmas trees halfway up the sheer white walls. High above, a frosted Perspex roof. The weak light of evening beyond. And birdsong. My first thought was that it was artificial, piped birdsong in a plastic Eden. But then I saw a bird flitting from one steel beam to another. It was beyond dusk outside and the birds had stopped singing by the river. I did not know then, though I soon discovered, that this shopping centre sited at the confluence of two buried streams had only just been completed, and was the pride of the town council, the result of many years of planning and the realisation of so many hopes to revitalise High Wycombe, a project that had once been called, quite appropriately perhaps, Phoenix.

Even now, when I call up High Wycombe on the satellite map on my computer this Eden is not there: instead there is only the wasteland of car parks around Desborough Road and Mendy Street, what was once Water-Up Lane and

Maundy's Meadow, once the site of those slums which Laurence Chadwick cleared after a century's efforts by a tiny few of the more conscientious members of the town's authorities. It had been suspected then by some vocal commentators that Chadwick's slum clearance was nothing more than a council land grab, that some master plan lay behind the dispossession. The car parks still vacant at what must be dawn on a sunny summer Sunday when seventy years later a satellite passed overhead give the lie to that idea. There was no real plan at all. Once hollowed out, Newland became and remained for years like the core of an ancient tree. Nor did I know on that evening in December that the exhumation of the river which flowed underneath had once been in the council's plans for the regeneration of this empty core. Not until I met Anne feeding her ducks did I realise that what had occurred to me as a thought beyond all hope might have occurred officially, collectively. But surely the very first thing you would do to revitalise a town is unearth the river that flows through it? And yet, if it ever was an aspiration, it hadn't happened. Phoenix had become Eden. Eden was complete. And yet still the River Wye flows under the streets.

As I write these notes now and my thoughts slip back to the disparate histories my meandering journey along the little River Wye has led me to, it seems that one after the other they have comprised the same incomplete fumbling towards a paradise never realised. And that this new Eden where birds chirrup in an electric twilight but no river flows is already just one more layer of dust and silt.

The High Wycombe Council offices are at the foot of Amersham Hill, opposite the police station and beside the river where it flows through a small park, meandering between boulders imported from some more igneous landscape. At the end of the park the stream drops through a galvanised steel grid, a baleen plate sieving from its flow plastic bottles and crisp packets but feeding a river to the underground; the Wye is lost again under Abbey Way. I walk through the sliding doors and explain to the girl at the desk that I'm trying to locate a particular minute from a council meeting that would have taken place in about 2003 or 2004, an item to do with Project Phoenix or the Eden Centre. She says she isn't sure about council minutes and that I'll need to ask Planning, pointing to a small machine further along the desk. For one uncomfortably long second it is as if I must talk to the machine. I look at it and back to her.

'You'll need to take a ticket,' she explains patiently. 'I'll call someone down for you. Take a ticket. Take a seat.'

I walk over, press the button on this machine marked Planning and take from it a small ticket of thin paper that

reads Welcome 0415 Planning, 15:13 18/7 2011. I take the ticket as the receptionist explains over the phone to someone in the back office that there is a gentleman in reception who needs to access some minutes from Planning meetings. She hangs up, looks past me out the window and says to her colleague, 'Is it raining outside?' I turn to look too. A lady in a flimsy dress is hurrying through the – quite obvious – rain, hunched under a coat which she holds over her head, and into the foyer where she stands up and shakes off the coat, her eyes wide in amazement. The bodybuilder who had been ahead of me in the queue, complaining over the phone at the reception desk to someone hidden within the bowels of the building that he had paid his parking fine already, stands hesitantly in the doorway. And now as I walk away to find a seat an elderly lady is at the desk complaining about the same thing. 'Your address. The reason why you shouldn't have to pay your ticket,' says the second receptionist, bored beyond all telling. And then without looking up or apparently changing who she is addressing she continues, 'Look at that rain!'

'I know,' says the first. 'Switchboard.'

A few moments later a lean, grey-haired man in a grey suit pushes through the doors from the back offices, leans forward and asks, 'Mr Wilson? Hello. I'm Peter.' He sits down opposite and asks how he can help. I explain that I'm trying to find out how the aspiration to de-culvert the River Wye dropped off the agenda of Project Phoenix. I explain how I have found a document online, a planning brief published in 2003 – you did well to find that, he says – which states in item 4.20 that de-culverting the Wye would be one of the benefits of the Western Sector's redevelopment. Somehow, not long after, the idea must have been dropped because I can find no more reference to it other than a few laments in the newsletters of the High Wycombe Society. I'm trying to find out what happened, I say.

'Yes . . .' says Peter. He looks distracted for a moment and gazes through the window as if surveying the world outside before giving his answer. 'It's a shame, isn't it? The river is down there, still under it all. But you know I am not the man to help you. Not really my department. I know someone who might know something. If you wait here I'll see if I can find him.'

A few minutes later Peter returns down the stairs walking beside another wiry, middle-aged man in a dark suit. He pushes through the doors and introduces me to Ian, who is holding a sheaf of buff-yellow papers.

'Ian has found some papers for you,' Peter says. 'But there's nothing I can add, so I'll leave you two.'

Ian has thick, curly hair, an aquiline nose.

'So tell me about your interest,' he begins, circuitously, guardedly. 'You want to find out about the river?'

I explain that I'm writing a history of the river. Sensing him tense at that news I add, 'So many have been built around, and then culverted. I'm interested in that whole . . . area. Here there was this moment when the de-culverting project was dropped. You know, it's there in the stated aspirations of Phoenix. It's there as one of the reasons why Phoenix will revive the town. But then somehow it gets dropped from the plans. I'd like to find out exactly what happened.'

'It's a funny coincidence that you came today,' he says. 'Because this document – the Delivery and Allocations, it is called – is going before committee tonight and it has the de-culverting in it, very much still part of the plan.'

'Okay . . .' I say, processing the news. 'So it was in the Phoenix plan. Then it got dropped. Since then I've seen it mentioned several times, still an aspiration, still in planning reports and studies. There's a feasibility study online too. By Peter Brett Associates. I've read that.'

'You have been doing your homework,' says Ian.

'And that report discusses a scheme to de-culvert two short sections and estimates that it would cost over ten million pounds.'

'So you see. It's not exactly cheap,' says Ian.

'This latest document, when is it proposing the work should be, or rather will be, done?'

'Well . . . this is a draft, first of all,' says Ian. 'It is a holding statement, if you like. A line in the sand ensuring that no development takes place that would actually compromise plans to de-culvert the river.'

'Does it specifically state when the river will be de-culverted?'

'It is very much a statement of aspiration. It is not any more an idea that we might unearth the whole river from top to bottom, all through the town centre. There's just too much . . . stuff on top of it. But when ideas come forward, you know when developers come forward, then we can try to build this into their strategies. We have no money as such. We have to work with developers.'

As for helping me discover why or when de-culverting the river came off the original Phoenix proposal, he can't help.

'Perhaps individual planning consents might be useful,' he suggests. 'Perhaps if you search them one by one, those that relate to Eden.'

'Can I do that here?' I ask.

'I think so,' he says, 'but I am not absolutely sure how. Reception should help.'

I wait in line again. A different receptionist sees me this time, tells me to take a Planning ticket again and wait to be called. I press the button and take ticket Welcome 0416

Planning, 15:40 18/7 2011. A few minutes later my number is called to desk number 4 and there I meet Daryl who gestures to the seat opposite and wearily asks me for my name and the nature of my enquiry.

'Wilson,' I say.

'First name? Or initial?'

'Charles.'

'Enquiry?'

'I want to look up planning applications relating to Phoenix or Eden, particularly the moment when the aspiration to de-culvert the river was dropped from the plans.'

Daryl looks up.

'I remember that,' he says. 'I joined the High Wycombe Society then. They were very agitated about the river.'

'I know,' I say. 'I've read all their newsletters. In one issue Phoenix is there with plans to uncover the river, the next it is not and the project has become Eden.'

'There was a line of cherry trees,' says Daryl, 'which I didn't want to see cut down.' He looks back at the screen. 'Too many hits, it says, under Eden. I'll try Phoenix . . . no hits at all. Must all be under Eden. You could try searching through the planning applications.'

'I thought that was what we were doing.'

'Over there.' He nods at a row of dead computers.

'On those computers?'

'Yes. I *think* that is what they are there for.'

'Okay. Thanks . . . Daryl.'

He smiles. I walk over and try to turn on a screen. It asks me for a username and password. I look back at Daryl.

'You'll have to ask at reception,' he says.

*   *   *

I gave up eventually, fearing that if I stayed in the building too long, if I took one more ticket from the machine marked Planning, I might never get out. Instead I walked to the library and found binders of council minutes in the shelving of the local history section, rows of lime-green volumes, year by year. The planning brief I had mentioned to Peter which spoke of uncovering the river had been published in 2003 and so I began there and reached Monday 8 September 2003 before I found a relevant reference. At a meeting presided over by Councillor Mrs L. M. Clarke it was resolved under item 46 pursuant to regulation 21(i)(b) of the Local Authorities Regulations 2000 that the press and public be excluded from the meeting during consideration of the minute nos. 47 and 48 because of their reference to matters which contained exempt information. And then against minute 47:

> The Cabinet had before it a detailed report which set out the background and issues surrounding the development agreement and lease in connection with the Project Phoenix development proposals. Members were reminded of . . . the negotiations which had been taking place with Stannifer Developments Limited . . . The Cabinet also received a confidential appendix to the report which set out further details excluded from the report because of their highly sensitive commercial nature.

Ten days later the full council met, and were presented with minute 47 as above and also minutes from 21 July, which included a question from Mrs F. W. Alexander: 'Why was the exclusivity agreement between the council and Stannifer entered into? . . . Local residents have no real knowledge of the terms except that the council will deal exclusively with Stannifer.' She was answered by Mrs L. M. Clarke who emphasised that the terms of the exclusivity agreement were and would remain confidential and would not be released to the general public, but assured Mrs Alexander that the project was of the utmost importance. 'We want it to be our flagship,' she said.

All I could discover therefore was that the council had dealt exclusively with one developer under terms they would not release to the public. I could find no reference in the minutes of 2003 or subsequent years to the uncovering of the river as a part of the Phoenix project. Even the newsletters of the High Wycombe Society, which in the spring of 2003 had argued that plans to unearth the river were very much part of the rival bid of the developers LXB and that the opportunity to de-culvert the river was the dominant concern of the public, came to mention the idea less often and less forcefully as the months and years passed.

Councillor Fulford had explained at a public meeting in the Guildhall that getting on with Phoenix was a matter of urgency and that uncovering the river was expensive and would use up too much land and that the river was too deep underground anyway. Getting rid of Abbey Way, he said, and opening up the Wye should be seen as a later phase of the ongoing regeneration of the town centre. In the spring of 2004 Stannifer commissioned the architects Benoys to prepare new plans and LXB left the contest, having been awarded a contract elsewhere. By the summer members were told that the project was not a Phoenix any more, that the council had responded to criticisms from various quarters and that now a longer-term master plan was taking shape that would include lively, vibrant open spaces, perhaps even coffee bars to rival Italian piazzas. By September 2004 Benoys and Stannifer had presented their new plans and the Society had responded with concerns which no longer included regret at the absence of the River Wye. By the spring of 2005 the High Wycombe Masterplan Vision had inherited the idea of 'rediscovering the River Wye' while on 24 March the riverless Stannifer plans were fully passed by Wycombe District Council. Finally on 9 May all the members of the Wycombe District Council were treated to the announcement that the new name for the development, following long consultation between Stannifer and marketing and branding consultants DS Emotion, was to be EDEN.

I could only guess that when it came down to it the developers, who must have had the upper hand with their exclusivity contract in their pockets, had decided that the river was too expensive to unearth, was an inconvenience in a shopping centre anyway and would in no way add to the profit.

Sensing I would get no closer to knowing the truth of the matter, I tried to find out instead why the river had been buried in the first place. I knew from the photographs I had discovered in the library that the stream had first been buried more or less when I was born, in the summer of 1965. I started to work backwards from 1965 through minutes which itemised such discussions as which contractors should be commissioned to culvert the River Wye, the closure of roads to allow the works to take place, the scheduling of when the works would take place, the compulsory purchase orders required, arriving finally at the very first mention of the need to culvert the river in minute 600 taken at a quarterly meeting of the town council held on 20 January 1959. No exclusion of the public had been deemed necessary when it was decided to bury a dirty, forgotten river. No regret expressed. The minute simply read: 'Your Committee have considered a report upon the question of widening Oxford Road, and to enable redevelopment to be carried out at the appropriate time it would appear essential for the length of the River Wye between Brook Street and Westbourne Street to be culverted in the immediate future.'

And I had come to the end of my journey, and discovered only this: the river was buried to widen a road.

A road that had once run hand in hand with the stream along a winding and marshy course from High Wycombe to West Wycombe, which had been raised and straightened with excavated chalk from Dashwood's caves, which had claimed all those lives and become finally the new voice of the valley, drowning out the sweeter sound of running water with the ceaseless grind of traffic, had finally buried its rival. In the next edition of the *Bucks Free Press* under a heading So River Wye to be Banished a reporter described how Councillor Brine had made a last-minute plea for the river. He asked if the suggestion that it could be kept as an attractive feature between the up- and down-lanes had been considered, but Councillor Wharton replied: 'How many motorists would find it an attractive feature in the middle of the road on a foggy night like this?' Alderman Lance added that culverting was the most economic proposition. And with these two sentiments uppermost and no one else to speak up for the stream, its subterranean fate was sealed. Mrs Dorothy Hoskins's letter to the paper, published the same day, only applauded the council's decision: the river is in such a revolting state there, she said, bright green and strewn with garbage and old boots and discarded utensils, that covering it up is the best solution.

Half a century on and the sheaf of buff papers which Ian gave me in the council office, the *Draft Delivery and Allocations Document* contains encouraging statements: an acknowledgement that chalk streams are a globally rare habitat, a statement that the de-culverting of the River Wye is part of the long-term vision and master plan for High Wycombe, that opportunities for de-culverting watercourses should be actively pursued and that planning proposals which prejudice the potential for de-culverting will not be allowed. Only time will tell whether the aspirations contained in these statements will ever be realised, or if instead the popular idea of de-culverting the lost river might serve simply to catalyse future development proposals, only to be shelved again and again when profit and loss charts are carefully analysed by developers with exclusivity contracts and the town council won't reveal why such documents were drawn up in the first place.

After all, this hopeful vision has been kicked down the road before, as John Scruton pointed out in 1971 when in despair at the sorry fate of the river he got together with thirty other like-minded people in a room above the old gaol in West Wycombe and formed a society to try to safe-guard what was left of it. There was once a widely publicised plan to make something of the river, he had said, with walkways through the town and trees, and this argument was used to persuade people that the Central Development Plan was a good idea. Then it was culverted and lost under-ground and there's no water feature at all. It's just lost, he said. Perhaps the most tragic loss the town has ever known.

As I finish these notes at a window table of the café overlooking the square outside the library in the Eden Centre I look down on the one water feature which the council and the developers of Eden did give to the people of High Wycombe as part of their vision of earthly Paradise. In the centre of the square and not more than fifty yards from the underground course of the river a steel column rises out of the ground as if through a hole in the pavement. At its top water in a shallow hollowed pool vibrates gently with the force of the pump working it and from there cascades in a thin film down the sides of the polished stainless steel. Though the sculpture hardly draws attention to itself, this column of shimmering water that falls seemingly without end never-theless pulls people in as they pass. Teenagers stand in front of it taking pictures of one another. A man walks up and lets his boxer dog drink from it by slurping at the vertical film of water as it falls. A crocodile of young children on a school outing walks past, shepherded by their teachers, and every single one of them touches the water, approaching with arms outstretched as if coming to some holy relic with a reverence and sense of awe beyond their years. And when two mothers with toddlers stop to talk a few feet away from it, their children are pulled to the pulsing water like iron filings to a magnet. They place their palms on the surface, move slowly around the sculpture dragging their hands across it, bewitched as the water cascades over their small fingers. They push their feet up against it. Flick the water at each other. One holds his tongue there for a second. Recoils when his nose gets wet. When the mothers finish talking and move away in opposite directions the toddlers are pulled back twice more by the water and leave reluctantly.

If it is ever possible to bring the river back to the surface of the town, said John Scruton, then that heart will come back too.

As the train built up speed, the engine drumming as if it might break at any moment, I rested my head against the cool of the carriage window and said goodbye to the River Wye and to the terraces of High Wycombe rising above it, bathed for a moment in the golden light of a summer sunset. I closed my eyes and dreamt of a silt road, of speeding in monochrome against a river of headlights. And I dreamt that the road and our journey along it are all that we carry within ourselves, all the pasts we have lived through, all the futures we have wished for.

ACKNOWLEDGEMENTS

I am truly grateful to all those who were so generous with their support, advice and friendship as I worked on this book.

Thank you to Andrew Kidd for encouraging me to pursue this idea and keeping me on task, to Juliet Brooke for so many hours of expert editing, and to both for their patience and guidance. Thank you to Rachel Cugnoni. Thank you to John Andrews, Jim Babb, Lydia Syson and Tristan Jones all of whom read drafts in various states of dreadfulness and were still encouraging. Thank you to the late Ray Klimeck and to Chris Bassano for making me so welcome down under. Thank you to Michael Youl for doing that, too, but also for so much help with research into the work of his great grandfather. Thank you to Dr. Haydon Bailey for help with fossils, to Allen Beechey for useful snippets on the River Wye, to Gareth Burnell for translating some Latin, to Jill Chambers for her research on the milling riots and the convicts, to Geoff Sharman for a letter and book from Tasmania, to James Rattue for help with sacred springs and for his fascinating book *High Wycombe Past*, to Ed Dashwood for his useful emails about the river's source and for letting me roam about his park and gardens, to Mary Hilder for waiting in when she was ill and being so friendly even though I was late, to Anne Pfisterer for chatting and telling me about the ducks, to Alistair and David Mackenzie and to Michael Tait for permission to use the quote from their film *The Last Great Wilderness*, to Jonathan Young for 'The Trout of the Empire' commission, to Robert Wilding for showing me where to find the Trench Royal.

Thank you to Steven de Joode at the Antiquariaat Forum for the image of Woodward's terraqueous globe on page 157, to Colin Seabright for the loan of his postcards of the Oxford Road and The Grange, to James Venn, old friend of Stanley Freese, for permission to use Stanley's photographs of the cart-horse and the empty field on page 184 and Stanley's notes on page 187, to Brian Flint whose photograph of Stanley Freese I photographed, to Michael Dewey who manages the wonderful photography archive Sharing Old Wycombe's Photographs, to the *Bucks Free Press* for permission to use the images on pages 70, 76, 83, 240, 263 and to the Wycombe Museum for permission to use the images on pages 66, 73, 82, 170, 175 and for permission to reproduce the Town Planning map on page 61, to the British Library for the image of Rowland Vaughan's Golden World taken from Ellen Wood's 1897 edition of *Most Approved and Long Experienced Water Workes* on page 35, to the Art Gallery of South Australia for John Glover's 1832 *A Corrobery of Natives in Mills Plains* on page 238, to the National Portrait Gallery for the image of John Woodward on page 160, to the Freshwater and Marine Image Bank for their image of a *galaxia* on page 234.

Thank you to the staff of High Wycombe Library, the Wycombe Museum, the Buckinghamshire Centre for

Studies, the British Library's rare books and maps rooms and the High Wycombe Council offices. Thank you to the staff of *Country Life* magazine who let me rummage around their archive.

More than anyone, thank you to Vicky.